Advance Praise for *A Theory of the Drone*

"In Chamayou's razor-sharp telling, drones fundamentally transform the psychic, moral, and physical space and art of killing. But it is his *theory* of the drone that is even more chilling. It demands that we consider the emergence of a new ethical and political norm of war that is neither war as we know it—nor peace. The 'principle of immunity for the imperial combatant' rests on a twisted logic: On the one hand is the achieved capacity of the drone operative (one of many newly installed masters of 'lethal surveillance') to move throughout a day between killing fields and coffee breaks, between combat zones and home. On the other hand is the enlisting of a citizenry to accept the 'moral obligation' to kill. In this compelling analysis, Amnesty International's classing of drone strikes as war crimes would be only part of the story. Chamayou's critical point is that drones alter the very terrain and logic of who deserves to die and implicates us all."

—Ann Stoler, Willy Brandt Distinguished University
Professor of Anthropology and Historical Studies
at the New School for Social Research

Also by Grégoire Chamayou

Manhunts: A Philosophical History

A THEORY OF THE DRONE

Grégoire Chamayou

Translated by Janet Lloyd

THE NEW PRESS

NEW YORK
LONDON

The New Press gratefully acknowledges the
Florence Gould Foundation for supporting publication of this book.

Originally published in France as *Théorie du Drone*
by La Fabrique Editions, Paris, 2013
Published in the United States by The New Press, New York, 2015

Distributed by Perseus Distribution

LIBRARY OF CONGRESS CATALOGING-IN-PUBLICATION DATA

Chamayou, Grégoire.
[Théorie du drone. English]
A theory of the drone / Grégoire Chamayou ; translated by Janet Lloyd.
pages   cm
Includes bibliographical references and index.
ISBN 978-1-59558-975-0 (hardcover)—
ISBN 978-1-59558-976-7 (e-book)   1. Drone aircraft—Moral and ethical
aspects.   2. Military ethics.   I. Lloyd, Janet, 1934–   II. Title.
UG479.C53   2013
172'.42—dc23   2014033225

The New Press publishes books that promote and enrich public
discussion and understanding of the issues vital to our democracy
and to a more equitable world. These books are made possible by
the enthusiasm of our readers; the support of a committed group of
donors, large and small; the collaboration of our many partners in the
independent media and the not-for-profit sector; booksellers, who often
hand-sell New Press books; librarians; and above all by our authors.

www.thenewpress.com

Composition by dix!
This book was set in Walbaum MT

Printed in the United States of America

2   4   6   8   10   9   7   5   3   1

In memory of Daniel

CONTENTS

III. Necroethics

IV. The Principles of the
Philosophy of the Right to Kill

V. Political Bodies

A THEORY OF THE DRONE

PRELUDE

That night, shortly before dawn rose in the Afghan mountains, they had noticed unusual behavior on the ground.

PILOT: Can you zoom in a little bit, man, let 'em take a look?

SENSOR OPERATOR: At least four in the back of the pickup.

PILOT: What about the guy under the north arrow? Does it look like he's holdin' something across his chest?

SENSOR OPERATOR: Yeah, it's kind of weird how they all have a cold spot on their chest.

PILOT: It's what they've been doing here lately, they wrap their [expletive] up in their man dresses so you can't PID [positively identify] it.

The pilot and the sensor operator scrutinize the scene on a monitor. They wear khaki uniforms with a shoulder badge—an owl with outstretched wings against a red background and flashes of lightning in the talons. Wearing earphones, they are sitting side by side on fake-leather seats. There are warning lights everywhere. But this place is unlike an ordinary cockpit.

They are shadowing something thousands of miles away. Images of vehicles, captured in Afghanistan, are relayed by satellite to Creech Air Force Base, not far from Indian

1

Springs, Nevada. In the 1950s, this was where the American nuclear tests were carried out. The atomic mushroom cloud rising in the distance could be seen from Las Vegas. Today, drivers on Highway 95 regularly catch sight of other shapes above their heads: oblongs with rounded heads, like fat, white blind larvae.

Creech AFB is the cradle of the U.S. Air Force fleet of drones. The soldiers call it "the home of the hunters." But the antiwar organization CODEPINK calls it "a place of disbelief, confusion and sadness." [1]

The work here is extremely boring. Men pass whole nights watching a screen on which, for the most part, appear unchanging images of another desert on the other side of the planet. Eating Doritos and M&Ms, they wait for something to happen: "months of monotony and milliseconds of mayhem." [2]

In the morning another team will come to take over the controls of the apparatus. The pilot and sensor operator will return to the steering wheels of their SUVs, which will take them back to their wives and children in a peaceful residential suburb of Las Vegas, forty-five minutes away.

The passengers traveling in three vehicles that, a few hours ago, left their little village in the province of Daikundi have no idea that for quite some time now, dozens of eyes have been watching them. Among those invisible spectators are not only the pilot and sensor operator but also a mission intelligence coordinator, a safety observer, a team of video analysts, and a ground force commander, the last of whom will eventually give the go-ahead for an aerial strike. This network of eyes remains in constant communication with one another. And on this night of February 20, 2010, their conversation is, as usual, recorded:

00:45 GMT (05:15 in Afghanistan)
PILOT: Is that a [expletive] rifle?

SENSOR OPERATOR: Maybe just a warm spot from where he was sitting. Can't really tell right now, but it does look like an object.

PILOT: I was hoping we could make a rifle out, never mind.

. . .

01:05

SENSOR OPERATOR: That truck would make a beautiful target. OK, that's a Chevy Suburban.

PILOT: Yeah.

SENSOR OPERATOR: Yeah.

. . .

01:07

MISSION INTELLIGENCE COORDINATOR: Screener said at least one child near SUV.

SENSOR OPERATOR: Bull [expletive] . . . where?

SENSOR OPERATOR: Send me a [expletive] still, I don't think they have kids out at this hour, I know they're shady but come on.

. . .

SENSOR OPERATOR: Well, maybe a teenager but I haven't seen anything that looked that short, granted they're all grouped up here, but . . .

MISSION INTELLIGENCE COORDINATOR: They're reviewing . . .

PILOT: Yeah, review that [expletive] . . . why didn't he say possible child, why are they so quick to call [expletive] kids but not to call a [expletive] rifle?

MISSION INTELLIGENCE COORDINATOR: Two children were at the rear of the SUV.

. . .

01:47

MISSION INTELLIGENCE COORDINATOR: Looks kinda like blankets, they were praying, they had like . . .

PILOT: JAG25 KIRK97 We get a good count, not yet?

SENSOR OPERATOR: They're praying, they're praying. . . . This is definitely it, this is their force. Praying? I mean seriously, that's what they do.

MISSION INTELLIGENCE COORDINATOR: They're gonna do something nefarious.

. . .

01:50

MISSION INTELLIGENCE COORDINATOR: Adolescent near the rear of the SUV.

SENSOR OPERATOR: Well, teenagers can fight.

MISSION INTELLIGENCE COORDINATOR: Pick up a weapon and you're a combatant, it's how that works.

. . .

01:52

SENSOR OPERATOR: One guy still praying at the front of the truck.

PILOT: JAG25 KIRK97 be advised, all pax [passengers] are finishing up praying and rallying up near all three vehicles at this time.

SENSOR OPERATOR: Oh, sweet target. I'd try to go through the bed, put it right dead center of the bed.

MISSION INTELLIGENCE COORDINATOR: Oh, that'd be perfect.

. . .

02:41

SENSOR OPERATOR: Well, sir, would you mind if I took a bathroom break real quick?

PILOT: No, not at all, dude.

. . .

03:17

UNKNOWN: What's the master plan, fellas?

PILOT: I don't know, hope we get to shoot the truck with all the dudes in it.

SENSOR OPERATOR: Yeah.

[The Predator drone has only one missile on board—not enough to target three vehicles—so two Kiowa helicopters, known as "Bam Bam 41," are ordered to take up an attacking position. A plan is agreed: the helicopters will fire first, then the drone will finish the job by firing its Hellfire missile at the survivors.]

. . .

03:48

MISSION INTELLIGENCE COORDINATOR [speaking to the drone pilot about the helicopters]: . . . at ground force commander's orders we may have them come up, action those targets, and let you use your Hellfire for cleanup shot.

PILOT: Kirk97, good copy on that, sounds good.

. . .

04:01

SENSOR OPERATOR: Sensor is in, let the party begin . . . Tell you what, they could have had a whole fleet of Preds up here.

PILOT: Oh, dude.

. . .

04:06

PILOT: As far as a weapons attack brief goes, man, we're probably going to be chasing dudes scrambling in the open, uh, when it goes down, don't worry about any guidance from me or from JAGUAR, just follow what makes the most sense to you. Stay with whoever you think gives us the best chance to shoot, um, at them. And I'm with you on that. So I'll brief you up on the launch profile, we'll hit a weapons attack brief when we know what we're going to shoot.

. . .

04:11

HELICOPTERS: Kirk97, Bam Bam four-one has you loud and clear.

PILOT: OK, Bam Bam 41, Kirk97 have you loud and clear as well. Understand you are tracking our three vehicles, do you need a talk on or do you have them?

HELICOPTERS: 41 has them just south side of the pass of the reported grid, white Highland[er] followed by two SUVs.

PILOT: Kirk97, that's a good copy. Those are your three vehicles. Be advised we have about twenty-one MAMs, about three rifles so far PIDed in the group and, ah, these are your three.

. . .

04:13

PILOT: It's a cool-looking shot.

SENSOR OPERATOR: Oh, awesome!

. . .

HELICOPTERS: [unintelligible] weapons and ICOM chatter with tactical maneuver. Break. Um, understand we are clear to engage.

PILOT: Okay, he's clear to engage so he has Type Three. I'm going to spin our missiles up as well.

. . .

04:16

SENSOR OPERATOR: Roger. And, oh, . . . and there it goes! [The helicopters fire at the convoy] . . . Have another guy . . . did they get him too? Yep.

PILOT: They took the first and, uh, the last out. They're going to come back around.

. . .

04:17

MISSION INTELLIGENCE COORDINATOR: Do we want to switch back to the other frequency?

PILOT: I tried, nobody was talking to me over there.

SENSOR OPERATOR: Looks like they're surrendering. They're not running.

. . .

04:18

SENSOR OPERATOR: That guy's laid down? They're not running.

SAFETY OBSERVER: Dude, this is weird.

SENSOR OPERATOR: They're just walking away.

. . .

SAFETY OBSERVER: You want to see if there's anybody at the back?

UNKNOWN: Yeah [unintelligible] outline.

SAFETY OBSERVER: By that third wreck.

SENSOR OPERATOR: A couple—two or three. Yeah, they're just chilling.

PILOT: Zoom in on that for a second for me. The third one.

SENSOR OPERATOR: The third one?

PILOT: Yeah. Did they blow that up? They did, right?

SAFETY OBSERVER: They did, yeah.

SENSOR OPERATOR: No, they didn't.

PILOT: They didn't.

SENSOR OPERATOR: They didn't. No, they're just out there.

PILOT: Yeah, that thing looks destroyed, though, doesn't it?

SAFETY OBSERVER: Yeah, they hit it. There's some smoke.

SENSOR OPERATOR: They hit it. You [unintelligible] . . .
These guys are just . . . [rocket attack on middle vehicle]

UNKNOWN: Oh!

PILOT: Holy [expletive]!

. . .

04:22

SENSOR OPERATOR: PID weapons, I don't see any . . .

SAFETY OBSERVER: Got something shiny on the one at the right . . .

SENSOR OPERATOR: Right. . . . That's weird. . . .

PILOT: Can't tell what the [expletive] they're doing.

SENSOR OPERATOR: Probably wondering what happened.

SAFETY OBSERVER: There's one more to the left of the screen.

SENSOR OPERATOR: Yeah, I see them.

SAFETY OBSERVER: Are they wearing burqas?

SENSOR OPERATOR: That's what it looks like.

PILOT: They were all PIDed as males, though. No females in the group.

SENSOR OPERATOR: That guy looks like he's wearing jewelry and stuff like a girl, but he ain't . . . if he's a girl, he's a big one.

. . .

04:32

SAFETY OBSERVER: One of those guys up at the top left's moving.

SENSOR OPERATOR: Yeah, I see him. I thought I saw him moving earlier, but I don't know if he's . . . is he moving or is he twitching?

SAFETY OBSERVER: Eh, I think he moved. Not very much, but . . .

SENSOR OPERATOR: Can't, can't follow them both.

MISSION INTELLIGENCE COORDINATOR: There's one guy sitting down.

SENSOR OPERATOR [talking to individual on the ground]: What you playing with?

MISSION COORDINATOR: His bone.

. . .

04:33

SAFETY OBSERVER: Oh, shit. Yeah, you can see some blood right there, next to the . . .

MISSION INTELLIGENCE COORDINATOR: Yeah, I seen that earlier.

. . .

04:36

MISSION INTELLIGENCE COORDINATOR: Is that two? One guy's tending the other guy?

SAFETY OBSERVER: Looks like it.

SENSOR OPERATOR: Looks like it, yeah.

MISSION INTELLIGENCE COORDINATOR: Self-aid buddy care to the rescue.

SAFETY OBSERVER: I forget, how do you treat a sucking gut wound?

SENSOR OPERATOR: Don't push it back in. Wrap it in a towel. That'll work.

. . .

04:38

PILOT: They're trying to [expletive] surrender, right? I think.

SENSOR OPERATOR: That's what it looks like to me.

MISSION INTELLIGENCE COORDINATOR: Yeah, I think that's what they're doing.

. . .

04:40

SENSOR OPERATOR: What are those? They were in the middle vehicle.

MISSION INTELLIGENCE COORDINATOR: Women and children.

SENSOR OPERATOR: Looks like a kid.

SAFETY OBSERVER: Yeah. The one waving the flag.

. . .

04:42

SAFETY OBSERVER: I'd tell him they're waving their . . .

SENSOR OPERATOR: Yeah, at this point I wouldn't . . . I personally wouldn't be comfortable shooting at these people.

MISSION INTELLIGENCE COORDINATOR: No.[3]

INTRODUCTION

In the official vocabulary of the U.S. Army, a drone is defined as "a land, sea, or air vehicle that is remotely or automatically controlled."[1] The drone family is not composed solely of flying objects. There may be as many different kinds as there are families of weapons: terrestrial drones, marine drones, submarine drones, even subterranean drones imagined in the form of fat mechanical moles. Provided there is no longer any human crew aboard, any kind of vehicle or piloted engine can be "dronized."

A drone can be controlled either from a distance by human operators (remote control)[2] or autonomously by robotic means (automatic piloting). In practice, present-day drones combine those two modes of control. Armies do not yet have at their disposal operational autonomous lethal robots, although as we shall see, there are already advanced plans for those.

The term "drone" is mainly used in common parlance. Military jargon refers to "unmanned aerial vehicles" (UAVs) or to "unmanned combat air vehicles" (UCAVs), depending on whether the contraption carries weapons.

This work will focus on the case of armed flying drones, the ones that are known as "hunter-killers" and used in the attacks regularly reported by the press. Their history is that of an eye turned into a weapon. "We've moved from using UAVs primarily in intelligence, surveillance, and re-connaissance roles before Operation Iraqi Freedom," said a U.S. Air Force general, "to a true hunter-killer role with the Reaper"—a name that "captures the lethal nature of this new weapon system."[3] The best definition of drones is prob-ably the following: "flying, high-resolution video cameras armed with missiles."[4]

David Deptula, an Air Force officer, identified their basic strategy: "The real advantage of unmanned aerial systems is that they allow you to project power without projecting vulnerability."[5] "Projecting power" should here be under-stood in the sense of deploying military force regardless of frontiers: a matter of making military interventions abroad, the problem of extending imperial power from the center over the world that constitutes its periphery. In the history of military empires, for many years "projecting power" meant "sending in troops." But it is precisely that equation that now has to be dismantled.

Self-preservation by means of drones involves putting vul-nerable bodies out of reach. This could be seen as the fulfill-ment of the ancient desire that inspires the whole history of ballistic weapons: to increase one's reach so as to hit the enemy from a distance before the opponent can launch its own attack.[6] But with drones, the weapon's range (the dis-tance between the weapon and its target) has been increased by the range of the remote control (the distance separating the operator from the weapon). Thousands of miles can now be interposed between the trigger on which one's finger rests and the cannon from which the cannonball will fly.

However, "projection of power" is also a euphemism that obscures the facts of wounding, killing, destroying. And to do this "without projecting vulnerability" implies that the only vulnerability will be that of the enemy, reduced to the status of a mere target. Underlying the palliative military rhetoric, as Elaine Scarry detects, the real claim is that the "successful strategy is one in which the injuring occurs only in one direction. . . . Thus, the original definition, which seems to posit noninjuring against injuring, instead posits one-directional injuring against two-directional injuring." [7] By prolonging and radicalizing preexisting tendencies, the armed drone goes to the very limit: for whoever uses such a weapon, it becomes a priori impossible to die as one kills. Warfare, from being possibly asymmetrical, becomes absolutely unilateral. What could still claim to be combat is converted into a campaign of what is, quite simply, slaughter.

The use of this new weapon is most marked by the United States. That is why I have borrowed from that country most of the facts and examples upon which my thesis is based. At the time of writing, the American armed forces had at their disposal more than six thousand drones of various kinds; more than 160 of these were Predator drones in the hands of the U.S. Air Force.[8] For both the military and the Central Intelligence Agency (CIA), the use of hunter-killer drones has become commonplace, to the point of being routine. These machines are deployed not only in zones of armed conflict, such as Afghanistan, but also in countries officially at peace, such as Somalia, Yemen, and above all Pakistan, where CIA drones carry out on average one strike every four days.[9] Exact figures are very hard to establish, but in Pakistan alone estimates of the number of deaths between 2004 and 2012 vary from 2,640 to 3,474.[10]

The use of this weapon has grown exponentially: the number of patrols by American armed drones increased by 1,200 percent between 2004 and 2012.[11] In the United States today, more drone operators are trained than all the pilots of fighter planes and bombers put together.[12] Whereas the defense budget decreased in 2013, with cuts in numerous sectors, the resources allocated to unmanned weapon systems rose by 30 percent.[13] That rapid increase reflects a strategic plan: the gradual dronization of an increasing portion of the American armed forces.[14]

The drone has become one of the emblems of Barack Obama's presidency, the instrument of his official antiterrorist doctrine, "kill rather than capture".[15] replace torture and Guantanamo with targeted assassination and the Predator drone.

In the American press, this weapon and this policy are the subject of daily debate. Militant anti-drone movements have sprung up.[16] The United Nations has set up an inquiry into the use of armed drones.[17] In other words, this has become a burning political issue.

The intention of this book is to subject the drone to a philosophical investigation. In this matter, I follow the precept expressed by Canguilhem: "Philosophy is a reflection for which all foreign material is good and, we would gladly say, in which all good material must be foreign." [18]

If the drone lends itself in particular to this kind of approach, it is because it is an "unidentified violent object": as soon as one tries to think about it in terms of established categories, intense confusion arises around notions as elementary as zones or places (geographical and ontological categories), virtue or bravery (ethical categories), warfare or conflict (categories at once strategic and legal-political). I should first like to explain these crises of intelligibility by bringing to light the contradictions they express. At the root of them all lies the elimination, already rampant but here absolutely radicalized, of any immediate relation of reciprocity.

That, in itself, might constitute an initial analytical dimension to this "drone theory." But over and above that formula, what might the theorization of a weapon signify? What might such an attempt involve?

A guiding thread is a thought expressed by the philosopher

Simone Weil in the 1930s: "the most defective method possible," she warned, would be to approach warfare and the
phenomena of armed violence "in terms of the ends pursued
and not by the nature of the means employed." [19] On the
other hand, "the very essence of the materialist method is
that, in its examination of any human event whatever, it attaches much less importance to the ends pursued than to the
consequences necessarily implied by the working out of the
means employed." [20] Rather than hastening to seek possible
justifications—in other words, rather than moralizing—
she advised doing something quite different: Begin by taking
apart the mechanism of violence. Go and look at the weapons,
study their specific characteristics. Become a technician, in a
way. But only in a way, for the aim here is an understanding that is not so much technical as political. What is important is not so much to grasp how the actual device works but
rather to discover the implications of how it works for the
action that it implements. The point is that the means adopted are binding, and a combination of specific constraints
is associated with each type of means adopted. Those means
not only make it possible to take action but also determine
the form of that action, and one must find out how they do
so. Rather than wonder whether the ends justify the means,
one must ask what the choice of those means, in itself, tends
to impose. Rather than seek moral justifications for armed
violence, one should favor a technical and political analysis
of the weapons themselves.

Analyzing a weapon might involve revealing what possession of it implies and seeking to know what effects it might
produce on its users, on the enemy that is its target, and on the
very form of their relations. But the central question would
be this: How do drones affect the war situation? To what do
they lead, not only in terms of their relation to the enemy
but also in terms of the state's relation to its own subjects?

The implications are tendentious, often intertwined, taking the form of dynamic sketches rather than unequivocal deductions. "Taking apart the mechanism of the military struggle" means making a strategic analysis of the "social relations it implies."[21] Such would be the program for a critical analysis of weaponry.

But studying a determinative relationship does not mean ruling out an analysis of intentionality—that is, attempting to identify the strategic projects that govern the technical choices while at the same time being determined by those choices. Contrary to what simplistic dualisms postulate, technical determinism (means) and strategic intentionality (ends), although conceptually opposed, are not in practice incompatible. On the contrary, it is possible for the two to interact harmoniously. The surest way to ensure the permanence of a strategic choice is to opt for means that implement it to the point of turning it into the sole practicable option.

Another important point is that amid the general uncertainty fueled by a created crisis, lurking within the fog of war, large-scale intellectual maneuvers are in the offing and semantic coups are being plotted. In fact, a whole collection of theoretical offensives are being launched with the aim of appropriating, twisting, and redefining concepts that, by naming and theorizing violence, allow it to be legitimately exercised. More than ever, philosophy is a battlefield. It is time to enter the fray. What I have to say is openly polemical, for, over and above the possible analytical contributions this book may make, its objective is to provide discursive weapons for the use of those men and women who wish to oppose the policy served by drones.

Let me start with the following questions: Where did the drone come from? What is its technical and tactical genealogy? And what are its consequent fundamental characteristics?

This weapon extends and radicalizes the existing processes

of remote warfare and ends up by doing away with combat. But in so doing, it is the very notion of "war" that enters into crisis. A central problem arises: if the "war of drones" is no longer quite warfare, what kind of "state of violence" does it amount to?[22]

The attempt to eradicate all direct reciprocity in any exposure to hostile violence transforms not only the material conduct of armed violence technically, tactically, and psychically, but also the traditional principles of a military ethos officially based on bravery and a sense of sacrifice. Judged by the yardstick of such classical categories, a drone *looks like* the weapon of cowards.

That does not prevent its supporters from declaring it to be the most ethical weapon ever known to humankind. Bringing about this moral conversion and transmutation of values is the task to which philosophers working within the confined field of military ethics today devote themselves.

They declare the drone to be the humanitarian weapon par excellence. Their discursive efforts are essential for ensuring the social and political acceptability of this weapon. In this discourse of legitimation, the elements of language provided by arms dealers and spokespeople for the armed forces are recycled, through the crude processes of discursive alchemy, into the guiding principles of an ethical philosophy of a new kind: a "necro-ethics" that calls urgently for critical assessment.

But the offensive is also and perhaps above all pushing into the field of legal theory. "Warfare without risk," in which the drone is probably the most effective instrument, critically undermines the meta-legal principles that underpin the right to kill in war. Against a background of fundamental destabilization such as this, formulas for redefining a sovereign power over life and death are being introduced. The aim is to accommodate the right to "targeted assassination" even if, in the process, the rights typically associated with being in armed conflict go up in smoke.

But that is not all. By inventing the armed drone one has also, almost inadvertently, discovered something else: a solution to the central contradiction that for several centuries has affected the modern theory of political sovereignty in matters of warfare. The generalization of such a weapon implies a change in the conditions that apply in the exercise of the power of war, this time in the context of the relations between the state and its own subjects. It would be mistaken to limit the question of weaponry solely to the sphere of external violence. What would the consequences of becoming the subjects of a drone-state be for that state's own population?

I

Techniques and Tactics

1

Methodologies for a Hostile Environment

> Better medicine is not the only way to achieve zero-loss warfare.
>
> —Robert L. Forward, *Martian Rainbow*

How could one intervene without danger in places as inhospitable as irradiated zones, in the depths of the sea, or on distant planets? In 1964, the engineer John W. Clark produced a study of "remote control in hostile environments": "When plans are being made for operations in these environments, it is usual to consider only two possibilities: either placing a machine in the environment or placing a protected man there. A third possibility, however, would in many cases give more satisfactory results than either of the others. This possibility employs a vehicle operating in the hostile environment under remote control by a man in a safe environment."[1] Rather than deep-sea divers or autonomous machines, one could use remotely controlled machines or what Clark, forging an awkward neologism based on ancient Greek roots, called "telechiric machines," or "technology of manipulation at a distance."[2]

He wrote: "In the telechiric system, the machine may be thought of as an alter ego for the man who operates it. In effect, his consciousness is transferred to an invulnerable mechanical body with which he is able to manipulate tools or

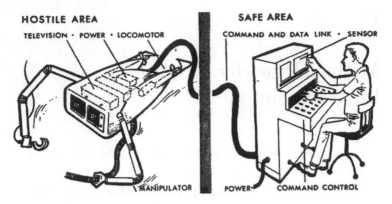

HOSTILE AREA

TELEVISION · POWER · LOCOMOTOR

SAFE AREA

COMMAND AND DATA LINK · SENSOR

MANIPULATOR   POWER   COMMAND CONTROL

The topography of the telechiric machine: the example of a bathyscape. From J.W. Clark, "Remote Control in Hostile Environments," *New Scientist* 22, no. 389 (April 1964).

equipment almost as though he were holding them in his own hands."[3] The only thing lacking in this second body is the living flesh of the first body. But therein lies the great advantage: the body that is vulnerable is removed from the hostile environment.

This device implies a specific topography, a particular way of thinking and of organizing space. And Clark, following the example provided by the bathyscape, produced the basic schema for it.

Space is divided into two: a hostile area and a safe one. The picture shows a sheltered power in a safe place operating in a dangerous place outside. This power, sometimes called "telearchic," implies a frontier.[4] But that border is asymmetrical: it must not only block intrusions from outside but also be able to open slightly in order to admit the mechanical pseudopods designed to intervene in the hostile environment.[5]

The hostile zone, for its part, remains a space that is left derelict but which, as a potentially threatening area, definitely needs to be kept under surveillance. It may even be exploited for its resources, but it is not, strictly speaking, to be occupied. One intervenes there and patrols it, but there is no suggestion of going to live there—except to carve out new secured zones, bases, or platforms in accordance with a general topographical schema and for reasons of security.

To the apostles of remote control, such an invention appeared to be a way to avoid the ordeals of working in extreme conditions. Even if one foresaw that in the age of atomic power and the conquest of space there would be "an increasing need for the performance of tasks in environments hostile to human beings," it was possible to announce joyfully: "With technology as advanced as it is today, it is unnecessary to require a man to expose himself to physical danger in order to earn a living. . . . There is no hazardous task performed by men today that cannot, in principle, be performed by remotely controlled machines." [6]

Remote control was thus a philanthropic device that would be able to relieve humankind of all perilous occupations. Miners, firefighters, and those working on the atom, in space, or in the oceans could all be converted into remote-control operators. The sacrifice of vile bodies was no longer necessary. Once living bodies and operative ones were dissociated, only the latter, entirely mechanized and dispensable, would now come into contact with danger: "There are no people to be hurt. A collapse or explosion would elicit no more response than, 'Well, it is very sad. We've lost six robots.'" [7]

In his enthusiastic list of the possible applications of telechiric machines, Clark had overlooked one obvious one, which a reader hastened to point out:

The minds of telechirists are grappling with the problems of employing remotely-controlled machines to do the peaceful work of man amid the hazards of heat, radiation, space and the ocean floor. Have they got their priorities right? Should not their first efforts towards human safety be aimed at mankind's most hazardous employment—the industry of war? . . . Why should twentieth-century men continue to be stormed at by shot and shell when a telechiric Tommy Atkins could take his place? All conventional wars might eventually be conducted telechirically, armies of military robots battling it out by remote control, victory being calculated and apportioned by neutral computers, while humans sit safely at home watching on TV the lubricating oil staining the sand in sensible simile of their own blood.[8]

It would be a utopia, with warfare converted into a tournament of machines—battles without soldiers, conflicts with no victims. However, the reader, who was no fool, concluded with a quite different scenario, one that, sad to say, was far more realistic: "Far-flung imperial conquests which were ours because we had the Maxim gun and they had the knobkerry will be recalled by new bloodless triumphs coming our way because we have telechiric yeomanry and they, poor fuzzy-wuzzies, have only napalm and nerve-gas."[9]

Once the remotely controlled machine becomes a weapon of war, it is the enemy who is treated as a dangerous material. He can be eliminated from afar as one watches on a screen, softly enclosed within a climatized "safe zone." Asymmetrical warfare becomes radicalized, unilateral. Of course people would still die, but only on one side.

A Radioplane factory worker, 1944. Photograph by David Conover for the U.S. Army.

2

The Genealogy of the Predator

> Humanity needed it and it made its appearance forthwith.
>
> —Hegel[1]

The girl who posed there, holding a drone propeller, was still called Norma Jeane Dougherty. She was immortalized by a photographer who had come to report on the Radioplane Company, founded in Los Angeles by Reginald Denny, a movie actor who had turned to aeromodelism. That was how the girl who was then still an ordinary worker but was to become Marilyn Monroe was discovered. The drone was born partly in Hollywood and thus, necessarily, under the sign of pretense.

Initially, the English word "drone" meant both an insect and a sound. It was not until the outbreak of World War II that it began to take on another meaning. At that time, American artillery apprentices used the expression "target drones" to designate the small remotely controlled planes at which they aimed in training. The metaphor did not refer solely to the size of those machines or the *brm-brm* of their motors. Drones are male bees, without stingers, and eventually the other bees kill them. Classical tradition regarded them as emblems of all that is nongenuine and dispensable.[2] That was precisely what a target drone was: just a dummy, made to be shot down.

However, it was a long time before drones were to be seen

cruising above battlefields. To be sure, the idea dates back quite a while: there were the Curtiss-Sperry aerial torpedo and the Kettering Bug at the end of World War I, and then the Nazi V-1s and V-2s unleashed on London in 1944. But those old flying torpedoes may be considered more as the ancestors of cruise missiles than as those of present-day drones. The essential difference lies in the fact that while the former can be used only once, the latter are reusable.[3] The drone is not a projectile, but a projectile-carrying machine.

It was during the Vietnam War that the U.S. Air Force, to counteract the Soviet surface-to-air missiles that had inflicted heavy casualties on it, invested in reconnaissance drones nicknamed "Lightning Bugs," produced by Ryan Aeronautical.[4] An American official explained that "these RPVs [remotely piloted vehicles] could help prevent aircrews from becoming casualties or prisoners. . . . With RPVs, survival is not the driving factor."[5]

Once the war was over, those machines were scrapped.[6] By the late 1970s, the development of military drones had been practically abandoned in the United States. However, it continued elsewhere. Israel, which had inherited a few of these machines, recognized their potential tactical advantages.

In 1973, the Israel Defense Forces (IDF), facing off against Egypt, ran up against the tactical problem of surface-to-air missiles. After losing around thirty planes in the first hours of the Yom Kippur War, Israeli aviation changed its tactics. They decided to send out a wave of drones in order to mislead enemy defenses: "After the Egyptians fired their initial salvo at the drones, the manned strikes were able to attack while the Egyptians were reloading."[7] This ruse enabled Israel to assume mastery of the skies. In 1982, similar tactics were employed against the Syrians in the Bekaa Valley. Having first deployed their fleet of Mastiff and Scout drones, the Israelis then sent out decoy planes that were picked up by enemy radar. The Syrians activated their surface-to-air missiles, to no effect whatsoever. The drones, which had been observing the scene from the sky, easily detected the positions of the antiaircraft batteries and relayed them to the Israeli fighter planes, which then proceeded to annihilate them.

The drones were used for other purposes as well:

Two days after a terrorist bomb destroyed the [U.S.] Marine Barracks in Beirut in October 1983, Marine Commandant Gen. P.X. Kelley secretly flew to the scene. No word of his arrival was leaked. Yet, across the border, Israeli intelligence officers watched live television images of Kelley arriving and inspecting the barracks. They even zoomed the picture in tight, placing cross hairs directly on his head. Hours later, in Tel Aviv, the Israelis played back the tape for the shocked Marine general. The scene, they explained, was transmitted by a Mastiff RPV circling out of sight above the barracks.[8]

This was just one of a series of minor events that combined to encourage the relaunch of American drone production in the 1980s. "All I did," confessed Al Ellis, the father of the Israeli drones, "was take a model airplane, put a camera in it, and take the pictures. . . . But that started an industry."[9]

At this point, however, the drones were simply machines for intelligence, surveillance, and reconnaissance. They were just eyes, not weapons. The metamorphosis came about almost by chance, between Kosovo and Afghanistan, as the new millennium began. As early as 1995, General Atomics had invented a new remote-controlled spy plane prototype, the Predator. Despite its disquieting name, the beast was not yet equipped with claws or teeth. In Kosovo, where it was deployed in 1999, the drone limited itself to filming targets and illuminating them by means of lasers, allowing the F-16 planes to strike.

But it would take a " 'different kind of war' to make the Predator into a *predator*." [10] No more than a few months before September 11, 2001, officers who had seen the Predator at work in Kosovo had the idea of experimentally equipping it with an antitank missile. Writes Bill Yenne in his history of the drone, "On February 16, 2001, during tests at Nellis Air Force Base, a Predator successfully fired a Hellfire AGM-114C into a target. The notion of turning the Predator into a predator had been realized. No one could imagine that, before the year was out, the Predator would be preying upon live targets in Afghanistan." [11]

Barely two months after the outbreak of hostilities in Afghanistan, George Bush was in a position to declare: "The conflict in Afghanistan has taught us more about the future of our military than a decade of blue ribbon panels and think-tank symposiums. The Predator is a good example. . . . Now it is clear the military does not have enough unmanned vehicles." [12]

3

The Theoretical Principles
of Manhunting

> Individual will research and incorporate current manhunt-
> ing experiences and procedures in order to provide an ed-
> ucational forum for manhunting issues. . . . Must possess
> a SECRET level clearance and be able to obtain a TOP
> SECRET/SCI security clearance.
>
> —Job description for a special operations manhunting
> program analyst in an advertisement published
> by the military contractor SAI in 2006

In 2004, John Lockwood set up an Internet site called Live
-Shot.com. The idea was at once simple and innovative. By
subscribing online for a few dollars, the Internet surfer could
become a "virtual hunter." Thanks to a camera fixed to a
mobile forearm, itself connected to a remote control device,
one could, without stirring from home, shoot live animals let
loose for the occasion on a ranch in Texas.

When it made the news, there was a rush to condemn it.
The editor-in-chief of the magazine *Outdoor Life*, acknowl-
edging the profound "ethical problems" that such a venture
presented, set out a fine definition of what hunting meant
for him: "To me, hunting isn't just about pulling the trigger
on an animal. It's about the total experience. . . . Hunting
is about being out there, not about pulling the trigger with
the click of a mouse." [1] A Wisconsin lawmaker took up the

theme, giving the definition a strangely environmentalist twist: "To me, hunting is being out in nature and becoming one with nature."[2] Even the extremely conservative National Rifle Association expressed its opposition, joining with the American Society for the Prevention of Cruelty to Animals in an unusual alliance: "We believe that hunting should be outdoors and that sitting in front of a computer three states away doesn't qualify as 'hunting.'"[3] A Houston police officer was even more adamant, saying, "It's not hunting. It's killing. . . . Someone gets a computer and pushes a button and something dies for no reason."[4]

Lockwood protested, claiming that his foremost purpose had been to allow handicapped people who were passionate about hunting to indulge in their favorite pastime and mentioning an American soldier in Iraq who had thanked him for offering such a fine opportunity, saying that he had no idea when he might be able to go hunting again. But it was all in vain. Hunting online was forbidden. Lockwood, disappointed, tried to salvage his scheme by suggesting that his clients should fire at cardboard targets representing Osama bin Laden. However, his intended Internet audience shifted to other, no doubt more exciting, online pleasures, and the little venture that had seemed so promising collapsed.

The triggers of moral indignation are quite mysterious sometimes. While the virtual hunting of animals was almost universally condemned as scandalous, the remote-controlled hunting of human beings was at the same moment taking off without any of those same people making any objections.

In the immediate aftermath of September 11, George W. Bush had predicted that the United States would embark upon a new kind of warfare, "a war that requires us to be on an international manhunt."[5] Something that initially sounded like nothing more than a catchy Texas cowboy slogan has since been converted into state doctrine, complete with experts, plans, and weapons. A single decade has seen the establishment of an unconventional form of state violence that combines the disparate characteristics of warfare and policing without really corresponding to either, finding conceptual and practical unity in the notion of a militarized manhunt.

In 2001, U.S. secretary of defense Donald Rumsfeld had become convinced that "the techniques used by the Israelis against the Palestinians could quite simply be deployed on a larger scale."[6] What he had in mind was Israel's programs of "targeted assassinations," the existence of which had recently been recognized by the Israeli leadership. As Eyal Weizman explains, the occupied territories had become "the world's largest laboratory for airborne thanatotactics," so it was not surprising that they would eventually be exported.[7]

But one problem remained. "How do we organize the Department of Defense for manhunts?" Rumsfeld asked. "We are obviously not well organized at the present time."[8] In the early 2000s, the U.S. military apparatus was not yet ready to roll out on a worldwide scale the sort of missions that normally are assigned to the police within a domestic framework: namely, the identification, tracking, location, and capture (but in actual fact the physical elimination) of suspect individuals.

Within the United States, not all the high-ranking officers who were informed of these plans greeted them with enthusiasm. At the time, journalist Seymour Hersh noted that many feared that the proposed type of operation—what one advisor to the Pentagon called "preemptive manhunting"— had the potential to turn into another Phoenix Program, the sinister secret program of murder and torture that had once been unleashed in Vietnam.[9]

Of course, there was the additional problem of how to legally justify these hybrid operations, the enfants terribles of the police and the army. At the levels of both warfare theory and international law, they seemed to be conceptual monstrosities. But we shall be returning to this point.

In any case, a new strategic doctrine became necessary. Researchers set about defining the "manhunting theoretical principles" that could provide a framework for such operations.[10] George A. Crawford produced a summary of these in a report published in 2009 by the Joint Special Operations University. This text, which set out to make "manhunting a foundation of US national strategies,"[11] in particular called for the creation of a "national manhunting agency," which would be an indispensable instrument for "building a manhunting force for the future."[12]

The contemporary doctrine of hunting warfare breaks with the model of conventional warfare based on concepts of fronts and opposed battle lines facing up to each other. In 1916, General John J. Pershing launched a vast military offensive in Mexico in an unsuccessful attempt to lay hands on the revolutionary Pancho Villa. For American strategists who cite this historical precedent as a counterexample, it was a matter of reversing polarity: faced with the "asymmetrical threats" posed by small mobile groups of "nonstate actors," they should use small, flexible units, either human or—preferably—remotely controlled, in a pattern of targeted attacks.

Contrary to Carl von Clausewitz's classical definition, the fundamental structure of this type of warfare is no longer that of a duel, of two fighters facing each other. The paradigm is quite different: a hunter advancing on a prey that flees or hides from him. The rules of the game are not the same. "In the competition between two enemy combatants," wrote Crawford, "the goal is to win the battle by defeating the adversary: both combatants must confront to win. However, a manhunt scenario differs in that each player's strategy is different. The fugitive always wants to avoid capture; the pursuer must confront to win, whereas the fugitive must evade to win." [13] The hostile relationship now boils down, as in a game of hide-and-seek, to "a competition between the hiders and the seekers." [14]

The primary task is no longer to immobilize the enemy but to identify and locate it. This implies all the labor of detection. The modern art of tracking is based on an intensive use of new technologies, combining aerial video surveillance, the interception of signals, and cartographic tracking. The profession of manhunters now has its own technocratic jargon: "Nexus Topography is an extension of the common practice of Social Network Analysis (SNA) used to develop profiles of HVIs. . . . Nexus Topography maps social forums or environments, which bind individuals together." [15]

In this model the enemy individual is no longer seen as a link in a hierarchical chain of command: he is a knot or "node" inserted into a number of social networks. Based on the concepts of "network-centric warfare" and "effects-based operations," the idea is that by successfully targeting its key nodes, an enemy network can be disorganized to the point of being practically wiped out. The masterminds of this methodology declare that "targeting a single key node in a battle-field system has second, third, n-order effects, and that these effects can be accurately calculated to ensure maximum success." [16] This claim to predictive calculation is the foundation of the policy of prophylactic elimination, for which the hunter-killer drones are the main instruments. For the strategy of militarized manhunting is essentially *preventive*. It is not so much a matter of responding to actual attacks but rather of preventing the development of emerging threats by the early elimination of their potential agents—"to detect, deter, disrupt, detain or destroy networks before they can harm"[17]—and to do this in the absence of any direct, imminent threat.[18]

The political rationale that underlies this type of practice is that of social defense. Its classic instrument is the security measure, which is "not designed to punish but only to preserve society from the danger presented by the presence of dangerous beings in its midst."[19] In the logic of this security, based on the preventive elimination of dangerous individuals, "warfare" takes the form of vast campaigns of extrajudiciary executions. The names given to the drones—Predators (birds of prey) and Reapers (angels of death)—are certainly well chosen.

Quo modo Deum.

The eye of God. From Horapollo, *Ori Apollinis Niliaci: De sacris notis et sculpturis libri duo* (Paris: Kerver, 1551), 222.

4

Surveillance and Annihilation

It's kind of like having God overhead. And lightning comes down in the form of a Hellfire.

—Colonel Theodore Osowski

Seeking the eye of God,
I saw only a socket,
huge, black and bottomless
where night which inhabits it
sends rays over the world
and always thickens.

—Gérard de Nerval, *Les Chimères*

The eye of God, with its overhanging gaze, embraces the entire world. Its vision is more than just sight: beneath the skin of phenomena it can search hearts and minds. Nothing is opaque to it. Because it is eternity, it embraces the whole of time, the past as well as the future. And its knowledge is not just knowledge. Omniscience implies omnipotence.

In many respects, the drone dreams of achieving through technology a miniature equivalence to that fictional eye of God. As one soldier writes, "Using the all-seeing eye, you will find out who is important in a network, where they live, where they get their support from, where their friends are."[1] Then all you have to do is "wait till these people have gone down a lonely stretch of road and take them out with a Hell-fire missile."[2]

The promoters of drones emphasize that these machines have "revolutionized our ability to provide a constant stare against our enemy."[3] Therein, it seems, lies their fundamental contribution: a revolution in sighting. But in what sense? Their innovations can be listed as several major principles.

1. *The principle of persistent surveillance or permanent watch.*

Freed from the constraints that a pilot's body imposed, a drone can remain in the air for a long time. For twenty-four hours its gaze can remain constant; a mechanical eye has no lids. While the machine patrols, its operators, on the ground, watch the screen in eight-hour shifts. The removal of crews from the cockpit has made it possible for their work to be thoroughly reorganized, and it is really this socialized reduction of the need for human eyes, over and above the technological powers of the machine, that ensures a "constant geo-spatial 'overwatch'" by the institutional eye.[4]

2. *The principle of a totalization of perspectives or a synoptic viewing.*

The second major principle makes the watch total as well as persistent. This is the notion of "wide area surveillance": see everything, all the time. This extension of the field of vision is likely to be entrusted to new and revolutionary optical devices still in the process of being developed. Equipped with such systems of synoptic imagery, a drone would have at its disposal not just one but dozens of high-resolution microcameras facing in every direction, like the multiple facets of the eye of a fly. A software system would aggregate the various images in real time into a single overall view that could be seen in detail when necessary.[5] The result would be the equivalent of a high-resolution satellite image, on the scale of an entire town or region, but transmitted both live and in streaming video. The teams of operators could, if they wished, zoom in on a particular area or a particular individual at any time. Equipped with such a system, a single hovering machine would be the equivalent of a network of video surveillance cameras positioned over an entire town. The drone would become "all-seeing."

In practice, however, there is still a long way to go. A current military report declares that existing "all-seeing" devices are neither efficient nor well adapted, with insufficient resolution, particularly for efficiently tracking individuals, and with worrying deficiencies in their locational system.[6] But what concerns me at the moment are the main principles of this kind of reasoning, without regard to their present efficacy.

3. *The principle of creating an archive or film of everyone's life.*

Optical surveillance is not limited to the present time. It also assumes the important function of recording and archiving. "The idea behind persistent surveillance is to make a movie of a city-size area, with the goal of tracking all the moving vehicles and people," says John Marion, director of the persistent surveillance program for Logos Technologies.[7] Once such a movie of every life and everything is completed, it could be rerun thousands of times, each time focusing on a different person, zooming in on him or her so as to reexamine that person's own particular history. One could select scenes, rewind, replay, or fast-forward, navigating as one wished through not only space but also time. Once an event had taken place, one could backtrack to study its genealogy. For example, "if a whole town could be surveilled at once, . . . car bombs could be traced back to their points of origin."[8] The total archive would ensure the retrospective traceability of all movements and all their past histories.

However, all this would presuppose capacities to store, index, and analyze data that the systems presently in place do not possess.[9] The press informs us that in the course of 2009 alone, American drones generated the equivalent of twenty-four years' worth of video recording.[10] And the new ARGUS-IS wide-area surveillance system promises "to generate several terabytes [of data] per minute, hundreds of times greater than previous-generation sensors."[11] But that is precisely the problem: a "data overload," an excess or avalanche of data, the profusion of which will end up making the information unusable.

In an effort to resolve this problem, the Pentagon went to the sports stadium. The production of football broadcasts has resulted in a variety of innovative technologies. In every game, dozens of cameras film the players from every angle. Every sequence is instantly indexed on a database. Thanks to efficient software, the control room staff can run replays from a variety of angles while displaying statistics on the screen. As Larry James, Air Force deputy chief of staff for intelligence, surveillance, and reconnaissance, explains, "When it comes to collecting and analyzing data, sports broadcasters are far ahead of the military."[12] After sending emissaries into ESPN's studios, the U.S. military decided to acquire a modified version of the software that it used.[13] After all, their concerns are similar: "While sportscasters want to collect and catalog video on a specific player or a winning shot, the military wants the same capacity to follow insurgents and bombings."[14] As Walter Benjamin long ago predicted, future warfare would present a new "face which will permanently replace soldierly qualities by those of sports; all action will lose its military character, and war will assume the countenance of record-setting."[15]

The next stage in technology would be to make the indexing of images automatic. Instead of having to enter "tags" or metadata manually, this painstaking task would be entrusted to machines. But for this to be possible, there would have to be software capable of describing things and actions, that is, automatically transcribing aggregates of pixels into names, verbs, and propositions. The Defense Advanced Research Projects Agency (DARPA) funds cognitive scientists to conduct this type of research, which is designed to construct "integrated cognitive systems for automatized video-surveillance." [16]

We should imagine eventual scribe-machines, flying robotized clerks that, in real time, would record the smallest actions occurring in the world below—as if, in parallel to the life of human beings, the cameras that already capture animated images would now set about producing a circumstantial account of them. But those lines of text, a meticulous chronicle of every fact and gesture, would at the same time constitute something more: a great index, an informative catalog of an immense video library in which everyone's life would become retrospectively researchable.

4. *The principle of data fusion.*

Drones have not only eyes but also ears and many other organs. For example, "Predator and Reaper drones also can interpret electronic communications from radios, cell phones or other communication devices." [17] The archival aim would be to fuse together these different layers of information and pin them all together so as to combine in a single item all the informational facets of one particular event: for example, associating a particular telephone call with a particular video sequence and particular GPS coordinates. This is the aim of data fusion. [18]

5. *The principle of the schematization of forms of life.*

Derek Gregory notes that the ability to integrate data produced by a variety of sources—"combining the where, the when, and the who"—into a three-dimensional array "replicates the standard time-geography diagrams developed by the Swedish geographer Torsten Hägerstrand in the 1960s and 1970s."[19] This extremely inventive development in human geography set out to draw maps of a new kind, spatio-temporal graphs that would show the course of lives in three dimensions, with all their cycles and itineraries but also their accidents and deviations. In a cruel perversion, this idea of a cartography of lives has today become one of the main epistemic bases of armed surveillance. The aim is to be able "to follow several individuals through various social networks in order to establish a form or pattern of life that conforms with the paradigm of 'information based on activity,' which today constitutes the heart of the counter-insurgency doctrine."[20]

Contrary to what one might imagine, the main objectives of these continuous surveillance devices is not so much to tail individuals already known, but rather to spot the emergence of suspect elements based on their unusual behavior. Because this model of information is predicated on an analysis of behavior patterns rather than the recognition of nominal identities, it claims to be able, paradoxically, to "identify" individuals who remain anonymous—in other words, to describe them by behavior that reflects a particular profile. This is identification that is not individual but generic.[21]

6. *The principle of the detection of anomalies and preemptive anticipation.*

Images are scanned in order to pick out, amid masses of activity, events that seem pertinent to the focus on security. These are detectable because of their anomaly or irregularity. Any behavior that diverges from the web of habitual activities may indicate a threat. "According to an Air Force intelligence analyst who spoke on condition of anonymity, analyzing imagery captured by drones is like a cross between police work and social science. The focus is on understanding 'patterns of life,' and deviations from those patterns. For example, if a normally busy bridge suddenly empties, that might mean the local population knows a bomb is planted there. 'You're now getting into a culture study,' says the analyst. . . . [You're] looking at people's lives."[22] Gregory sums this up as follows: "Essentially, the task consists in distinguishing between 'normal' and 'abnormal' activity in a kind of militarized rhythm-analysis that takes on increasingly automatized forms."[23]

Automatic detection of abnormal behavior operates by predicting the possible developments resulting from different types of behavior.[24] Having noted the characteristic features of a familiar sequence in a particular situation, analysts claim to be able to make probable inferences about future developments, and intervene so as to prevent those developments from ever occurring. Thus recognition of particular scenarios can serve as the basis for early threat detection.[25]

Predicting the future is based on knowledge of the past. The archives of lives constitute the basis for claims that, by noting regularities and anticipating recurrences, it is possible both to predict the future and to change the course of it by taking preemptive action. Such claims are clearly founded upon very fragile epistemological bases, which in no way prevents them from being extremely dangerous but, on the contrary, ensures that they are.

The names given to these devices are very revealing: Argus[26] and Gorgon Stare.[27] In Greek mythology, Argus, the figure with a hundred eyes, was also known as Panoptes, "the one who sees all." Jeremy Bentham's panopticon, analyzed by Michel Foucault, was originally an architectural contraption. In a carrying forward of this pattern, in recent decades cities have been stuffed with video surveillance cameras. Surveillance by means of drones is more economical, as it involves no spatial alterations, nor does it require anything to be affixed to walls. Air and sky are all that are needed. As in the film *Eyeborgs*, the cameras are detached from walls and thereupon acquire wings and weapons.[28] We are entering into the era of winged and armed panoptics. As for the gaze of the Gorgon, it turned to stone all those unfortunate enough to encounter it. It was a gaze that killed. At this point, it is a matter no longer of surveillance and punishment but of *surveillance and annihilation*.

David Rohde, a *New York Times* journalist kidnapped in 2008 and held in Waziristan for seven months, was one of the first Westerners to describe the effects that this lethal continuous surveillance produced upon the populations subjected to it. Evoking a "hell on earth," he added: "The drones were terrifying. From the ground, it is impossible to determine who or what they are tracking as they circle overhead. The buzz of a distant propeller is a constant reminder of imminent death."[29]

The accounts collected in this region by the authors of a 2012 report titled "Living Under the Drones" are in a similar vein:

They're always surveying us, they're always over us, and you never know when they're going to strike and attack.[30]

Everyone is scared all the time. When we're sitting together to have a meeting, we're scared there might be a strike. When you can hear the drone circling in the sky, you think it might strike you. We're always scared. We always have this fear in our head.[31]

Drones are always on my mind. It makes it difficult to sleep. They are like a mosquito. Even when you don't see them, you can hear them, you know they are there.[32]

Children, grown-up people, women, they are terrified. . . . They scream in terror.[33]

One inhabitant of Datta Khel—a place hit more than thirty times by drones in the course of the past three years—says that his neighbors "have lost their mental balance . . . are just locked in a room. Just like you lock people in prison, they are locked in a room."[34]

Drones are indeed petrifying. They inflict mass terror upon entire populations. It is this—over and above the deaths, the injuries, the destruction, the anger, and the grieving—that is the effect of permanent lethal surveillance: it amounts to a psychic imprisonment within a perimeter no longer defined by bars, barriers, and walls, but by the endless circling of flying watchtowers up above.

5

Pattern-of-Life Analysis

Enemy leaders look like everyone else; enemy combatants look like everyone else; enemy vehicles look like civilian vehicles; enemy installations look like civilian installations; enemy equipment and materials look like civilian equipment and materials.

—American Defense Science Board

"It is the strangest of bureaucratic rituals," write two *New York Times* reporters. "Every week or so, more than 100 members of the government's sprawling national security apparatus gather, by secure video teleconference, to pore over terrorist suspects' biographies and recommend to the president who should be the next to die."[1] In Washington, this weekly meeting has been labeled "Terror Tuesday." Once established, the list of nominees is sent to the White House, where the president orally gives his approval to each name. With the "kill list" validated, the drones do the rest.

The criteria that go into making these lists of people condemned to death without trial remain unknown. The administration refuses to provide any information on this subject. Harold Koh, the State Department's legal adviser, nevertheless tried to be reassuring: "Our procedures and practices for identifying lawful targets are extremely robust, and advanced technologies have helped to make our targeting even more precise."[2] In short: *Trust us, even blindfolded.*

Apart from these "personal strikes," there are also "signature strikes," here meaning strikes authorized on the basis of traces, indications, or defining characteristics. Such strikes target individuals whose identity remains unknown but whose behavior suggests, signals, or signs membership in a "terrorist organization."

In such cases, the strike is made "without knowing the precise identity of the individuals targeted." It depends solely on their behavior, which, seen from the sky, appears to "correspond to a 'signature' of pre-identified behavior that the United States links to militant activity."[3] Today, strikes of this type, against unknown suspects, appear to constitute the majority of cases.[4]

To locate these anonymous militants, targeters "rely on what officials describe as 'pattern of life analysis,' using evidence collected by surveillance cameras on the unmanned aircraft and from other sources about individuals and locations. . . . The information then is used to target suspected militants, even when their full identities are not known."[5] As one Reaper drone operator explains, "We can develop those patterns of life, determine who the bad guys are, and then get the clearance and go through the whole find, fix, track, target, attack cycle."[6]

Each and every person has a particular form or pattern of life. Your daily actions are repetitive, your behavior has certain regularities. For example, you rise at roughly the same hour and regularly make the same journey to work or elsewhere. You frequently meet up with the same friends in the same places. If you are placed under surveillance, it is possible to record all your movements and establish a spatiotemporal map of all your usual doings. Furthermore, by intercepting your telephone calls, observers can superimpose your social network upon this map, determine which are your personal links, and calculate the importance of each one in your life. As an American army manual explains: "While the enemy moves from point to point, reconnaissance or surveillance tracks and notes every location and person visited. Connections between those sites and persons to the target are built, and nodes in the enemy's network emerge."[7] Once this network of places and links in your life is established, it will be possible to predict your behavior: if it is not raining, on Saturday you will probably go jogging in a particular park at a particular time. But an observer may also perceive suspicious irregularities: today you have not followed your usual route, and you have met with someone in an unusual place. Any interruption of the norm that you yourself have established by your habits, any departure from your regular behavior, can sound an alarm bell: something abnormal and therefore potentially suspect is happening.

An analysis of the pattern of a person's life may be defined more precisely as "the fusion of link analysis and a geospatial analysis."[8] For some idea of what is involved here, imagine a superimposition, on a single map, of Facebook, Google Maps, and an Outlook calendar. This would be a fusion of social, spatial, and temporal particulars, a mixed mapping of the *socius*, *locus*, and *tempus* spheres—in other words, a combination of the three dimensions that, not only in their regularities but also in their discordances, constitute a human life.

This method stems from activity-based intelligence, or ABI. From the mass of information collected about a particular individual, group, or place gradually emerge patterns, or traceable themes. Activity becomes an alternative to identity. Once a target has been named, instead of trying to localize it, do quite the opposite. Start by establishing surveillance and gathering information. Next, make large-scale graphs to do an analysis of "big data," picking out nodular points that, by reason of the position and scale they occupy on the diagram, can be identified as threats that need to be neutralized.

"By compiling activity-based association data with its meta-data over time and adding analysis and reporting from many analysts," wrote Keith L. Barber of the National Geospatial-Intelligence Agency, "a rich archive will be formed to harvest patterns of life, networks and abnormalities which may have been overlooked otherwise."[9] The tools of human geography and the sociology of social networks are now enlisted in the service of a policy of eradication in which "persistent surveillance" makes it possible to pick out dangerous individuals. The painstaking work of establishing an archive of lives progressively gathers together the elements of a file that, once it becomes thick enough, will constitute a death warrant.

Officials claim that these methods ensure selective targeting. "You can track individuals and—patiently and carefully—build up a picture of how they move, where they go and what they see," noted a U.S. counterterrorism official.[10] Those who end up being killed "are people whose actions over time have made it obvious that they are a threat," added another.[11]

But the whole problem—at once epistemological and political—lies in this claimed ability to be able to correctly convert an assembly of probable indices into a legitimate target.

Both the means and the methodology are patently limited. As a former CIA officer admits, "You can only see so much from 20,000 feet."[12] A drone can distinguish shapes only more or less imprecisely. For example, in April 2011, American drones were "unable to discriminate the highly distinctive combat outline of two Marines (with full battle equipment) from the irregular enemy."[13] A telling joke made in the corridors of American power went, "When the CIA sees three guys doing jumping jacks, the agency thinks it's a terrorist training camp."[14]

On March 17, 2011, an American strike decimated a group
of men meeting in Datta Khel, Pakistan, on the grounds that
"they acted in a manner consistent with AQ [al-Qaeda]-
linked militants." [15] The manner of their gathering corre-
sponded to that predefined as resembling terrorist behavior.
But the meeting observed from the skies was actually a traditional assembly, a *jirga*, convoked to resolve a disagreement
in the local community. Seen from the sky, a village meeting
looks just like a gathering of militants. Between nineteen and
thirty civilians are estimated to have perished in the attack.

On September 2, 2010, the American authorities announced that they had eliminated an important Taliban
leader in Afghanistan. But in actual fact the missiles had
killed Zabet Amanullah, a civilian engaged in an electoral
campaign, as well as nine other people. That confusion was
possible only because of the excessive faith placed in quantitative analysis (necessary, however, for this kind of device):
the analysts had concentrated on SIM card data, the interception of phone calls, and graphs of social networks. Special
forces troops told journalist Kate Clark that "they were not
tracking the name, but targeting the telephones." [16]

As for establishing the truth, quantity of indications cannot be converted into quality. And that is certainly the problem since, as Gareth Porter explains,

> the link analysis methodology employed by intelligence
> analysis is incapable of qualitative distinctions among
> relationships depicted on their maps of links among
> "nodes." It operates exclusively on quantitative data—in
> this case the number of phone calls to or visits made to
> a pre-existing JPEL target or to other numbers in touch
> with that target. The inevitable result is that more num-
> bers of phones held by civilian non-combatants show up
> on the charts of insurgent networks. If the phone records

show multiple links to numbers already on the "kill/ capture" list, the individual is likely to be added to the list.[17]

In short, according to this theory, group membership and identity can be deduced from the number and frequency of contacts, regardless of their nature. Thus it is inevitable that, as one officer concluded, "if we decide [someone is] a bad person, the people with him are also bad." [18]

This profiling method works only with schemas. And a single schema may, by definition, correspond to a number of heterogeneous phenomena. Imagine that you see a shadow resembling a huge dog. If you have access only to the shadow, how can you tell with certainty what object created it? It may simply have been made by an arrangement of someone's hands as part of a shadow play.

It is nevertheless on the strength of such epistemological bases that "signature strikes" are today made by American drones. The authorities have built themselves a theater of shadows, but "the result, way too often, is firing blind based on 'pattern of life' indicators, without direct confirmation that the targets are, in fact, who we think they are— killing innocent people in the process." [19]

That echoed the words of a young Pakistani man, a victim, together with his family, of a drone strike, when he was asked why he thought they had been attacked: "They say there were terrorists, but it was my home. . . . There are no terrorists. It's just common people with beards." [20]

6

Kill Box

Nothing man can do on the surface of the earth can interfere
with a plane in flight, moving freely in a third dimension.
— Giulio Douhet

With the concept of a "global war against terror," armed
violence has lost its traditional limits: indefinite in time, it
is also indefinite in space.[1] The whole world, it is said, is a
battlefield. But it would probably be more accurate to call
it a hunting ground. For if the scope of armed violence has
now become global, it is because the imperatives of hunting
demand it.

While warfare is defined, in the last analysis, by combat, hunting is essentially defined by pursuit. Two distinct
types of geography correspond to the two activities. Combat
bursts out wherever opposing forces clash. Hunting, on the
other hand, takes place wherever the prey goes. As a hunter-
state sees it, armed violence is no longer defined within the
boundaries of a demarcated zone but simply by the presence
of an enemy-prey who, so to speak, carries with it its own
little mobile zone of hostility.

In order to elude its pursuers, the prey endeavors to render itself undetectable or inaccessible. Now, inaccessibility
is a matter not simply of the topography of the landscape—
bushy heaths or deep crevices—but also of the asperities of
political geography. As the theorists of manhunting remind

us, "borders are among the greatest allies" that a fugitive can have.[2] Out in the countryside, English common law used to authorize "the hunting of ravenous prey, such as badgers and foxes, in another man's land, because destroying such creatures is said to be profitable to the Public."[3] That is the kind of right that the United States today would like to claim in the case of human prey worldwide.[4] As Paul Wolfowitz has put it, we need "to deny them sanctuaries."[5]

What is emerging is the idea of an invasive power based not so much on the rights of conquest as on the rights of pursuit: a right of universal intrusion or encroachment that would authorize charging after the prey wherever it found refuge, thereby trampling underfoot the principal of territorial integrity classically attached to state sovereignty. According to such a concept, the sovereignty of other states becomes a contingent matter. Full enjoyment of that sovereignty is recognized only if those states take imperial tracking to heart. If they do not—"failed" states cannot, "rogue" states will not—their territories can legitimately be violated by a hunter-state.

The drone counters the terrestrial forms of territorial sovereignty, founded upon the enclosure of land, with the continuity of the air above. In doing so, it extends the great historical promises of aerial power. As Douhet puts it, the aerial weapon, unaffected by harsh landscapes, "moves freely through a third dimension."[6] It draws its own lines in the sky.

By becoming stratospheric, an imperial power alters its relationship to space. It now becomes a matter not so much of occupying a territory as of controlling it from above by ensuring its mastery of the skies. Eyal Weizman has explained a whole sector of contemporary Israeli strategy in those terms, describing it as a politics of verticality. In this "technology versus occupation model,"[7] the point is to "maintain domination of the evacuated areas by means other than territorial control."⁸ This verticalization of power implies a form of above-the-ground authority, in which everything—every individual, every house, every street, even the smallest event—"can thus be monitored, policed or destroyed from the air."⁹

The question of sovereignty now assumes an aeropolitical dimension¹⁰: who is it that holds the power over the air, and over the airwaves as well?¹¹ Alison Williams, who emphasizes the importance of thinking of political geography as a three-dimensional phenomenon, speaks of "a crisis of aerial sovereignty."¹² The repeated violations of subordinate aerial spaces by U.S. drones constitute one of today's most striking examples. Just as sovereignty is no longer flatly territorial but instead volumetric and three-dimensional, so too are the ways to challenge or deny it.

Stephen Graham explains that classical military doctrines used to rely on "the horizontal projection of power across an essential 'flat' and featureless geopolitical space."¹³ Today that mode of projection has been replaced or supplemented by another. To put that in very schematic terms, we have switched from the horizontal to the vertical, from the two-dimensional space of the old maps of army staffs to geopolitics based on volumes.

In contemporary doctrines of aerial power, operational space is no longer regarded as a homogeneous and continuous area. It has become "a dynamic mosaic where insurgent objectives and tactics may vary by neighborhood."¹⁴ We should see it as a patchwork of squares of color, each of which corresponds to specific rules of engagement.

But those squares are also, and above all, *cubes*. This is the central concept of the "kill box," a notion that emerged in the early 1990s: "The kill box is graphically portrayed by a solid black line defining the area with diagonal black lines within." [15] One should imagine a theater of operations portrayed on a screen in 3-D as a set of cubes laid out on a surface divided into squares.

A "kill box" has a particular life cycle: it is opened, activated, frozen, and then closed. One can follow these developments on a screen, rather like the defragmentation of a hard disc: small clusters that are activated and change color as they are used.

"When established, the primary purpose of a kill box is to allow air assets to conduct interdiction against surface targets without further coordination with the establishing commander." [16] Once one recognizes that "the mosaic nature of COIN [counterinsurgency] is ideally suited to decentralized execution," [17] each cube becomes "an autonomous zone of operations" for the combat units assigned to it.[18] To put this more clearly: within a given cube, one may fire at will. A kill box is a temporary autonomous zone of slaughter.

In this model, the conflict zone appears as a space fragmented into a provisional multitude of kill boxes that can be activated in a manner both flexible and bureaucratic. As General Richard P. Formica explained, with undisguised enthusiasm, in an e-mail: "Kill boxes enable us to do what we wanted to do for years . . . rapidly adjust the delineation of battlespace. . . . Now with automation technology and USAF [U.S. Air Force] employment of kill boxes, you really have a very flexible way of delineating battlespace both in time and on the ground." [19]

In a memo addressed in 2005 to secretary of defense Donald Rumsfeld, the president of the RAND Corporation advised him that "a non-linear system of 'kill boxes' should be adopted, as technology permits," for counterinsurgency operations.[20] He stressed the following essential point: "Kill boxes can be sized for open terrain or urban warfare and opened or closed quickly in response to a dynamic military situation." [21]

This twofold principle of intermittence and scalar modulation for the kill box is of capital importance: it makes it possible to envisage extending such a model beyond the zones of declared conflict. Depending on the contingencies of the moment, temporary lethal microcubes could be opened up anywhere in the world if an individual who qualifies as a legitimate target has been located there.

When American army strategists imagine what drones will be like in twenty-five years, they begin by getting an infographist to create a composite image of a typical Arab town, complete with mosque, other buildings, and palm trees. In the sky are what appear to be dragonflies, but they are actually nano-drones, autonomous robotic insects capable of marauding in a swarm and "navigating in increasingly confined spaces."[22]

With devices such as these, armed violence could be unleashed in tiny spaces, in microcubes of death. Rather than destroy an entire building in order to eliminate one individual, a miniaturized could be sent through a window, and the impact of the resulting explosion could be confined to one room or even one body. Your room or study could become a war zone.

Even before the advent of the micromachines of the future, drone partisans are already emphasizing the technological precision of their weapons. But the paradox is that they use this supposed gain in precision to extend the field of fire to take in the entire world. What we find here is a double movement that seizes upon the spatiolegal notion of an armed conflict zone in a way that tends to dislocate it almost completely. The two principles of this paradoxical dismemberment are the following: (1) The zone of armed conflict, having been fragmented into miniaturizable kill boxes, tends *ideally* to be reduced to the body of the enemy or prey. That is, his body becomes the battlefield. This is the principle of

precision or *specification*. (2) In order for the pursuit and surgical strikes to be carried out, this mobile microspace must
be able to be aimed wherever necessary—so the whole world
becomes a hunting ground. That is the principle of *globalization* or *homogenization*. According to the military and the
CIA, it is because we can aim at our targets with precision
that we can strike them down wherever we choose, even outside any war zone.

Similarly, a whole contingent of U.S. lawyers today claim
that the notion of a "zone of armed conflict" should no longer
be interpreted in a strictly geographic sense. That geocentric
concept, supposedly out of date, is now opposed to a target-
centered one that is attached to the bodies of the enemy prey.
The conflict zone now "goes where they go, irrespective of
geography," [23] and "the boundaries of the battlefield are not
determined by geopolitical lines but rather by the location of
participants in an armed conflict." [24]

One of their principal arguments, of a pragmatic rather
than legal nature, is borrowed directly from the discourse of
the American administration. The geocentric interpretation
of the laws of warfare must be thrown overboard, they obedi
ently insist, because to extend it would in effect "create sanctuaries for terrorist organizations in any state . . . in which
law enforcement is known to be ineffective." [25] But that argument, lurking beneath the semantic debate, also reveals
what is at stake politically: it aims to justify the use of lethal
policing powers regardless of borders.

As Derek Gregory points out, one of the problems is that
the "legal logic through which the battlespace is extended
beyond the declared zone of combat in Afghanistan is itself
infinitely extendable." [26] By redefining the notion of armed
conflict as a mobile place attached to the person of the enemy, one ends up, under cover of the laws of armed conflict, justifying the equivalent of a right to execute suspects

anywhere in the world, even in zones of peace, illegally and without further procedures, one's own citizens included.[27] Where will all this end? That is the question that the NGO Human Rights Watch put to Barack Obama in 2010: "The notion that the entire world is automatically by extension a battleground in which the laws of war are applicable is contrary to international law. How does the administration define the 'global battlefield' . . . ? Does it view the battlefield as global in a literal sense, allowing lethal force to be used, in accordance with the laws of war, against a suspected terrorist in an apartment in Paris, a shopping mall in London, or a bus station in Iowa City?"[28]

Reacting to the dangers of such an interpretation, critics defend a more classical notion of a zone of armed conflict, emphasizing the fundamental idea that armed violence and the laws that govern it operate within the context of space. That is, as a legal category, warfare is and should be a *geographically defined object*. Is one feature of armed conflict the fact that it occupies a particular place, a definable zone? Despite its apparent abstraction, this ontological question has decisive political implications. If the answer to that question is affirmative, a succession of truisms follow: war and peace have a legal geography if they are conceived to be states that succeed one another not only in time but also within definable spaces. A zone is a zone, a portion of space that is circumscribed, with limits, having an inside and an outside; an armed conflict is an armed conflict, characterized by a certain intensity of violence. But these simple definitions have extremely important normative implications, starting with the following: if the special laws of war apply only in the place where the fighting takes place, then beyond that place one has no right to behave as a warrior.

As the jurist Mary Ellen O'Connell, who describes the present-day drone strikes in Pakistan, Somalia, and Yemen as illegal, reminds us: "Drones launch missiles or drop bombs, the kind of weapons that may only be used lawfully in armed conflict hostilities."[29] The fact is that "there was no armed conflict on the territory of Pakistan because there was no intense armed fighting between organized armed groups. International law does not recognize the right to kill with battlefield weapons outside an actual armed conflict. The so-called 'global war on terror' is not an armed conflict."[30] These strikes therefore constitute grave violations of the laws of war.

It is immediately clear that the proposed globalized man-hunts stand in contradiction to this traditional interpretation of the law. Hence their promoters' intensive attempts to contest that view of the situation and to dismiss the notion that armed conflicts presuppose an implicit geographical ontology.[31] In the present struggle to extend the hunting domain, jurists stand in the front line, and the ontology that they apply constitutes their field of battle.[32] The question "What is a place?" becomes a matter of life or death. Perhaps the time has come to remember that by geographically confining the licit exercise of violence, the fundamental legal aim was to *circumscribe* it.

7

Counterinsurgency from the Air

Air power contains the seeds of our own destruction if we do
not use it responsibly. We can lose this fight.

—General Stanley A. McChrystal

When Ernesto "Che" Guevara wrote these lines, in 1960,
they were still true:

> One of the favorite arms of the enemy army, supposed
> to be decisive in modern times, is aviation. Nevertheless,
> this has no use whatsoever during the period that guer-
> rilla warfare is in its first stages, with small concentrations
> of men in rugged places. The utility of aviation lies in the
> systematic destruction of visible and organized defenses;
> and for this there must be large concentrations of men
> who construct these defenses, something that does not ex-
> ist in this type of warfare.[1]

Up until very recently, in what used to be called the "im-
perialist camp," strategists of counterinsurgency warfare
subscribed to Guevara's opinion. Against bunches of furtive
combatants, as skilled at hiding in the mazes of the landscape
as in the recesses of society, aerial weapons were considered
totally impotent or—worse still—counterproductive. In the
absence of concentrations of troops detectable from the sky,
bombing inevitably implied a bloodbath among the civilian

population. But in reality the reasons for rejecting this doctrine were less moral than strategic: while the declared objective of counterinsurgency warfare was to rally the civilian population, the use of blind violence was likely to have the opposite effect, driving civilians into the arms of the enemy. Hence the theoretical marginalization of aerial weaponry in this form of strategy. As late as 2006, the American army's *Counterinsurgency Field Manual* devoted no more than a few pages to aerial weaponry, relegating them to an appendix.

In practice, however, the situation was already beginning to swing the other way. With the use of drones rapidly spreading, from the 2000s onward aviation was becoming one of the essential weapons in American counterinsurgency operations. A few strategists set about theorizing this silent changeover: their aim was to make military practice self-aware, whatever the cost of a major doctrinal upset.

Deploring the time lag between theory and practice, Air Force strategists began to call for the explicit adoption of a doctrine of aerial counterinsurgency. These supporters of airpower clashed head-on with the orthodox theorists of ground-centered counterinsurgency, "an outworn paradigm . . . too narrowly focused," which "relegates airpower to the support role while the ground forces do the real work."[2] In opposition to that archaic world, it would be necessary to accept the evidence and fully come to terms with the new air-centered strategy in which drones have already become the foremost instrument. However much certain insurgents remained, as Carl Schmitt put it, essentially "telluric,"[3] contemporary counterinsurgents had become "stratospheric."

Guerrilla warfare has always posed problems for major powers, which regularly become bogged down in asymmetrical conflicts. Instead of direct confrontation, insurgents, in order to compensate for their provisional weakness, favor skirmishes and ambushes. By striking, then immediately withdrawing, they remain elusive. The drone seems to provide a tardy resolution to this historical problem: in a radically absolute form, it turns against the guerrillas their own long-established principle, namely, *deprive the enemy of an enemy*. An insurgent confronted by an army of drones no longer has any target to attack. "We pray to Allah that we have American soldiers to kill. These bombs from the sky we cannot fight," said Maulvi Abdullah Haijazi, an Afghan villager reacting to American strikes.[4] American officers delight in those words; they consider the statement as confirming the implacable efficacy of their new weapon.

In making combat impossible and transforming armed combat into execution, the aim is to annihilate the very willpower of those opposing them. As Charles Dunlap, a major general in the U.S. Air Force, explains, "Death per se does not extinguish the will to fight in such opponents; rather, it is the hopelessness that arises from the inevitability of death from a source they cannot fight."[5] He goes on to say, "The precision and persistence of today's airpower creates opportunities to dislocate the psychology of the insurgents."[6] The idea is not a new one. In the twentieth century, Sir John Bagot Glubb had already expressed it in very similar terms when speaking of the aerial bombing by means of which the British put down native rebellions in the interwar period: "Their tremendous moral effect is largely due to the demoralization engendered in the tribesman by his feeling of helplessness and his inability to reply effectively to the attack."[7]

It is fighting by means of terror, and no attempt is made to disguise the fact. Says Dunlap, "American precision airpower is analogous (on a much larger and more effective scale) to the effect that insurgents try to impose . . . through the use of improvised explosive devices."[8] The point could not be made more clearly: at a tactical level (and setting aside technological sophistication), drone strikes are equivalent to bomb attacks. They constitute the weapons of state terrorism.

Air force strategists are well aware of the objections that theorists of the "historical channel" of counterinsurgency never fail to raise. What the latter urge, in so many words, is to remember the lessons of the past: what is being presented as a new strategy has already been tried out, with remarkably disastrous results. The doctrine of "air control" is no different from that behind the Royal Air Force (RAF) air raids used after World War I to "disrupt and destroy villages to force the local populace to adhere to British mandates." [9]

That policy ended in bitter failure. An assessment made by a British officer in 1923 describes perverse effects strangely similar to those seen today, three generations later, in the same regions of the world: "By driving the inhabitants of the bombarded area from their homes in a state of exasperation, dispersing them among neighboring clans and tribes, with hatred in their hearts at what they consider 'unfair' methods of warfare, these attacks bring about the exact political results which it is so important, in our own interests, to avoid, viz. the permanent embitterment and alienation of the frontier tribes." [10]

As Angelina Maguinness, an intelligence officer at U.S. Special Operations Command, somewhat prophetically pointed out, in view "of the historical lessons from the implementation of RAF air control, it is *interesting* that prominent airpower theorists would offer airpower as an alternative to large ground forces in COIN strategy." [11] In more emphatic terms, she goes on to reproach the partisans of the air-centered model for making a fundamental mistake about the very essence of counterinsurgency strategy: "[Airpower theorist Phillip] Meilinger fails to consider the nature of insurgency and COIN. If the center of gravity is the population and the population resides, operates, and identifies itself in the ground dimension, then it is foolish to assume the US can modify the nature of COIN warfare to that which it wants to fight and still succeed. . . . Insurgencies are by nature primarily ground-oriented; thus, effective COIN campaigns are primarily oriented in this manner as well." [12]

This debate over the respective merits of ground and air warfare is of a quasi-metaphysical nature: can counterinsurgency rise to the level of an aero-policy without losing its soul? There is of course a risk that in the course of the operation, the strategy—together with politics—may be lost in the clouds.

The partisans of counterinsurgency with drones claim to have succeeded in avoiding the mistakes of the past, and all thanks to the progress of technology. To be sure, in the past "the negative effects of imprecise weapons and collateral damage appear to have more than counteracted the tactical advantages" of aviation. In fact, they go on to say, it was those unfortunate historical experiences that lent credibility to "the truism that COIN is about boots on the ground and that airpower is counterproductive." [13] But all that is now behind us: the drone is a highly technological instrument. The twofold revolution in persistent surveillance and in the precision of targeting, they declare, has consigned those old objections to the dustbins of history.

As Hannah Arendt warned us, the problem of political lying is that the liar himself ends up believing his lies. [14] Certainly the overall impression here seems to be that of a discursive self-intoxication. As a result of repeatedly proclaiming that drones and other surgical strikes are so accurate that they cause no more than negligible collateral damage, supporters of that strategy seem truly to have come to believe that all serious adverse effects have been eliminated. However, the facts won't go away, and their message is quite the opposite.

David Kilcullen is certainly no pacifist. This former advisor to General David Petraeus in Iraq is today considered to be one of the United States' most eminent experts in the doctrine of counterinsurgency. In 2009 he, alongside Andrew McDonald Exum, co-signed an op-ed piece in the *New York Times* calling for a moratorium on drone strikes in Pakistan.[15] Their diagnosis was simple: those operations were dangerously counterproductive for American interests. People were congratulating themselves on short-term tactical successes without seeing that they would pay dearly for them at a strategic level.

In the first place, they pointed out, the end effect of such strikes was to drive the civilian population into the arms of the extremist groups that on the whole appeared "less ominous than a faceless enemy that wages war from afar and often kills more civilians than militants."[16] They went on to declare: "The drone strategy is similar to French aerial bombardment in rural Algeria in the 1950s, and to the 'air control' methods employed by the British in what are now the Pakistani tribal areas in the 1920s. The historical resonance of the British effort encourages people in the tribal areas to see the drone attacks as a continuation of colonial-era policies."[17]

Second, this anger and tendentious radicalization of public opinion were not limited to the region suffering such strikes. In a globalized world, armed violence produces transnational repercussions, and the widely shared perception is that of a hateful power that is both cowardly and contemptuous. Beware of a backlash.

Third, and perhaps above all: "The use of drones displays every characteristic of a tactic—or, more accurately, a piece of technology—substituting for a strategy."[18] Their final diagnosis was that by resorting on a massive scale to a technological gadget that took the place of a genuine strategy, the state ran the risk of a rapid stupefying political effect.

What is in fact at stake here, deep down in these internal debates within the U.S. military apparatus, is nothing less than an understanding of politics. To understand this fully, a very brief and partial genealogy of the doctrines being torn apart here may be necessary.

This genealogy starts with a number of French strategists who were attempting to elaborate a counterrevolutionary strategy and had dipped into the works of Mao Zedong, Che Guevara, and many others. From their cursory reading of theories of revolutionary warfare they had, for their own purposes, noted the following fundamental thesis: the struggle is above all political. David Galula, who taught in military schools across the Atlantic after serving in Algeria, condensed those theories into a canonical formula: "The battle for the population is a major characteristic of the revolutionary war." [19] Like guerrilla warfare, counterinsurgency warfare is above all political. Its center of gravity is the local population, who must be disconnected from the enemy and won over to one's cause. The strategic aim is to marginalize the enemy and deny it its popular base.[20] Once that is achieved, the victory is won.

For those who adhere to this notion—Kilcullen, for example—the antagonism between insurgency and counterinsurgency is seen as "a struggle to control a contested political space." [21] This cannot be engineered from outside; in order to reconquer the terrain, which is both geographical and political, you have to be there, on the spot. A terrain cannot be controlled vertically, from the skies, only horizontally, on the ground. This is particularly true when the actual "terrain" is human, namely, the population itself, starting with what it thinks, believes, and perceives. The art of counterinsurgency, meanwhile, is " 'political warfare' in which the perception of the action and its political results are more important than tactical successes on the field of battle." [22] What is at stake are the perceived political effects of the military operations upon the population, and it is those effects that determine the pertinence of the tactics and weapons employed. As the time-honored expression has it, conquering the "hearts and minds" of the population presupposes mobilizing a whole vast spread of "military, political, economic, psychological and civic" means, among which open force is not always necessarily the principal component. [23] Those fine words, of course, should be set in comparison to the corresponding historical practices.

The fact remains that it is this fundamentally politico-military understanding of counterinsurgency, paradoxically inherited from a revolutionary Marxist understanding of armed violence, that today causes the advocates of the demographic- and territory-centered orthodox doctrine to reject the promotion of the drone to the position of being the almost exclusive weapon of American-style counterinsurgency. When Kilcullen opposes the technological fetishism of the drone, it is in the name of that strategic conception, following directly in the footsteps of Galula. "At the operational level counterinsurgency remains a competition between several sides, each seeking to mobilize the population in its cause," he writes. "The people remain the prize." [24]

As the counterinsurgency specialists see it, what is happening is a dangerous paradigm switch that undermines both the strategy of the American armed forces and their own institutional position within those forces. To those specialists, the dronization of operations signals the preeminence of the antiterrorism paradigm over that of counterinsurgency.

Originally, they explain, the two expressions were virtually synonymous, differing only in the way they were used.

The "antiterrorism" label was, on account of its negative connotations, used mostly as a rhetorical means of delegitimizing adverse insurrectional movements.[25] It was in the 1970s in Europe, faced with the actions of the Red Army Faction and the Red Brigades, that antiterrorism progressively turned itself into an independent paradigm, founded upon different principles that broke away from the classic doctrinal framework of counterinsurgency. The differences are significant.

Whereas counterinsurgency is essentially politico-military, antiterrorism fundamentally has to do with policing and security. This fundamental divergence in orientation is reflected in several other distinctive features.

First, there is a difference in the way that the enemy is conceived. Whereas the first paradigm regards insurgents as the "representatives of deeper claims at the heart of society"[26] (and it is important to understand the reasons for this, in order to counteract them effectively), the second one, by labeling them "terrorist," regards them above all as "aberrant individuals," dangerous figures, quite simply mad, or as incarnations of pure evil.

With these new labels, the targets are no longer political adversaries to be opposed, but criminals to be apprehended or eliminated. Whereas counterinsurgency strategy aims above all to "defeat the insurgents' strategy, rather than to 'apprehend the perpetrators' of specific acts,"[27] antiterrorism adopts a strictly opposite way of proceeding: its policing logic individualizes the problem and reduces its objectives to neutralizing, on a case-by-case basis, as many suspects as possible. Whereas counterinsurgency is population-centered, antiterrorist action is individual-centered. It is a matter not of cutting the enemy off from the population but solely of rendering it impossible for him personally to do any more harm. In these circumstances, the solution lies in tracking such people down one by one, regardless of the social or geo-political reasons for the antagonism they express. Within the categories of policing, political analysis dissolves.

Antiterrorism, which is both moralizing and Manichean, abandons any real analysis of the roots of hostility and its own effects upon it. The binary nature of good and evil is no longer just a rhetorical ploy but is imposed as an analytical category, to the detriment of any consideration of the complexity of strategic relations. Whereas counterinsurgency strategy implies (apart from brute force) compromise, diplomatic action, pressure, and agreements, all of which operate under constraint, antiterrorism excludes any political impact upon the conflict. "We do not negotiate with terrorists" is the key phrase in radically nonstrategic thought.

Dronized manhunting represents the triumph, both practical and doctrinal, of antiterrorism over counterinsurgency. According to this logic, the total body count and a list of hunting trophies take the place of a strategic evaluation of the political effects of armed violence. Successes become statistics. Their evaluation is totally disconnected from their real effects on the ground.

The partisans of orthodox doctrine are uneasy: as they see it, in the middle or long term, this reorientation is bound to produce effects that are strategically catastrophic for American interests. Drones are without doubt excellent at pulverizing bodies from a distance but are totally unsuited to winning over "hearts and minds." As Peter Matulich writes, "The current use of drones in counter-terrorism strikes in Pakistan is contrary to the effective COIN doctrine the US has developed over the past ten years. . . . [D]rone operations as they currently stand are of limited use if not counterproductive. Drones alone are incapable of facilitating the population-centric goals of COIN. Their use in 'clearing' operations produces negative effects including collateral damage and the militarization of local populations. This not only alienates populations but can fuel further insurgency." [28]

Evidence provided by a Pakistani Taliban leader, Baitullah Mehsud, illustrates the apparent truth of that thesis: "I spent three months trying to recruit and only got 10–15 persons. One US attack and I got 150 volunteers." [29] This pattern seems to have been forgotten by the American forces, which is particularly surprising since it appears printed in black and white in the military's own handbooks: "Confrontational military action, in exclusion, is counter-productive in most cases; it risks generating popular resentment, creating martyrs that motivate new recruits, and producing cycles of revenge." [30] But is it really a case of forgetfulness?

Perhaps, but perhaps not; for, as defenders of the orthodox doctrine fear, it is perfectly possible that the proposed reorganization of airpower may in fact be far more radical, purely and simply doing away with the political aspects of classic counterinsurgency theory. Thus Dunlap insistently stresses that the official doctrine tends to "overemphasize what 'hearts and mind-winning' efforts by occupying troops can achieve." [31] Furthermore, he pleads that it is important not to "undervalue the function of force in suppressing intractable insurgents." [32] "Where historically there was much discussion about the effect, or the lack thereof, of airpower on the civilian populations of hostile nations, now the issue is very different: it focuses on the psychological impact on the insurgents themselves, not the civilian population." [33]

What we are witnessing here is a redistribution of priorities: the yield from a policy designed to terrorize and eradicate now takes precedence over any consideration of its political effects on the population. So what if the drones make the population turn away from us? Who cares? What do the "hearts and minds" of villagers in Waziristan or anywhere else matter? And in any case, unlike in the old colonial wars, the objective is no longer to conquer a territory but simply to eliminate from afar the "terrorist threat."

Seen in this light, the intensive recourse to drones takes on new meaning. Richard Andres, an Air Force special advisor, reports that the tactical limitation of the old air weapons was that "they could not kill or suppress insurgents fast enough to overcome enemy recruiting."[34] Reading between the lines, we should understand that an armada of hunter-killer drones at last does possess that capacity: it can win that race and eliminate individuals at least as fast as new ones are recruited. The strategic plan of air counterinsurgency is now clear: as soon as a head grows back, cut it off. And never mind if, in a spiraling development of attacks and reprisals that is hard to control, the perverse effect of that prophylactic measure is to attract new volunteers. From this point of view, the objection that drone strikes are counterproductive because they allow the enemy, in a classic pattern of action and repression, to recruit more volunteers no longer applies. Never mind if the enemy ranks thicken, since it will always be possible to neutralize the new recruits as fast as they emerge. The cull will be repeated periodically, in a pattern of infinite eradication. Once antiterrorism overtakes counterinsurgency, we are led to understand, the sufficient aim becomes a regular elimination of emerging threats, which takes the form of a periodic reaping: "Kill enough of them and the threat goes away. . . . However, the 'kill list' . . . never gets shorter, the names and faces are simply replaced."[35] Caught up in an endless spiral, the eradication strategy is, paradoxically, destined never to eradicate. The very dynamics of its perverse effects prevent it from ever fully decapitating a hydra that regenerates itself ceaselessly as a result of the strategy's own negativity.

The partisans of the drone as a privileged weapon of

"antiterrorism" promise a war without losses or defeats. What they fail to mention is that it will also be a war without victory. The scenario that looms before us is one of infinite violence, with no possible exit; the paradox of an untouchable power waging interminable wars toward perpetual war.

8

Vulnerabilities

These imposters sold charms that made people invulnerable in warfare and fortunate in hunting and preserved them from all danger.

—Charles-Etienne Brasseur de Bourbourg

The great myths of invulnerability are almost all accounts of failure. The heroes are invulnerable, except at one point. Achilles' body is entirely "impenetrable by iron," with the exception of his heel. Siegfried, who was bathed in the entrails of a dragon, has a body covered "with skin as hard as scales, unaffected by the blows of an axe," except for his right shoulder, on which the leaf of a lime tree had alighted.[1] Heracles envelops the child Ajax in the pelt of a Nemean lion, and this makes Ajax's body invulnerable except in his armpits, which were not in contact with the wild beast's hide. In Persian mythology, Zoroaster pours enchanted water over the head of Isfendiyar, but the latter makes the mistake of closing his eyes, so Rustam will be able to fell him by shooting an arrow into his right eye. In the Nordic fables, Frigga, the mother of Baldur, makes all beings, both animate and inanimate, swear to spare her son. All swear the oath except for one puny plant, mistletoe, which she had omitted to invite to the meeting.

The message of these myths is that invulnerability is precisely that, a myth. There is always one unforeseen weak point, one flaw. He has felled a dragon but will die from a fallen leaf. The lesson is not only that invulnerability can never be total, but also that any attempt to achieve invulnerability in turn engenders a corresponding vulnerability. It is by grasping Achilles' body in order to plunge it into the river that Thetis makes it invulnerable and at the same time produces its vulnerable point, which is the spot at which she grasped it. With regard to invulnerability and vulnerability, these two, far from excluding one another, each summon up the other.

This warning may also be read as a prescription: when faced with an enemy who is seemingly invulnerable or who wishes to be so, find the fault, seek out the Achilles' heel. Everything depends upon discovering in what way the seemingly invulnerable one is vulnerable. Combat presupposes an inquiry, and that inquiry concerns the body of the enemy.

In the Middle Ages, before gunpowder upset the socio-technical conditions for life and death in battle, it was said that the knights had managed "to render themselves almost invulnerable by thinking of joining together their pieces of armor so closely that neither spear nor sword nor dagger could penetrate easily to their bodies and making that armor so hard that no piece could be pierced."[2] Consequently, however, "part of the skill of combatants, both in battles and in single combat, lay in finding a fault in the armor."[3]

There is a time lag between what happens on the ground and when the drone operators see the image of that on their screen. The problem lies with the signal's latency. Space, which it was claimed could be suppressed by technical means, made a comeback in the form of an incomprehensible time lag. All that the operators have to aim at is the slightly obsolete image of an earlier situation. The *New York Times* reports that targets now make the most of this asynchrony:

when individuals think that they are being hunted by a drone, they adopt zigzag movements.[4]

A far cry from the all-powerful image that they wish to convey, drones are fragile weapons, riddled with faults and deep contradictions. They have multiple vulnerabilities. First are the technological ones. Their use presupposes mastery over the airspace in which they move. If this condition, automatically acquired in the context of asymmetrical warfare in which the enemy lacks effective antiair defenses, should disappear, most of the present-day drones would, as David Deptula himself admits, simply "start falling from the sky like rain."[5]

Mastery over the airwaves is also necessary. In 2009, the press reported that Iraqi insurgents had managed to intercept the video feeds transmitted by Predator drones.[6] To accomplish this, all they needed was a satellite antenna and software that could be purchased on the Internet for $26. Convinced of their own technological superiority, the American military had apparently not taken the elementary precaution of effectively encrypting their transmissions.

The Israeli army recently realized that as a result of similar negligence, Hezbollah had over the past ten years developed the capacity to intercept video feeds from Israeli drones, which enabled that organization to, among other things, pinpoint the position of the Israeli battalions on the ground, the better to ambush them.[7] Armed surveillance was, without the Israelis knowing it, lending its eyes to the enemy. One of the classic principles of guerrilla warfare is to supply oneself with weapons taken from the enemy camp. It is a rule that today is equally valid for the electromagnetic components of one's arsenal.

If the signals emitted by the drones have been so easily intercepted, it is not beyond the bounds of possibility that the flows of data that control them could likewise be hacked. The air pirates of the future will use software to crack codes and take control from a distance. In 2011 *Wired* magazine revealed that malware had infected the Creech Air Force Base computers, including those handled by drone operators.[8] This involved a software spy of the keylogger variety, capable of recording keystrokes and transmitting them to a third party in such a way as to make it possible to recover passwords. That threat remained relatively benign, but it is obviously possible to envisage other scenarios. Just like any other connected computer system, the drone is vulnerable to intrusions. A computer army can be paralyzed by a viral attack more efficiently than by bombs.

The option of having totally robotized drones would certainly eliminate any problems involving humans in the command centers. However, it would have another security weakness: these machines would be dependent upon GPS data, which can easily be jammed or manipulated. In the course of a test organized by the American authorities in June 2012, a group of researchers from the University of Texas demonstrated how easily a drone could be brought down in this way. Thanks to an apparatus put together at the cost of a few thousand dollars' worth of material, "we fooled the UAV into thinking that it was rising straight up."[9] The drone's autopilot immediately compensated, sending the drone toward the ground. If no one had intervened, it would have crashed.

However, the faults are not solely technical. They are also politico-strategic. In 1999, two Chinese strategists suggested that the American preference for "zero dead" offered the United States' adversaries a rapid, easy, and low-cost means of thwarting the world's greatest power: "These common American soldiers who should be on the battlefield have now become the most costly security in war, like precious china bowls that people are afraid to break. All of the opponents who have engaged in battle with the American military have probably mastered the secret of success—if you have no way of defeating this force, you should kill its rank and file soldiers." [10] The dronization of the armed forces further radicalizes this strategic fault. If the military withdraws from the battlefield, enemy violence will turn against targets that are easier to reach. Even if the soldiers are beyond reach, civilians are not. As one American soldier explains, "We must understand that attempts to armorize our force against all potential enemy threats ... shifts the 'burden of risk' from a casualty-averse military force onto the populace. In doing so, we have lifted the burden from our own shoulders and placed it squarely upon those who do not possess the material resources to bear it—the civilian populace." [11] The paradox is that hyperprotection of military personnel tends to compromise the traditional social division of danger, in which soldiers are at risk and civilians are protected. By maximizing the protection of military lives and making the inviolability of its "safe zone" the mark of its power, a state that uses drones tends to divert reprisals toward its own population.[12]

This type of scenario is all the more probable given that the viability of the security model associated with the principle of "projecting power without projecting vulnerability" rests upon very fragile assumptions. It postulates that the establishment of an effective domestic "safe zone" is possible—that the danger, the threat, the enemy can be absolutely confined to the space outside.[13] This assumption runs up against the problem of the irreducible porosity of frontiers. There is no wall high enough, no barrier sufficiently impassable to guarantee the absolute isolation of a national "gated community."

The military drone is a low-cost weapon—at least in comparison to classic fighter planes. That has long been one of the principal selling points for such a weapon. But of course the contradiction lies in the fact that it is in the nature of such a weapon to proliferate.

What does Francis Fukuyama do after the end of history? In his leisure hours, he puts together little drones in his garage and then proudly exhibits them on his blog.[14] He is part of an rapidly developing subculture: that of the homemade drone. Following in the footsteps of the model enthusiasts of the 1960s, there today exists a whole little community of amateurs who buy or construct drones at the cost of a few hundred dollars. With their microcameras on board, these machines make it possible to produce unofficial little films, some of which are strikingly beautiful. I am thinking in particular of a flight over New York in which, once over the Brooklyn Bridge, the camera scans the facades of the skyline, ending up by gliding past the flame on the Statue of Liberty.[15] Proof enough of the validity of Walter Benjamin's thesis that technology, today used for death-dealing purposes, may eventually recover its emancipating potential and readopt the playful and aesthetic aspirations that secretly inspire it.

But even if the drone can and should be demilitarized, it is also perfectly possible to convert such homemade machines into daunting unconventional weapons at little cost. The Russian researcher Eugene Miasnikov sees in amateur drones a "suicide bomber on steroids": unlike a suicide bomber, an amateur drone "can easily penetrate security and threaten otherwise safe areas (e.g., the Green Zone) or reach crowded public places like sports stadiums."[16]

In November 2006, a confidential report produced by the U.S. military noted that a new technique was being used by the insurgents in Iraq. Suicide bombers were now equipped with a camera that transmitted images directly to their superiors. Thanks to this equipment, "a second member of a terrorist cell is able to observe the activities of the suicide bomber via a miniature camera installed in the vest. The second member will ensure the bomber approaches the intended target and actually conducts the detonation. Should the bomber fail to detonate the device, the observer is able to detonate the device remotely." [17]

A human drone is thus invented: a man, remotely controlled by others, who can be blown up at any moment, thanks to a long-distance detonating device. The irony is that commanders in the opposite camp might, thanks to the video cameras installed on the helmets of their own soldiers, be watching as some individual approaches and makes suspicious gestures. From the snow that simultaneously covers their respective screens, those on both sides will instantly know that their men have perished. Once this stage is reached, the next step in perfecting the art of assassination is to do without the man carrying the bomb: move on from a dronized partisan to, quite simply, a drone.

II

Ethos and Psyche

9

Drones and Kamikazes

To me, the robot is our answer to the suicide bomber.

—Bart Everett

Walter Benjamin did some thinking about drones, radio-controlled planes that the military thinkers of the mid-1930s were already imagining.[1] He used this example to illustrate the difference between what he called the "first technique," which could be traced back to prehistoric art, and the "second technique," which was characteristic of modern industry. As he saw it, the distinction between them was not so much the inferiority or archaism of the one in comparison to the other but rather a "difference of trends." "The first technique," he wrote, "engages the human being as much as possible, the second as little as possible. The great technological feat of the first technique is, in a manner of speaking, the human sacrifice; that of the second lies along the lines of remote-controlled airplanes that don't require any human crew." [2]

On one hand, the techniques of sacrifice; on the other, those of play. On one hand, integral engagement; on the other, total disengagement. On one hand, the uniqueness of a living action; on the other, the limitless reproducibility of a mechanical gesture. Wrote Benjamin, "*Once and for all* is the motto that applies to the first technique (it deals with the forever irreparable lapse or the eternal vicariousness of the sacrificial death). *Once is nothing* is the motto of the second technique (it has to do with the experimentation and its tireless variations of the test set-up)."[3]

On one hand, the kamikaze or the suicide bomber, who crashes once and for all in a single explosion; on the other, the drone, which fires its missiles repeatedly, as if nothing happened.

Whereas the kamikaze implies a total fusion of the fighter's body and weapon, the drone ensures their radical separation. The kamikaze: *My body is a weapon.* The drone: *My weapon has no body.* The former implies the death of the agent. The latter totally excludes it. Kamikazes are those for whom death is certain. Drone pilots are those for whom death is impossible. In this sense, they represent two opposite poles on the spectrum of exposure to death. In between the two are classic fighters, those for whom death is a risk.

One speaks of "suicide bombing" or of "suicide assassination," but what would be the antonym? There is no specific expression to designate those who kill by explosion without ever risking their lives. Not only is it not *necessary* for them to die in order to kill, but it is *impossible* for them to be killed as they kill.

Contrary to the evolutionist schema that Benjamin, in truth, only suggested, the better to subvert it, the kamikaze and the drone—the weapon of sacrifice and the weapon of self-preservation—did not succeed each other chronologically, one following from the other as history follows from prehistory, On the contrary, they emerged together, as two opposed but historically simultaneous tactics.

In the mid-1930s, an engineer working for the RCA read an article about the Japanese army that greatly alarmed him. From that article he learned that the Japanese were training squadrons of pilots for suicide aircraft. Long before the tragic surprise attack on Pearl Harbor, Vladimir Zworykin understood the scale of this threat: "The efficiency of this method, of course, is yet to be proven but if such a psychological training of personnel is possible, this weapon will be of the most dangerous nature. We hardly can expect to introduce such methods in our country and therefore have to rely on our technical superiority to meet the difficulty."[4] At that time the United States already possessed prototypes of "radio-controlled planes" that could be used as air torpedoes. Bur the problem was that these remote-controlled devices were blind. Noted Zworykin, "They lose their efficiency as soon as they are beyond visual contact with the directing base. The solution to this problem was evidently found by the Japanese." That solution was the kamikaze: since the pilot has eyes and is ready to die, he is able to guide the machine right to its target.

However, Zworykin was also one of the pioneers of television. And therein, of course, lay the solution: "One possible means of obtaining practically the same results as the suicide pilot is to provide a radio-controlled torpedo with an electric eye."[5]

The operator would be able to watch the target right to the end and, through radio control, visually guide the weapon to the point of impact.

Coupling television with the remote-controlled plane, Zworykin had discovered the formula that, much later, would become that of both "smart bombs" and armed drones: remove from the plane any part of the pilot save an electronic retina, with the pilot's actual body remaining elsewhere, out of range of the enemy antiair defenses.

Zworykin's text is remarkable because, though his was one of the very first theoretical formulations, he recognized the ancestor of the drone as an anti-kamikaze, and did so not only from the logical point of view of his definition but also and above all at a tactical level. This was the weapon that responded to the kamikaze both as its antidote and as its twin. The drone and the kamikaze constituted two opposed practical options for resolving one and the same problem, that of guiding the bomb to its target. What the Japanese intended to bring about through psychological training and their mores of sacrifice, the Americans would achieve through material technology and purely technical procedures.

The conceptual genesis of the drone takes place within the framework of an ethico-technical economy of life and death in which technological power takes over from a form of undemandable sacrifice. While on one side there were to be courageous combatants ready to sacrifice themselves for the cause, on the other there were to be nothing but ghostly machines.

This antagonism between the kamikaze and remote control reappears today: suicide bombings versus phantom bombings. The polarity is primarily economic. It sets those who have nothing but their bodies with which to fight in opposition to those who possess capital and technology. But these two regimes, the one tactical, the other material, also correspond to two different ethical regimes: the ethic of heroic sacrifice, on one hand, and the ethic of vital self-preservation, on the other.

The drone and the kamikaze stand in contrast as two opposed forms of moral sensibility, two forms of ethos that reflect each other but are each other's antithesis and nightmare. What is at stake in this difference, at least on the face of it, is a particular concept of one's relationship to death, both one's own and that of others; to sacrifice or self-preservation; to danger and to courage and to vulnerability and destructiveness. Involved here are two political and affective economies regarding one's relationship to death, both the death that one deals and that to which one exposes oneself; but also two opposed concepts or visions of horror.

Richard Cohen, a columnist at the *Washington Post*, sets out his view of the situation: "As for the Taliban fighters, they not only don't cherish life, they expend it freely in suicide bombings. It's difficult to envisage an American suicide bomber."[6] He asserts: "There is really no such thing as an American suicide bomber. We don't extol the bomber and parade his or her children before the TV cameras so that other children will envy them for the death of a parent. This is odd to us. This is chilling to us. This is downright repugnant." Then he adds complacently, "Maybe we have come to cherish life too much."[7]

So what is "odd," "chilling," and "repugnant" is being ready to die in the struggle and find glory in so doing. The old idol of martial sacrifice, falling directly from its pedestal into the enemy clutches, has become utterly repellent, the epitome of moral horror. Sacrifice, at once incomprehensible and ignoble and immediately interpreted as scorn for life (without any sense that it may, on the contrary, imply scorn for death), is opposed by an ethic based on a love of life—of which the drone surely represents the ultimate expression. As an ultimate affectation, we admit that we love life so much that we do perhaps overprotect it. This excessive love would certainly be excusable were it not that so much self-complacency hints at self-love. For, contrary to Cohen's claims, it is certainly *our* lives, not life in general, that we hold so dear. If the case of an American kamikaze seems to be inconceivable, that is because it would be an oxymoron. Here life could not possibly be denied, for the very good reason that the only life that is denied is that of others.

When questioned by a journalist in order to find out if it was "true that Palestinians were not concerned about human life, not even that of those close to them," Eyad El-Sarraj, the director of the mental health program in Gaza, replied, "How can you believe in your own humanity if you do not believe in the humanity of the enemy?" [8]

In what respect might it be less horrible to kill without exposing oneself than to share the fate of one's victims? In what respect might a weapon making it possible to kill without danger be less repugnant than the opposite? Jacqueline Rose, amazed that "dropping cluster bombs from the air is not only less repugnant: it is somehow deemed, by Western leaders at least, to be morally superior," asks herself why "dying with your victim should be seen as a greater sin than saving yourself." [9]

Hugh Gusterson adds that an "anthropologist from Mars might note that many people in the Middle East feel about U.S. drone attacks the way that Richard Cohen feels toward suicide-bombers. The drone attacks are widely perceived in the Middle East as cowardly, because the drone pilot is killing people on the ground from the safety of an air-conditioned pod in Nevada, where there is no chance that he can be killed by those he is attacking." [10]

Talal Asad suggests that the horror provoked in Western societies by suicide bombings lies in the fact that the author of the attack, through his action, a priori rules out any kind of retributive justice. By dying with his victim, coagulating both crime and punishment within a single action, he makes punishment impossible and thereby deactivates the fundamental resort of a form of justice conceived in the penal mode. [11] He will never be able "to pay for what he has done."

The horror aroused by the idea of death administered by pilotless machines is perhaps connected to a similar perception. Gusterson goes on to say, "The drone operator is also a mirror image of the suicide bomber in that he too deviates, albeit in the opposite direction, from our paradigmatic image of combat." [12]

Death in combat. From Jean de Vauzelles, *Imagines mortis* (Cologne: Birckmann, 1555), ill. 40 (detail).

10

"That Others May Die"

You can run . . . but you'll only die tired.
                        —T-shirt glorifying the Predator drone

In the early twentieth century one military author provided
a glimpse into the state of mind of the crews of the first military submarines at a time when, without sonar, surface vessels were totally incapable of detecting their presence: "They
were invulnerable. For them, the war became a game, a sport,
a kind of hunt in which, having dispensed and distributed
murder, they needed to do nothing but enjoy the spectacle
of the agony of their victims. They, meanwhile, would be
sheltered from any attacks and, once back in port, they could
busy themselves recounting their hunting prowess." [1]

Using new means, the drone procures for its operators an
even greater sense of invulnerability. Today as yesterday, the
radical imbalance in exposure to death leads to a redefinition
of relations of hostility and of the very sense of what is called
"waging war." Warfare, by distancing itself totally from the
model of hand-to-hand combat, becomes something quite
different, a "state of violence" of a different kind. It degenerates into slaughter or hunting. One no longer fights the
enemy; one eliminates him, as one shoots rabbits.

In the sixteenth century, a book of images of death represented an armed warrior fighting against a skeleton—death
itself. It was an allegory of a derisory struggle, a vain combat

lost in advance, since death never dies. It has time on its side, and the eyes of the soldier confronting it seem already empty.

Today, drone operators have been happy to take over that classical imagery. The badge of the MQ-9 Reaper drone shows the reaper, with its disturbing grin and blood dripping from its blade, accompanied by the motto "That others may die."

This is by no means unprecedented. Every time that, as Voltaire put it, "whoever was rich became almost invulnerable in war," warfare turned into one-sided killing.[2] As soon as one camp made itself practically untouchable through an overwhelming superiority in weaponry, life and death took

The badge of the Reaper.

up their positions in an exclusive fashion on one or the other side of the front line.

But every time such situations arose, certain contemporaries were troubled. Faced with a spectacle of armed violence that so manifestly contravened "the conventional understanding of war as an activity in which human dying and killing are exchanged," it was not long before they expressed their indignation.[3] But when these people began to express their objections too openly, they were often faced with a very ancient discursive strategy used to calm uneasy consciences and silence the most vociferous: the reassuring discourse of historical permanence. It is a matter of showing, with the backing of many historical examples, that there is nothing fundamentally new about this kind of situation, so it is perfectly acceptable.

In an article entitled "In Defense of Drones: A Historical Argument," David Bell criticizes those who regard these weapons as "something altogether new—a fantasy of science fiction that has become reality" and he points out that "if our technology is new, the desire to take out one's enemies from a safe distance is anything but."[4] That is no doubt true, but how such a "historical" reminder could possibly constitute a "defense of drones" remains more mysterious.

Bell might well have added that the desire to take out one's enemies from a safe distance was never better satisfied than in the "glorious" episodes of colonial wars, in which natives were felled en masse while the armies of the whites were hardly scratched. On the evening following the "battle" of Omdurman, in Sudan, on September 2, 1898, there were forty-eight dead on the side of the Anglo-Egyptian forces under Kitchener's command, as against the nearly ten thousand dervishes cut down by the bursts of bullets from Maxim machine guns. Many other examples could be given.

The current use of drones, in its own way, falls into place

in the continuous line of such "asymmetrical wars" involving machine guns marshaled against spears or rusty old guns, in "little wars" that are already no longer heroic or even really "wars" in the same sense that a Westerner who saw himself as a Greek warrior would give to that word. If there was any repugnance felt at the use of ignoble means, it was present only in situations where the conflict was between equals, rather than simply a matter of putting down inferiors. As Jünger reflects, "In every age a distinction has been drawn between two styles, a superior and a barbaric form of the law and the conventions of war. . . . In the Middle Ages, the Christian fleets could fire red hot cannon balls only when they encountered Turkish vessels. In the twentieth century, dum-dum bullets, proscribed in European theatres of operation, were used in colonial wars and the reason for this was said to be that lead bullets did not halt the frenzy of attacks by the 'savages.' "[5]

It would be strange to present these historical antecedents as a possible justification for their contemporary reincarnations. Yet that is the gist of the subtext to arguments of the "there is nothing new under the sun" type. They are designed to assuage the present troubled situation by referring to a past considered to set a legal precedent. However, the soothing invocation of history comes at the price of mutilating the real meaning of historical continuity. As Talal Asad explains, it comes down to playing on two different scenarios: if "the psychological effect of this unequal killing is mitigated by the fact that there exists a long-standing tradition of fighting peoples militarily and ethnically inferior in which it is proper that the latter die in much greater numbers," nevertheless "the growing literature on new military technologies and strategies pays very little attention to the continuities of the new wars with earlier colonial wars."[6] The specter of colonial violence is tacitly called upon in order to revitalize present violence by setting it within the tranquil continuity of a past tradition, and then it is immediately covered up, for no attempt is made to spell out the real content of that tradition. The drone is the weapon of an amnesiac postcolonial violence.

11

A Crisis in Military Ethos

Technical progress, by encouraging the hope of killing in safety and without danger, threatens to make us forget that the primary quality of a soldier is his scorn of death.

—Captain Boucherie, 1914

On the naked body of a giant discovered in a crevice in the ground, Gyges, a Lydian shepherd, by chance found a gold ring that made him invisible. Confident in his new power and sure that he would escape the watchful eyes of men, he multiplied his misdeeds, killed the king, and seized the throne with impunity. His enemies could neither avoid his attacks nor defend themselves against him. Invisibility conferred upon him a kind of invulnerability.

What the *Republic* suggested by this thought experiment finds technical realization in the drone. As John Kaag and Sarah Kreps write, given that "remote-controlled machines cannot suffer the consequences [of their actions] and the humans who operate them do so at a great distance, the myth of Gyges is more a parable of modern counterterrorism than it is about terrorism." [1] Freed from the constraints imposed by reciprocal relations, will the drone masters be able to continue to demonstrate virtue and to resist the temptation to commit injustice with virtually no sanction imposed? That question, to which we shall return, raises the matter of moral hazard.

But there is another way of posing the problem. If it remains true that "the strongest is never strong enough to be always the master, unless he transforms his strength" into virtue,[2] we may ask ourselves the following question: what kind of right or virtue is needed by these modern Gyges? Let us put that question another way: not whether the invisible man can be virtuous, but what redefinition of virtue will he need if he wishes to persist in calling himself virtuous and considering himself to be so even in his own eyes.

Traditional military morality had its own cardinal virtues: courage, sacrifice, heroism, and so on. Those values had a clear ideological function: to make the butchery acceptable—or, even better, glorious. And the generals were well aware of this: "We must find a way of guiding men to death, otherwise this war will be impossible; and I know that way; it lies in a spirit of self-sacrifice, and nowhere else."[3]

Being "ready to die" seemed to be one of the main factors in victory, the very heart of what Clausewitz had called "moral strength." That was the ultimate horizon: "We should not forget that our mission is to kill and be killed. We should never close our eyes to that fact. Making war by killing without being killed is a chimera; making war by being killed without killing is inept. So one must know how to kill, while being ready to die oneself. A man who is committed to death is terrible."[4] According to classic philosophical ideals, warfare continued to be the moral experience par excellence: to make war was to be ready to die.

But one problem remained. "How then do we justify the encouragement of heroic sacrifice in war? Every war exacts a price, sometimes an extremely high one. Is this not in contradiction with 'preserving oneself'?" asked Mao, and then replied to his own question: "In fact, there is no contradiction at all; to put it more exactly, sacrifice and self-preservation are both opposite and complementary to each other. For

such sacrifice is essential not only for destroying the enemy but also for preserving oneself—partial and temporary
'non-preservation' (sacrifice, or paying the price) is necessary for the sake of general and permanent preservation."[5]
It is within this dialectic between preservative exposure and
conservative destruction that the value of sacrifice found its
place: heroically forfeiting some parts made it possible for
the whole to endure. For Hegel too, "true courage," that of
civilized people, lies not so much in scorn for death but rather
in their "readiness for sacrifice in the service of the state."[6]

But what happens when all that is no longer necessary?
When there is no need to expose living forces in order to inflict losses on the enemy? The dialectic of sacrifice thereupon
dissolves into the simple imperative of self-preservation,
with the consequence that heroism and the courage that goes
with it become impossible.

There is nothing new about such a diagnosis. For more
than two decades, we have been told that we have entered the age of "virtueless war,"[7] a "post-heroic age."[8] If
a few traces of such values linger here or there, they merely
result from outdated nostalgias, ideological residues that are
fast decomposing—except that those old values, now struck
by obsolescence, may yet raise a protest against their predicted burial. So long as the superstructures survive, they can
still prove bothersome, the effect of their own inertia being
to slow down the development of the infrastructure that is
actively working to undermine them.

The problem here is that in the light of traditional values,
killing by drones—crushing the enemy without ever risking
one's own skin—is still seen as the highest degree of cowardice and dishonor. The clash between the technical reality of
the conduct of the war and its residual ideology presents a
powerful contradiction even for the personnel of the armed

forces. For them, the clash between these new weapons and the old frameworks that may be outmoded but are nonetheless influential produces a crisis in military ethos.

A revealing symptom of this is the fact that initially the most virulent criticisms of the drones came not from hopeless pacifists but from Air Force pilots, in the name of the preservation of their traditional warrior values.[9] Today, these toppled knights of the sky, the last representatives of a military caste on the wane, strum on their guitars as they sing songs aimed against their mechanical competitor. For instance, Dos Gringos, a "duet of fighter-pilots who have revived the genre of fighter-pilot songs," composed the following requiem:

> They shot down the Predator
> That's one less shot for me
> They have shot down the Predator
> And it fills my heart with glee . . .
>
> They shot down the Predator
> I wonder how that feels
> For that operator who has lost his set of wheels
> It must be so defenseless
> Like clubbing baby seals.[10]

Despite their bravado, the pilots have lost out. Lieutenant Nick "Goose" Bradshaw is dead and Lieutenant Pete "Maverick" Mitchell, who already knew he was sitting on an ejector seat, is being eclipsed in the air by a quite different kind of figure, no doubt far harder to idealize.

In English one uses the expression "unmanned aerial vehicle" to refer to a crewless plane. But one of the troubles with unmanned aerial vehicles is literally the peril of becoming "un-manned" in every sense of the term, including "emasculated." That also is why those Air Force officers initially put up such resistance to the general adoption of the drones. Obviously the drones threatened their own employment, their professional qualifications, and their institutional position, but the threat was also to their own virility, which was largely associated with the taking of risks.[11]

But that warrior heroism, whose swan song we have just recorded, is something that was already largely moribund even before the drones stuck their noses in. In his day, Walter Benjamin was already waxing ironic on the subject of the illusory and inconsequential glorification of the "heroism" of imperialistic wars by reactionary thinkers: "These authors nowhere observe that the new warfare of technology and material which appears to some of them as the highest revelation of existence, dispenses with all the wretched emblems of heroism that here and there have survived the World War."[12] Thus, when Edward Luttwak attaches the label "post-heroic" to this form of contemporary warfare in which it is insisted that no national soldier should be put at risk in external interventions, we might well ask ourselves whether "we" have ever been heroic. However that may be, the already questionable ideal of sacrificial heroism finds itself so openly proved false by the facts that it should, as a matter of urgency, be repudiated as an official value. One must get rid of it and find a way of replacing it by other notions of warrior virtue.

If the drone is represented as being virtuous, that is because it makes it possible to rule out any possibility of casualties in one's own camp. That argument was recently summed up in a British report: "the use of unmanned aircraft prevents the potential loss of aircrew lives and is thus in itself morally justified."[13] A comparison between this thesis of drones, which are deemed virtuous because they spare their agents any confrontation with death, and the classic maxims according to which military virtue is the precise opposite, is enough to reveal the scope of the revolution taking place in the field of values.

The concern to preserve one's forces and avoid senseless losses is certainly in itself nothing new or specific. In the traditional military ethos, scorning death in no way implied not striving to preserve one's life. What is new is that preserving the lives of one's own soldiers is regarded as a quasi-absolute state imperative, which in the last analysis excludes any sacrifice at all. An army that exposes the lives of its troops is bad; one that preserves them at all costs is good. Exposure to risk is to be condemned; killing without danger is to be commended. Dying for one's country was certainly a fine thing, but killing for it, given that it now offers us a dispensation from the heavy toll of our own death, is finer by far.

What is taking place before our very eyes is a switch from one official ethic to another: from an ethic of self-sacrifice and courage to one of self-preservation and more or less assumed cowardice. This major inversion of values demands that one trample underfoot what one previously worshipped and look up to what one despised just yesterday. What one used to call cowardice becomes bravery, and what one used to call a spirit of sacrifice becomes an object of disgust now that it is the privilege of an enemy faced with certain death. Baseness has to be set up as greatness. To this extent, what we have before us is not so much the spectacle of "virtueless war" as a vast redefinition of warrior virtues.

However, can armed violence really do without its morale-boosting dose of heroism? To wean it off that dose would be difficult. In order to preserve the effects while renouncing the drug, a substitute is needed. In this case, it would be a matter of retaining the words but altering their meaning.

In September 2012, the Pentagon considered the possibility

of allotting military medals to drone operators.[14] The problem, of course, lay in what claim the operators could possibly have to decorations that are supposed to reward bravery in battle. But, after all, what is bravery? Everything depends on how it is defined. Let us pose the question to the Lacheses and Niciases (those ancient Athenian generals) of today. Colonel Eric Mathewson, a drone pilot emeritus, offered his own personal interpretation of the notion. "Valor, to me, is not risking your life," he said, "Valor is doing what is right. Valor is about your motivations and the ends that you seek. It is doing what is right for the right reasons. That, to me, is valor." [15] With this kind of definition—irrelevant, tautological, and reduced to a flatly jesuitical justification of ends that justify means—all that can be said is that it does not get us very far.

Luther Turner, a retired colonel who piloted fighter planes before switching to drones at the end of his career, suggested a different definition that at least throws a little light upon the situation: "I firmly believe it takes bravery to fly a UAV [unmanned aerial vehicle], particularly when you are called upon to take someone's life. In some cases you are watching it play out live and in color." [16]

It takes courage to be an assassin. At any rate, the idea is that killing involves a kind of bravery, particularly when one has a graphic view of its effects. One has to make an effort to force oneself to overcome one's original repugnance at doing it and seeing it and, perhaps above all, seeing oneself doing it.

Combining the statements of those two drone pilots, one arrives at the idea that it may be valorous to do something that at first seems repugnant and not at all valorous, provided one does it in the line of duty, in the name of superior aims that are good and just in themselves. In other words, bravery consists in doing the dirty work.[17]

To those who rebelled against such a perversion of vocabulary, protesting against such an Orwellian twisting of the meanings of words—spawned by a new military language that labeled as "bravery" the act of killing without risking one's own skin, an act that for centuries had always been called "cowardly" or "ignominious"—the answer was "I just don't think that the pilots are really 'safe.' *Wired* and NPR both report that pilots are experiencing high levels of stress and PTSD [post-traumatic stress disorder] that takes a toll on their families. The soldiers are safe from physical damage and death, but psychological wounds cannot be written off." [18]

As for post-traumatic stress disorder, we shall be examining that further in the next chapter, but another important claim arises at this point: if drone operators are not "brave" in the classic sense of exposing their physical life in battle, they are brave in that they do indirectly expose their psychic life. Although they do not risk their bodies in those operations, they do risk their mental health. This would be a specific form of bravery, defined no longer by the exposure of one's physical vulnerability to enemy violence, but by exposure of one's psychic vulnerability to the effects created by one's own destructiveness.

By shifting what is sacrificed from the physical plane to the mental, such a redefinition would make it possible to restore to drone operators their lost share of heroism. Purely psychic heroism is a tendentious invention of a new kind of military bravery or virtue.

Alfred de Vigny wrote, "The paid man, the soldier, is a glorious pauper, victim, and executioner." [19] A soldier wields violence and is also exposed to it; he is both an executioner and a victim. But what does he become once the very possibility of being exposed to violence is removed? The fatal conclusion is that he becomes a mere executioner. And that is why he must somehow continue to be a victim if he wishes to continue to be called a soldier. There is a difficulty, though: what could he be the victim of? The only possibility is that he is psychically the victim of having to act as an executioner. That is the only way he can be defined in his own eyes, as in those of society, as the fighter that he no longer is.

But where does this theme of the psychic vulnerability of the agents of violence come from? What is its genealogy? It can be seen to emerge historically in the twentieth century, in reaction to the great butchery of 1914–18 and appears in both pacifist and feminist literature as a central theme in criticism of the military institution: armies force their soldiers to commit acts of violence that drive them mad, ravaging them psychically and brutalizing and traumatizing them. Jane Addams developed this critical theme in a 1915 address titled "The Revolt Against War." She cited the evidence provided by a nurse who told of the nightmares of "delirious soldiers. . . . again and again possessed by the same hallucination—that they are in the act of pulling their bayonets out of the bodies of the men they have killed." [20] In the same account, Addams considers cases where rank-and-file soldiers refused to fire. One said, "I have escaped the horror of killing anyone." [21] She also described how armies tried to neutralize such resistance by distributing stimulants before an attack so as to "inhibit the sensibilities of this type of man" and make the killing possible. [22] Initially, this theme of soldiers as victims of the violence they were forced to commit served as a direct criticism of the institution that produced such effects. But what used to be an antimilitarist argument is now being recycled, in a modified form, in order to promote the legitimization of dronized homicide. For that is certainly the theme that is mobilized in a back-to-front way so as to gild the drone operators' badge, at least in the eyes of the public. Whereas the attention drawn to the soldiers' psychic wounds was in the past aimed at contesting their conscription by state violence, nowadays it serves to bestow upon this unilateral form of violence an ethico-heroic aura that could not otherwise be procured.

12

Psychopathologies of the Drone

In the case of war neuroses, . . . what is feared is nevertheless an internal enemy.

—Sigmund Freud

"The trauma of drone pilots" has become a common theme in the media. An early appearance was in an Associated Press article in 2008: "Long-distance warriors are suffering some of the same psychological stresses as their comrades on the battlefield."[1] But the rest of the article produced nothing to corroborate that statement. In fact, quite the contrary: the journalist reported that in the course of various interviews with drone operators, "none said they had been particularly troubled by their mission."[2] The same procedure—an announcement followed up discreetly by a vague denial—seems to have been adopted in most press articles devoted to the matter.

Many American soldiers did not hesitate to vent their scorn and anger toward the drone pilots and their supposed trauma: "Fricken cry babies, that's what they are. . . . Fire them and get somebody new if they can't take the stress of the air-conditioned trailer and going home every night."[3] Or, in a similar register, "I simply scoff at the idea of some computer nerds whining about 'battle fatigue' or 'PTSD' when they not only know what they're getting into but aren't even in same country getting shot at. It's a slap in the face to those who *really* deploy, who *really* get shot at and who *really* have to deal with the psychological effects of war."[4]

By making it a point of honor to distance themselves from those whom they consider to be a bunch of wimps, those self-appointed spokesmen for "classic" soldiers indirectly illuminated the role that this media-promulgated theme played in the debate. The emphasis placed on the supposed traumas suffered by drone operators made it possible to assimilate them, via a common psychic vulnerability, to classic soldiers (fighters suffer from the stress of fighting and so do drone operators, so drone operators must be fighters too) and to humanize them as agents of armed violence (despite the technical nature of their weapon, they were not just cold killers).

The emphasis placed on the psychic agony of the drone operators also made it possible to dismiss the "PlayStation mentality," according to which putting murder on the screen involves a virtualization of the consciousness of homicide. Before the drones became the subject of daily arguments in the American press, there was a time when drone pilots could still reply more or less honestly to the questions put to them, such as "How do you feel about killing through the intermediary of a screen?" Here is a brief record of the replies:

Oh, it's a gamer's delight.[5]

Almost like playing the computer game Civilization, in which you direct units and armies in battle.[6]

It's like a video game. It can get a little bloodthirsty. But it's fucking cool.[7]

In the aftermath of such public relations disasters, press officers must have reframed their aim and rebriefed the troops, for nowadays there is no longer any sign of such statements in their interviews. On the contrary, when in 2012 a *New York Times* reporter visited a drone base, he noted, "As more than one pilot told me, a bit defensively, 'We are not just playing video games here.'"[8]

This is how the website Airforce-Technology.com, affiliated with the defense industry, describes this discursive U-turn: "While it was initially thought that those operating drones would be more callous about their actions than personnel operating in the battlefield, the opposite now appears to be true. Some analysts argue that UAV operators may almost care too much and that they are experiencing higher levels of combat stress than some units in Afghanistan, with significantly increased fatigue, emotional exhaustion and burnout."[9] We have come full circle: far from living through an experience of murder made unreal, the operators are affected by it so much that there is a serious concern that they "almost care too much" about their victims.

Clearly, if they felt nothing at all, this would raise a moral problem. But given that they kill with sensitivity and even with "care," they can continue to do so with our blessing. This sensitivity and care, this supposed empathy with the victims, is, paradoxically, what now makes a public rehabilitation of homicide by drones possible. The theme of empathy here undergoes a reversal similar to that of the psychic vulnerability mentioned above. Whereas empathy for the enemy was classically understood as a ferment of possible resistance to murder, as a possible premise for a refusal to kill, in the discourse that we are now considering it serves to apply a layer of humanity to an instrument of mechanized homicide. In the face of this vast operation involving the instrumentalization of ethico-affective categories for military ends, however, there is another image that comes to mind: that of the crocodile shedding tears, the better to devour its prey.

Nevertheless, there is a shadow darkening the media picture of empathetic drone operators suffering psychic trauma: it has no empirical basis. The military psychologist Hugo Ortega recently conducted a vast investigation into the subject. He subjected drone operators to psychological tests in order to determine their levels of stress and discover whether they might be affected by post-traumatic stress disorder. His conclusion:

> We haven't diagnosed any pilots with PTSD—that's right, that's right. We had, I think, one sensor operator that we thought maybe . . . but what is one? . . . The major findings of the work so far have been that the popularized idea of watching the combat was really not what was producing the most day-to-day stress for these guys.[10]

On the other hand,

> shift work, schedule changes—those are the top number-one issue for stress. And then they have long hours, low manning. It's really kind of a boring job to be vigilant on the same thing for days and days and days. It's really boring. It's kind of terrible. And maintaining relationships with their families—these were the kinds of things that they reported as stressful for them. And if you look through that stuff, they don't say "Because I was in combat." They don't say "Because we had to blow up a building." They don't say "Because we saw people getting blown up." That's not what causes their stress—at least subjectively to them. It's all the other quality-of-life things that everybody else would complain about too. If you look at nurses who work night shift, anybody who does shift work, they complain of the same things.[11]

Warfare becomes tele-work with shifting timetables, and the symptoms its agents present are all connected with this.

Apart from that, adds Ortega,

> they have more of an existential conflict. It's more of a guilt feeling, perhaps, or a "Did I make the right decision?" . . . So a lot more second-guessing in this, as opposed to the classic PTSD description of symptoms, which is really related to a physical threat event. . . . One was the feeling of a sort of guilt, that they were watching a battle take place and they could see it in extraordinary detail.[12]

However, that "guilt" is not something that Ortega studies. It lies outside his field of competence. At a theoretical level, it is relegated to the domain of existential matters that lie outside the framework of psychological research. So at a practical level, the notion of guilt is entrusted to the care of military social workers specifically assigned to take care of this kind of moral distress on drone bases—murder being considered as one of these spiritual problems.[13]

So the media buzz around the suffering of drone operators was without foundation. Military psychologists discovered no trace of post-traumatic stress disorder. But it should be pointed out that it would have been impossible for them to find any such traces, for one very simple reason that stems from the categories of disease at their disposal. Let us take a look at their bible, the *Diagnostic and Statistical Manual of Mental Disorders* (*DSM*), published by the American Psychiatric Association. What exactly is PTSD? The *DSM* is of the opinion that the patient must have been exposed to "an extreme traumatic stressor involving direct personal experience of an event that involves actual or threatened death or serious injury or other threat to one's physical integrity."[14] Drone operators are by definition excluded from that kind of situation, for there is no threat to their physical integrity. Perhaps it could be argued that the drone operators are nevertheless in a position of "witnessing an event that involves death or a threat to the physical integrity of another person," [15] but the truth is that they are far more than just *witnesses*: they are the *authors* of that death, that injury, that threat. The *DSM*'s category of PTSD is too indeterminate to cover the particular form taken by their experience. Once again, the drone upsets the available categories, to the point of rendering them inapplicable. As for the more general notion of "combat stress"—defined as stress that is "the result of exposure to the same conditions during military actions that cause physical injury and disease in battle" or to conditions close to those of battle in an "area of operations characterized by continuous action and high danger" [16]—short of deciding somehow or other to change the meaning of the words, one is bound to conclude that that notion too is inapplicable to drone operators.

Military psychologists could well save themselves both time and money, as there is no point in carrying out lengthy and costly inquiries in order to discover whether these pathologies, thus defined, are to be found among drone operators. For it is, by definition, impossible: the technology radically rules out or substantially modifies the only stress factors that are covered by the existing categories of disease.

As is often the case, in order to understand this matter more clearly, it is helpful to reread some of the psychoanalytic literature. In the aftermath of World War I, in a conference on war neuroses that gathered together most of the great names of the period, Karl Abraham made the following comment: "It is not only demanded of these men in the field that they must tolerate dangerous situations—a purely passive performance—but there is a second demand which has been much too little considered; I allude to the aggressive acts for which the soldier must be hourly prepared, for besides the readiness to die the readiness to kill is also demanded of him." [17]

Abraham was particularly interested in the case of soldier-patients for whom "the anxiety as regards killing is of similar significance to that of dying." [18] So now the question seems to become: what does the fact of killing, of becoming a killer, threaten to kill within the subject himself? Freud, who wrote the preface to the conference proceedings, suggested a reply to that question: "In the case of war neuroses, . . . what is feared is nevertheless an internal enemy." [19] What the violent subject sees developing within him in the course of the war is a new self, a "war-ego." This is a threat that does not come from outside but from within, for what this emerging self endangers is the old "peace-ego." A war neurosis is a response to that inner conflict; it is an attempt to find a pathological form of resolution. [20]

Closer to our own times, the psychologist Rachel McNair has suggested expanding the overly narrow notion of PTSD by defining a condition called "Perpetration-Induced Traumatic Stress" (PITS). [21] Noting that recent literature has focused almost exclusively on the traumas inflicted on passive victims by external forces, she tries to isolate the active component of the anxiety, the one that stems from the fact of having been the agent of violence, in fact a perpetrator of it. Within the mixed experience of a soldier, it is hard to sort out one particular element from the rest, but McNair studies cases of pure perpetration, for example the nightmares of executioners haunted by images of the last moments of their condemned prisoners. She does not cite the case of drone operators, as her book was published too early for that, but it looks as if that might be a good means by which to test out her idea, for it presents a case of pure perpetration, armed violence reduced solely to its active aspect and without any vital threat to its perpetrator. It is this emerging category of PITS that needs to be tested empirically if one wishes to illuminate debates about trauma suffered by drone operators.

The rapid development of new techniques of violence at a distance will doubtless reorient the psychoethical modes of problematizing the experience of war in Western societies. The first signs of such a reorientation are already detectable. In a state supplied with largely dronized armed forces, one will probably move on inexorably from a study of psychic traumas linked to violence personally suffered to a study of psychic wounds linked to violence personally perpetrated. A kind of clinic for executioners would thus develop alongside psychotherapies for assassins, all of which would be designed to deliver them from their unease.

We are thus faced, for the moment, with two hypotheses regarding the psychic life of drone operators: either this weaponry creates insensitive killers, or else it produces a mental process that involves being tormented by guilt, potentially to the degree of inducing neurosis. In practice, the truth about any given individual probably falls somewhere between those two poles. As for which of the two options is the more desirable, that is a question that remains open.

13

Killing from a Distance

"Honey, you seem a million miles away," Trish would notice.

"Sorry. Not quite that far away. Sometimes it's hard to keep switching on and off. Back and forth. It's like living in two places at the same time. Parallel universes."

—Matt J. Martin, *Predator: The Remote-Control Air War over Iraq and Afghanistan: A Pilot's Story*

Harun Farocki tells us that the technology of military vision produces not so much representations as " 'operative images,' images that do not represent an object, but instead are part of an operation."[1] Here, vision is a *sighting*: it serves not to represent objects but to act upon them, to target them. The function of the eye is that of a weapon.[2]

The link between the two is the image on the screen, which is not so much a figurative representation as an operative function. You can click the apparatus, and when you click, you kill. Here, though, the act of killing is in effect reduced to positioning the pointer or arrow on little "actionable images," tiny figures that have taken the place of the old flesh-and-blood body of the enemy.[3]

That gesture evokes the ancient procedure of "nailing," "the practice of sticking pins or needles into a waxen image of the person against whom . . . witchcraft was directed." Originally this probably involved "sticking them actually into the body of the individual . . . but as this process was no doubt sometimes attended with inconvenience and danger to the operator, the easier and safer method was devised of substituting a waxen proxy, instead of the true man. This practice was known under the name of *defixio*."[4] That hypothesis of the origin of wax dolls is no doubt rather farfetched, but it provides food for thought. The metaphors of targeting used in the vocabulary of drone operators in any case do raise distressing echoes of that archaic practice. What used to be a magical practice has been converted into a high-tech procedure. But perhaps the element of bewitching has not altogether disappeared.

The psychologist and former soldier Dave Grossman has elaborated a theory of the repugnance generated by killing. The closer the human target, the greater the initial resistance that needs to be overcome in order to kill it; conversely, the greater the distance, the less difficult it is to perform the act. On the basis of this hypothesis, he constructs a psychic diagram of a range of different weapons.

Grossman comments that when there is a great distance between the soldiers and the victims and when the soldiers cannot see those victims, the soldiers "can pretend they are not killing human beings,"[5] which is why bomber pilots who have massacred thousands of civilians have been able to feel not the slightest regret.[6] As the distance becomes shorter, the possibility of a psychic denial diminishes. "At close range the resistance to killing an opponent is tremendous. When one looks an opponent in the eye, and knows that he is young or old, scared or angry, it is not possible to deny that the individual about to be killed is much like oneself. It is here that many personal narratives of nonkilling situations occur."[7]

It is a theory that can be criticized from a number of angles, but at this point it interests me for its heuristic impact. Where should the drone be positioned in the diagram?

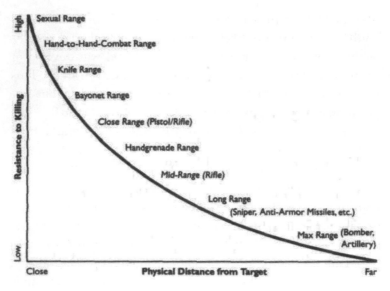

Spectrum of aggression. From Dave Grossman, *On Killing: The Psychological Cost of Learning to Kill in War and Society* (New York: Back Bay Books, 1995), 98.

According to the criterion of the range of the weapon and the physical distance involved, it should appear at the extreme right, at the most distant pole. But cameras allow the operator to see the target as if it were very close. So because of the perceptual proximity, the drone should be positioned further to the left on the distance axis. The problem is that what we call "distance" covers several dimensions that are confused in our ordinary experience but which technologies both disaggregate and redistribute spatially. So it is now possible to be both close and distant, according to dimensions that are unequal and that combine a pragmatic co-presence.[8] Physical distance no longer necessarily implies perceptual distance. In order to position the drone in this diagram, it would be necessary to disaggregate what the unitary term "distance" covers and diffract a horizontal axis that has become too crude.

The operators can see their victims: that is the first specific characteristic of their experience of violence from a distance. Surveillance may last for weeks while the operators are shadowing their targets. They follow them in all their daily occupations, sometimes even to the point of developing a strange sense of intimacy with them: "You see them wake up in the morning, do their work, go to sleep at night";[9] "I see mothers with children, I see fathers with children; I see fathers with mothers; I see kids playing soccer."[10]

Their video view then allows them to see the effects of the strike. That is a very important difference from the experience of traditional pilots: " 'When you come in at 500–600 miles per hour, drop a 500 pound bomb and then fly away, you don't see what happens.' . . . But when a Predator fires a missile, you watch it all the way to impact, and I mean it's very vivid, it's right there and personal. So it does stay in people's minds for a long time."[11] This new combination of physical distance and ocular proximity gives the lie to the classic law of distance: the great distance no longer renders the violence more abstract or more impersonal but, on the contrary, makes it more graphic, more personalized.[12]

However, those factors are counterbalanced by others that are likewise a result of the instrument's technology. Although the operators can see what they are doing, that perceptual proximity nevertheless remains partial. It is filtered through the interface. Quite apart from the fact that the sensory gamut is reduced to the optical dimension,[13] the resolution, although detailed enough to allow the operator to aim, is not good enough to distinguish faces.[14] All that the operators can see are little figures blurred into facelessness. A former CIA officer declares, "You could see these little figures scurrying and the explosion going off and when the smoke cleared, there was just rubble and charred stuff."[15] This figurative reduction of human targets helps to make the homicide easier: "There's no flesh on your monitor, just coordinates."[16] One is never spattered by the adversary's blood. No doubt the absence of any physical soiling corresponds to less of a sense of moral soiling.

Another important point is that the operator sees without being seen. As psychologist Stanley Milgram suggested, "possibly it is easier to harm a person when he is unable to observe our actions than when he can see what we are doing." [17] The fact that the killer and his victim do not appear in reciprocal perceptual fields makes it easier to administer violence. The agent is spared the embarrassment or shame that may be prompted by seeing one's actions with the eyes of one's victim. Grossman goes on to say, "The price most killers have to pay for a close-range kill—the memory of the 'face, terrible, twisted in pain and hate, yes, such hate'—this price need never be paid if we can simply avoid looking at our victim's face." [18] And this is made possible by the drone. It shows just enough to make it possible to take aim, but not enough to get a clear view. Above all, it ensures that *the operator will never see his victim seeing him doing what he does to him.*

The psychic discomfort is further mitigated by what Milgram called the break in the "phenomenological unity" of the act. I press a button here and a silhouette disappears in an explosion over there. "There is a physical and spatial separation of the act and its consequences," Milgram says. "The subject depresses a lever in one room, and protests and cries are heard from another. The two events are in correlation, yet they lack a compelling phenomenological unity. The structure of a meaningful act—I am hurting a man—breaks down because of the spatial arrangements." [19] The separation of the action into two distant points, as if between the two points of gigantic compass, slicing through the unity of its apprehension, decimates the immediate phenomenological meaning of it. In order to think of the action as a whole, the subject would have to manage to reunite the two sides of a shattered phenomenon. As one drone pilot writes about his first strike, "It would take some time for the reality of what happened so far away to sink in, for 'real' to become real."[20] Though intellectually the operator knows the strike to be real, for it to take on the reality of a unified act, there needs to be that period of time in which the work of realization takes place. The unity of the action is not a given, so in order to come about it needs to become the object of a mental endeavor of reunification or reflective synthesis. However, the probably insurmountable difficulty is that only one side of this hemiplegic action has now become accessible to the lived consciousness of the drone operator.

The filtered nature of perception, the figurative reduction of the enemy, the nonreciprocity of the fields of perception, and the dislocation of the phenomenological unity of the action are all factors that, when combined, produce a strong "moral buffering" effect.[21] Thus, offsetting the visual proximity, the device presents its operators with powerful means of distancing. But this form of experience also presents a second important characteristic: the fact that the violence of warfare is being exercised from a peaceful zone.

For classic soldiers, the transition from war to peace is a notoriously delicate phase. In this switch from one moral world to another difficulties in adaptation or reintegration may surface, for the return to civilian life requires periods of decompression. The fact is that even if they never leave their country, drone operators who "telecommute to the war-zone" have to manage the equivalent of such a switch twice a day, very fast and almost without transition.[22] The problem lies in the ceaseless to-ing and fro-ing between two worlds that are opposed in every way. Colonel Michael Lenahan, a Predator pilot and operations director for the 196th Reconnaissance Squadron, says, "It's bizarre, I guess. It is quite different—going from potentially shooting a missile, then going to your kid's soccer game": a killer in the morning and a father in the evening, a daily switch from the "peace ego" to the "war ego." [23]

Drone operators frequently mention this feeling of duality: "There is a cognitive difference. . . . In a physical aircraft your mind automatically switches. For us, I think, it was really more of a cognitive choice—that I'm at war right now. So deployment served as a wall of separation—not just physically, but cognitively, and one of the problems that we kept running back into is that you need to actually create this cognitive space as a factor of will. Well, there was no point at which we were ever in peacetime. We were just permanently somewhere between war and peace." [24] Another operator, describing the collision between family life at home and the violence of war at the office, and his own constant efforts to maintain a mental separation between the two spheres, explains: "Sometimes it's hard to keep switching on and off. Back and forth. It's like living in two places at the same time. Parallel universes. . . . It was enough to make a Predator pilot schizophrenic." [25]

In this kind of experience, psychic viability lies in the agent's ability to compartmentalize. As another drone operator confides, "You have to be able to turn it on and turn it off." [26] But that ability is most fragile when agents of violence are repatriated from a zone of war to a zone of peace. A military man who came to the rescue of drone operators his soldier colleagues were attacking in an online discussion, calling them "wimps" and other demeaning names, wrote: "Being 'at home' is hard right now. The hippies are getting louder and bolder in their hatred for what we do and what we have done in Iraq. Think of how many anti-war bumper stickers they see on the beltway on the way into work or the way home." [27] His comment points out a central contradiction in the whole system: relocating agents of armed violence to a domestic zone of peace places them in a social environment that may well not be able to understand them and which may actively, before their very eyes, contest the violence of which they are the agents.

Men at war need to forge for themselves a special moral world in which, unlike in the civilian world, killing is a virtue, not something prohibited.[28] There is always a latent contradiction between these normative regimes, but in the case of drone operators it is rendered manifest and permanent as a result of the superimposition of two worlds separated on every count. The drone operators are in a sense both in the rear and at the front, caught up in two very different moral worlds that pull their lives this way and that. They epitomize the contradiction of societies at war outside but living inside as though they are at peace. Only they are in both worlds, exactly at the hinge of contradiction, pulled asunder between the two poles. They live out the duplicity of the moral regime of so-called democratic states that are also imperial military powers. Perhaps what the military historian John Keegan wrote about modern conscripts will end up happening to drone operators: "At first acquaintance with the weapons the state foists on [them, they will begin to think] that its humanitarian code is evidence either of a nauseating hypocrisy or of a psychotic inability to connect actions with their results."[29]

That is indeed what is starting to happen. Brandon Bryant, a drone operator for over five years, decided to leave the air force, and he has spoken openly of his decision. The memory of one day in particular haunts him:

There were 16 seconds left until impact. "These moments are like in slow motion," he says today. . . . Bryant could still have diverted the missile at that point. Then it was down to three seconds. Bryant felt as if he had to count each individual pixel on the monitor. Suddenly a child walked around the corner, he says.

Bryant saw a flash on the screen: the explosion. Parts of the building collapsed. The child had disappeared. Bryant had a sick feeling in his stomach.

"Did we just kill a kid?" he asked the man sitting next to him.

"Yeah, I guess that was a kid," the pilot replied.

"Was that a kid?" they wrote into a chat window on the monitor.

Then, someone they didn't know answered, someone sitting in a military command center somewhere in the world, who had observed their attack. "No. That was a dog," the person wrote.

They reviewed the scene on the video. A dog on two legs? . . .

Bryant completed 6,000 flight hours during his six years in the Air Force. "I saw men, women and children die during that time," says Bryant. "I never thought I would kill that many people. In fact, I thought I couldn't kill anyone at all." . . .

On uneventful days in the cockpit, he would write in his diary, jotting down lines like: "On the battlefield there are no sides, just bloodshed. Total war. Every horror witnessed. I wish my eyes would rot." . . .

At some point he no longer enjoyed seeing his friends. He met a girl, but she complained about his bad moods. "I can't just switch and go back to normal life," he told her. When he came home and couldn't sleep, he would exercise instead. He began talking back to his superior officers.

One day he collapsed at work, doubling over and spitting blood. . . .

There was one day, he says, when he knew that he

wouldn't sign the next contract. It was the day Bryant walked into the cockpit and heard himself saying to his coworkers: "Hey, what motherfucker is going to die today?"[30]

This kind of testimony is extremely rare. More often active drone operators give a quite different account. "I feel no emotional attachment to the enemy," one operator said. "I have a duty, and I execute the duty."[31] The journalist's comment was that this soldier "compartmentalizes."

The military psychologist Hernando Ortega emphasizes the importance of such compartmentalization: "I think at Beale [Air Force Base] they have a sign on the door that goes in that says 'Welcome to the AOR [area of responsibility],' and it's in desert cam[o], and when they walk through there, [they] put their game on, go to the combat zone. When they walk out, they're going back home. So even those simple rituals like that would actually help them, but there are probably selection standards that we could come up with, the same as we finally came up with medical standards 11 years after the aircraft was invented."[32] When recruiting, one should select agents who spontaneously manifest a strong ability to compartmentalize, who "can switch off work and switch on home," put things to one side and not think about them—agents capable of not thinking.[33]

And what if drone psychopathology lay not where it is believed to be, in the possible traumas of the drone operators, but in the industrial production of compartmentalized psyches, immunized against any possibility of reflecting upon their own violence, just as their bodies are already immunized against any possibility of being exposed to the enemy?

In Chapter 3 I posed the question of what sort of redefinition of virtue would be necessary for a modern Gyges to consider himself virtuous. Military psychology provides an

answer: it would involve a practical skill, the ability to compartmentalize, *to set aside*.

In the darkest years of the twentieth century, Simone
Weil offered a very fine interpretation of the Platonic myth
and reformulated it definitively for the present day. What
is invisible, she said, is not the person who wears the ring,
but the ring itself. "The ring of Gyges that has itself become
invisible—that is precisely in what consists the act of setting
apart. It is setting apart oneself and the crime one commits;
not establishing the connection between the two." [34] What
Gyges says is, "I have become king and the other king has
been assassinated. The two things are totally unrelated. Here
is the ring." One sets something aside and forgets that one
has set it aside, one compartmentalizes—and "that faculty of
setting apart makes all crimes permissible." [35]

III

Necroethics

14

Combatant Immunity

The air war over Serbia offered airmen a glimpse of the future.

—Air Force report

"No body bags," "a phobia of losses," "an aversion to risk": in the late 1990s, massive use was made of all these expressions in the United States. They all conveyed the same idea: the tendency to subordinate the use of military force to a political imperative in order to preserve American military lives. What is specific about contemporary imperial violence has less to do with the asymmetry of force and the resulting unequal distribution of vulnerability—a classic feature of all the "small wars" of history—than with the type of norms that now shape the great Western "democratic" powers' exercise of that violence. If there is anything new about the situation, it might lie in the fact that the practical quasi-invulnerability of the dominant camp was, at the end of the twentieth century, set up as the dominant ethical and political norm.

It was probably at the moment of NATO's intervention in Kosovo, in 1999, that the clearest recognition of this phenomenon came about. As General Wesley Clark, who was in charge of the allied forces' operation, later explained, the prime concern had been "not to lose equipment and minimize the loss of airships": "I was motivated by a larger political-military rationale: If we wanted to keep this campaign going indefinitely, we had to protect our air fleet. Nothing would hurt us more with public opinion than headlines that screamed, 'NATO LOSES TEN AIRPLANES IN TWO DAYS.' "[1] Eighteen dead could well be enough to lose a war: the lesson had been learned in Mogadishu. And in the mind of the Clinton administration, the "Black Hawk Down" syndrome had revived the lesson learned in Vietnam. The fear was that losses, even if minimal from the point of view of the military balance of forces, would, through their supposed effect upon public opinion, carry an exorbitant political price. So they had to be avoided at all costs.

To this end, pilots were forbidden to fly below an altitude of 15,000 feet, a security distance that meant they were nearly out of reach of the enemy antiaircraft defenses and were almost untouchable. William Cohen, Bill Clinton's defense secretary, later declared: "The paramount lesson learned from Operation Allied Force is that the well-being of our people must remain our first priority."[2] The NATO planes carried out 38,004 raids in seventy-eight days without sustaining a single loss among the members of their crews.[3] The Americans had indeed managed to invent warfare that inflicted zero deaths in their own camp. However, this did not rule out contradictions. For the very altitude that ensured that the lives of the pilots were not exposed also meant a potential loss of accuracy for the air strikes. NATO officials questioned on this matter by Amnesty International acknowledged this: "An aircrew flying at 15,000 feet would be able only to identify whether the objective was the intended one according to the planning preparations, but would be unable to tell whether, for example, civilians had moved within its vicinity. The 15,000-feet rule thus effectively made it impossible for NATO aircrews to respect the obligation to suspend an attack once circumstances had changed on the ground rendering the objective no longer legitimate."[4]

Could one risk the lives of civilians whom one was claiming to be saving in this "humanitarian operation" simply because one was not prepared to risk "our lives" for "theirs"? The question presented all the features of a case of conscience, in the purest tradition of moral philosophy. It was a tension that journalist Michael Ignatieff summed up as follows: "High tech warfare is governed by two constraints—avoiding civilian casualties and avoiding risks to pilots—that are in direct contradiction. To target effectively you have to fly low. If you fly low, you lose pilots. Fly high and you get civilians."[5] Which of those two imperatives should win out? It was a problem of priorities, a hierarchization of norms. NATO responded with little hesitation, awarding priority to the lives of pilots, even if it increased the "collateral" risk of wounding and killing civilians. In the name of preserving military lives, the risk of producing more casualties among the civilians was accepted, even though it was those very civilians whom the operation was designed to protect. This amounted to admitting that, in military-political reasoning, the life of a Kosovar civilian was of less value than that of an American service member.

Philosophers familiar with theories of "just warfare" were faced with this upsetting aspect of "warfare without risk." Among those who detected a fundamental normative swing here, reactions were strong, even scandalized. The fact was that such a choice overturned the very principles of the standard war ethic. Wrote Jean Bethke Elshtain: "American officials described that intervention as a moral imperative. Yet before the conflict had even ended, observers were wondering if the United States had turned moral tradition on its head, with combatants rather than non-combatants provided immunity from the effects of fighting."[6] In her indignation, she had seized upon an essential point. What had emerged here, very clearly, was the preeminence of a tacit normative principle that was alien to the law of armed conflicts but implicitly regarded as superior to it, namely a sui generis principle of the immunity of imperial combatants. Elshtain went on, "We violated the norm of discrimination in a strange up-ended kind of way by devising a new criterion, it seems: *combatant immunity* ranked higher as a consideration than did non-combatant immunity for Serbian—or Albanian Kosovar—civilians, with our determination to keep NATO soldiers—in other words, American soldiers—out of harm's way, we embraced combatant immunity for our own combatants."[7]

This was no mere digression. A decade later, Alex J. Bellamy produced a similar diagnosis, this time of the kinds of interventions that the American army carried out on the ground in Afghanistan and Iraq: "It seems a clear pattern has emerged whereby the protection of US combatants takes precedence over the protection of non-combatants near the areas of operation. . . . Non-combatants will be protected so long as their protection does not require taking measures that may endanger the lives of soldiers." This came down to valuing "the lives of combatants more than non-combatants."[8]

That principle of immunity for the imperial combatant, which was presented in a more or less implicit, pragmatic fashion in the 1990s, has since been theoretically formalized. The doctrine was elaborated by Israel: "When senior Israeli Defense Forces [IDF] officers are asked about the killing of hundreds of Palestinian civilians during the fighting in the Gaza strip, they almost all give the same answer: The use of massive force was designed to protect the lives of the soldiers, and when faced with a choice between protecting the lives of Israeli soldiers and those of enemy civilians . . . , the soldiers take precedence."[9] That response was by no means merely improvised but was based on "an ethical theory, developed several years ago, that justifies its actions." What's the use of moral philosophy? Among other things, it facilitates the waging of war.

Asa Kasher, a professor at Tel Aviv University, has for many years worked closely with the Israeli army, for which he produced an "ethical code" in the mid-1990s. He has justified the campaigns of "targeted assassinations" and their inevitable "collateral damage" to the Palestinian population in densely populated zones. He has organized meetings propounding his revised military ethic among the staff of the IDF and Israel's internal security service, the Shin Bet.[10] In interviews he boasts, not without reason, that "what we are doing is becoming the law."[11]

In 2005, he, together with Major General Amos Yadlin, coauthored an article entitled "Military Ethics of Fighting Terror."[12] Their aim was to revise, from top to bottom, the established principles underlying the ethics and law of armed conflicts. The most radical of their attacks concerned the principle of noncombatant immunity: "According to the ordinary conception underlying the distinction between combatants and non-combatants, the former have a lighter package of state duties than the latter. Consequently, the duty to minimize casualties among combatants during combat is last on the list of priorities. . . . We reject such conceptions because we consider them to be immoral. A combatant is a citizen in uniform. . . . His blood is as red and thick as that of citizens who are not in uniform. His life is as precious as the life of anyone else."[13] From this, one was supposed to conclude that the preservation of the lives of the subjects of the nation-state is the supreme duty, which must in all cases and at whatever cost be placed above the duty to minimize the losses of noncombatants in the enemy camp. This meant that in a war situation, minimizing risks for an Israeli soldier took precedence over the duty to minimize "collateral risks" for a child in Gaza. The life of the former, armed to the teeth though he was, was ruled to matter more than the life of the latter. This was established in the style of cold violence peculiar to this kind of "ethical" discourse, which mimes the formal rigor of analytical philosophy.

The argument is paradoxically supported by a rhetorical reminder of the equal value of all lives. Because, however, that equality holds only among *citizens*, the result is a hierarchization of bodies based on whether they are subjects of the nation-state or not. The operation consists in replacing the primacy of the structural distinction between civilians and combatants by another that simultaneously redefines it, one that boils down to a hierarchical separation between nationals and foreigners—and all in the name of an "ethic" that is just a polite euphemism for a nationalism of the most ferocious kind.

The duties of the nation-state thus override the universal obligations declared by international humanitarian law. Or rather, it is assumed to be acceptable to revise the universal obligations imposed by that law because the fundamental normative threshold it is based on has shrunk to the *particular* duties of a state toward its own subjects. The law on armed conflicts applies limitations to the exercise of armed violence based on the universal rights of civilians, whoever they are. However, Kasher and Yadlin's revisionist architectonic reshapes the map of the relevant categories, making the limit of state sovereignty the separation line. On one side of that line certain lives must be preserved as a priority, even at the price of carnage for civilians who find themselves on the other side of that line. This involves a complete disproportion, since the preservation of the life of a single national soldier may justify forsaking an indefinite number of foreign civilians: "According to our norm of priorities on grounds of duties, the state should give priority to saving the life of a single citizen, even if the collateral damage caused in the course of protecting that citizen is much higher, which may seem unacceptable." [14] In Kasher and Yadlin's theoretical assault, the principle of distinction drags along with it the principle of proportionality, which will be sacrificed in the name of saving national lives.

Theorists of just warfare considered this doctrine a monstrosity. Michael Walzer and Avishai Margalit energetically rejected Kasher and Yadlin's position: "Their claim, crudely put, is that in such a war the safety of 'our' soldiers takes precedence over the safety of 'their' civilians. Our main contention is that this claim is wrong and dangerous. It erodes the distinction between combatants and non-combatants, which is critical to the theory of justice in war (*jus in bello*)." [15] Pointing out that "the crucial means for limiting the scope of warfare is to draw a sharp line between combatants and non-combatants," they added: "For Kasher and Yadlin, there no longer is a categorical distinction between combatants and non-combatants. But the distinction should be categorical, since its whole point is to limit wars to those— only those—who have the capacity to injure. . . . This is the guideline we advocate: conduct your war in the presence of non-combatants on the other side with the same care as if your citizens were those non-combatants." [16]

The president of the Israeli Academy of Sciences, Menahem Yaari, expressed himself more boldly: "A military code of conduct that discriminates, in cases of hazards being inflicted upon innocent civilians, on the basis of whether these civilians are 'ours' or 'theirs' is all the more worrisome when viewed against a general background of growing ethnocentric and xenophobic attitudes in Israel's traditional establishment. We see an ongoing drift from universalism and humanitarianism toward parochialism and tribalism." [17]

We need to assess the full scale of this assault. The project is nothing less than a dynamiting of the law of armed conflict as it was established in the second half of the twentieth century: an evisceration of the principles of international law in favor of a nationalism of self-preservation. And, as we shall see, that is also the primary principle of the necroethics of drones.

15

A Humanitarian Weapon

There's a war going on and drones are the most refined, accurate and humane way to fight it.
> —Jeff Hawkins, U.S. State Department,
> Bureau of Democracy, Human Rights, and Labor

We never said to ourselves, "Let's build a more humane weapon."
> —Henry A. Crumpton, CIA, Counterterrorism Center

The partisans of the hunter-killer drone claim that it represents "a major step forward . . . in humanitarian technology."[1] By this they do not mean that this machine could, for example, be used to deliver food or medicines to devastated areas. They mean something quite different, namely that the drone is humanitarian *as a weapon, as a means of killing.*

The meaning of words is so twisted in discourse such as this that those using them seem no longer even to notice how strange their formulations are. How can one claim that war machines with no human being aboard are a "more humane" means of destroying life? How can one describe as "humanitarian" procedures designed to annihilate human life? If humanitarian action is characterized by the imperative of taking care of humans in distress, it is hard to see how a lethal weapon could in any sense be said to conform to that principle.

Avery Plaw, a professor of political science at the University of Massachusetts, answers that question this way: "Drones save lives, American and other." [2] We need to elucidate the twisted logic that makes it possible to claim that an instrument of death saves lives.

It is clear enough that by making it unnecessary to expose American lives to combat, the drone indeed spares them. However, it is less clear to see how it might at the same time "save" any lives other than those. In a moment we shall see how, but let us begin by examining the first point in the argument.

In the first place, drones save "our lives"; in this respect, we are told, they are already "moral." That is a thesis that in the late 1990s one magazine summed up in an even more effective way with the following arresting subtitle, positioned between two photographs of clean-lined drones seen against an azure background: "Nobody dies—except the enemy." [3] According to this view of military morality, to kill while exposing one's own life is bad; to take lives without ever endangering one's own is good. That first principle of drone necroethics is, paradoxically, vitalist. And it is in accordance with this logic that the drone can be said to be a "humanitarian" weapon: the humanitarian imperative is to save *lives*. And the drone does indeed save *our* lives. It is therefore a humanitarian technology. QED.

Bradley Jay Strawser is the foremost herald of this thesis of the drone as a moral weapon. On the basis of two articles he has written on the matter, he was hired as a professor of philosophy at the U.S. Naval Postgraduate School in Monterey, California. The *Guardian* regards this as a sign: this American military institution is convinced that "drones and military ethics are set to become ever more fraught topics." [4] Strawser himself comments: "The school wanted a voice in that conversation, so they hired me. . . . I wanted to be a working philosopher and here I am. Ridiculous good fortune."[5]

According to him, the drone is not just morally acceptable but "morally obligatory."[6] If you wish to kill in conformity with moral law, you have to use a drone. His thesis is based on what he calls the "principle of unnecessary risk," according to which it is "wrong to command someone to take on *unnecessary* potentially lethal risk."[7] His reasoning runs as follows: "I argue that we have a duty to protect an agent engaged in a justified act from harm to the greatest extent possible, so long as that protection does not interfere with the agent's ability to act justly. UAVs afford precisely such protection. Therefore, we are obligated to employ UAV weapon systems if it can be shown that their use does not significantly reduce a warfighter's operational capacity."[8]

Again we find the principle of vital self-preservation, but here it is accompanied by a limiting condition: only if it is possible to replace warplanes by drones without incurring any "significant loss of capability" is there a moral obligation to do so.[9] The introduction of that condition comes down to admitting that "the just warrior's increased protection (which a UAV provides) should not be bought at an increased risk to noncombatants."[10] In other words, unlike Kasher and Yadlin, Strawser subordinates the principle of the preservation of the national combatant, if not to a principle of the minimization of risks for noncombatants, at least to a principle of nonaggravation of those same risks in comparison to earlier weaponry systems.

If, on the contrary, it turned out that this weapon made us "unable to properly adhere to the *jus in bello* principles of discrimination and proportionality, then such drones should not be used."[11] However, Strawser is confident that this is not the case, for he has read in the promotional materials put out by an Israeli arms maker that this kind of technology "*increases* a pilot's capability to discriminate": "The beauty of this seeker is that as the missile gets closer to the target, the picture gets clearer. . . . The video image sent from the seeker via the fiber-optic link appears larger in our gunner's display. And that makes it much easier to distinguish legitimate from non-legitimate targets." [12]

All that drone morality is doing here is recycling the old talk of "surgical strikes," for it assumes that that old military dream has now become a reality. It therefore assumes it is now free from the contradiction that rendered the Kosovo war immoral in the eyes of just-war theorists. Back then Walzer conceded that an army would obviously "embrace technologies that were said to be risk-free for its own soldiers, and the embrace would be entirely justified so long as the same technologies were also risk-free for civilians on the other side. This is precisely the claim made on behalf of 'smart bombs': they can be delivered from great distances (safely), and they never miss. But the claim is, for the moment at least, greatly exaggerated." [13]

However, what if technical progress and new weapons made it possible *materially* to overcome this tension? If the lives of national soldiers could be preserved with no additional risk for noncombatants in the opposite camp, the contradiction would fade away. The immunity of the former would be harmoniously matched by the safety of the latter. The moral dilemma would evaporate, resolved by the miracle of technology. And that is indeed the claim being made today by drone supporters. According to them, given that setting the drone operator at a distance implies no loss at all of operational capacity, the tension is de facto deactivated. That is why, in this discourse, there is no need to subscribe to Kasher and Yadlin's theoretical subordination of noncombatant immunity to the safeguarding of national military lives:

if one admits that the problem has been resolved in practice, there is no need for any related theory.

In similar fashion, one can claim that drones save not only "our lives" but also "theirs," thanks to their increased precision. Given that they would cause less "collateral damage" than other weapons, they would potentially be more ethical.

What is emerging here, more fundamentally, is a regime of military violence that claims to be humanitarian but might equally be called *humilitarian*.[14] It is a power that both kills and saves, wounds and heals, and it performs those double tasks in a single gesture, in an integrated manner: an immediate synthesis of a power of destruction and a power of caring, *murder* at the same time as *care*.[15]

Lives are saved. But saved from what? From oneself, from one's own power of death. The violence could have been worse, and since one tried in good faith to limit its deadly effects, one acted morally.

As Eyal Weizman has shown, this type of justification is essentially based on a *logic of the lesser evil*: "the essence of our humanitarian present, obsessed with the calculations and calibrations that seek to moderate, ever so slightly, the evils that it has largely caused itself."[16] He notes that Hannah Arendt too warned against this type of argument: "Politically, the weakness of the argument has always been that those who choose the lesser evil forget very quickly that they chose evil."[17]

16

Precision

If that is not being virtuous, I should be glad to know what is.
                                    —Thomas De Quincey

"It is very precise and it is very limited in terms of collateral damage," the former director of the CIA Leon Panetta declared when speaking of armed drones.[1] That argument turns up everywhere: the drone, by reason of its precision, is said to reduce "collateral damage" and encourage better respect for the principle of discrimination.[2] That erroneous commonplace rests upon a veritable nest of conceptual confusions. We should pick them out methodically, that is to say with *precision*.

Can the drone be presented as a more precise weapon? It all depends on what it is compared to. Strawser writes: "Drones . . . have the potential for tremendous moral improvement over the aerial bombardments of earlier eras."[3] A CIA agent expands his meaning: "Look at the firebombing of Dresden and compare what we're doing today."[4]

But if Dresden (or, let's say, Hiroshima) is considered a pertinent standard as far as precision is concerned, any military procedure will successfully pass the test.[5] The fact is that when it comes to selecting pertinent terms of comparison, there is a confusion between the *form* of the weapon and its *function*. Given that the drone is a flying object, one automatically compares it to the military flying machines

that preceded it. Compared to a World War II bomber, the
drone undeniably gains in precision. However, that type of
comparison is erroneous. To evaluate it properly, the drone
should be set alongside weapons currently available for the
same tactical function. For liquidating Osama bin Laden, the
choice was between a drone and a commando raid, not between a drone and a Dresden-like bombing of Abbottabad.
If one avoids being misled by some external attribute, the
right form of comparison involves not a similarity of forms
but an equivalence of functions. The drone is not a means of
carpet bombing, and World War II bombers were not weapons designed for targeted assassination. The useful comparison here is not between a present-day flying weapon and
an aerial weapon of the past, leading to the conclusion that
progress has been made, but rather between this weapon and
other present-day means for functions of the same order.

But the matter is still muddled on account of another confusion, a semantic one. Three close but not synonymous notions are blithely confused under the term "precision": the
accuracy of the firing, the extent of its impact, and the ad-
equacy of the identification of its target.

A laser-guided strike is extremely precise in terms of firing accuracy: the ballistic device explodes at the exact spot
designated. But that does not mean that its impact is necessarily reduced. Everything depends on the "kill radius" of
the projectile, that is to say the perimeter of the explosion. A
strike may be completely precise in the first sense but not in
the least precise in the second sense. There is a crucial difference between hitting the target and hitting only the target.

As a military play on words puts it, the drone makes it
possible "to put warheads on foreheads."[6] It is estimated that
the AGM-114 Hellfire fired by the Predator drone has a "kill
zone" of 15 meters—which means that all those who happen
to be within a radius of 15 meters around the point of impact,

even if they are not the designated target, will die together with the target. As for the "wound radius," that is estimated to be 20 meters.[7]

The replacement of troops on the ground by drones equipped with missiles clearly leads to "a significant loss of operational capacities" in view of the fact that by contrast, the lethal radius of a grenade is 3 meters (not to mention the even smaller lethal radius of a classic weapon such as a rifle). One cannot help wondering in what fictitious world killing an individual with an antitank missile that annihilates every living being within a radius of 15 meters and wounds all those within a radius of 20 meters can be reputed to be "more precise." As militant Pakistani transsexuals explained when interviewed in a demonstration protesting against drone strikes: "If terrorists were to enter a school in the US and take students hostage, the US would not send drones to fire missiles on the school, but would find the safest way to kill or arrest the terrorists without harming the children."[8]

But the thesis of the drone as an ethical precision device also rests upon another confusion, this time between the technical precision of the weapon and its capacity to discriminate in the choice of targets. This conceptual confusion leads to a crude paralogism that has nonetheless been repeated so often that one no longer even notices it. Here is an example, drawn from a speech by the former White House antiterrorism consultant and current CIA director John Brennan, whom the American press has dubbed the "assassination czar" in recognition of the key role that he played in implementing drone programs: "With the unprecedented ability of remotely piloted aircraft to precisely target a military objective while minimizing collateral damage, one could argue that never before has there been a weapon that allows us to distinguish more effectively between an al Qa'ida terrorist and innocent civilians."[9]

This official "truth," that the drone's increased precision turns it into an ethical weapon because it is better able to discriminate between civilians and combatants, is repeated, with not the least sign of any critical examination, in dozens of press articles and academic publications. However, endlessly drumming it in does not make it logically consistent.

The fact that your weapon enables you to destroy precisely whomever you wish does not mean that you are more capable of making out who is and who is not a legitimate target. The precision of the strike has no bearing on the pertinence of the targeting in the first place. That would be tantamount to saying that the guillotine, because of the precision of its blade—which, it is true, separates the head from the trunk with remarkable precision—makes it thereby better able to distinguish between the guilty and the innocent. The sophism is flagrant, and Brennan's carefully conditional phrasing seems to indicate that those who wrote his speech were conscious of the paralogism, in that they settle for suggesting the point rather than going so far as to affirm it. It was surely enough merely to insinuate it into the public mind.

However, there also exists a more subtle version of this same argument, which claims that "the real factor that allows discrimination in the use of force consists in the degree of accuracy of the visual identification of the target," that "the real enabler of discriminate application of force is accurate visual identification," and that, "insofar as superior imagery enables more discriminate use of force, the use of armed drone technology ought generally to be an ethically superior mode of warfare." [10]

So much for theory. In practice, drones' persistent surveillance is not, as we have seen, particularly brilliant when it comes to drawing distinctions. But it is also important to clarify the underlying argument. The matter boils down to this: by what means can one visually spot whether an individual has or has not the status of a combatant? By what means can a drone operator *see* the difference on his screen?

When, as is the case today in the context of anti-insurgent operations, drone operators target enemies without uniforms (and often beyond the zones of armed conflict), the status of combatant can no longer be ascertained by any distinctive conventional sign. As for carrying weapons, that criterion cannot be applied in a country where everybody carries a weapon. As a Yemeni official comments, "Every Yemeni is armed . . . so how can they differentiate between suspected militants and armed Yemenis?"[11]

The law on armed conflict prohibits the direct targeting of civilians. The only temporary exception to this rule is a case in which a civilian "participates directly in hostilities."[12] If a man dressed as a civilian suddenly aims his weapon, making it clear that he is taking part in the battle and that he poses an immediate threat, he now constitutes a legitimate target for the military of the opposing camp.

However, those two criteria, direct participation in the hostilities and posing an imminent threat, are rendered completely ineffective by the exclusive use of drones. How can there be any direct participation in hostilities if there is no longer any fighting? How can there be any imminent threat if there are no longer any troops on the ground? By depriving the enemy of any possibility of participating directly in hostilities, one also deprives oneself of the surest means of recognizing an enemy as such. The paradox is that the drone, so highly praised for its great ability to make out the difference between combatants and noncombatants, in practice abolishes the very condition for that differentiation, namely combat. It is rather as if one were using an extremely powerful microscope whose visualization techniques deactivate the phenomenon it is supposed to be observing.

How could it be possible to see combatants by means of a

weapon that rules out combat? There is a profound contradiction here. By depriving the military of the manifest criteria that make it possible to detect the difference between combatants and noncombatants, this weapon threatens the very applicability of the principle of distinction.

Once the detection of direct participation in hostilities becomes almost impossible for the pure and simple reason that there is no longer any combat, it becomes necessary to mobilize other techniques of detection and also other categories to designate the enemy. The status of combatant tends to be diluted in such a way as to extend to any form of membership of, collaboration with, or presumed sympathy for some militant organization, whether or not there is any link with its armed branch. What we now have is an insidious switch from the category of "combatants" to that of "suspected militants." This combatant = militant equivalence has the effect of extending the right to kill well beyond the classic legal boundaries and conferring an indefinite elasticity on the concept of a legitimate target.

Furthermore, in determining that status, one slips from an epistemology of manifest observation and statements of fact into an epistemology of suspicion in which a targeting decision is based on the identification of behavior or a pattern of life that suggests membership in a hostile organization. For example, your pattern of life might suggest a 70 percent chance that you are a militant, in other words a combatant, and we accordingly have the right to kill you.

Despite that alarming diagnosis, John Brennan reassured the public in June 2011 that American drones had triumphed over their structural limitations and accomplished a feat previously unknown in the history of war: "In fact, I can say that the types of operations . . . that the US has been involved in, in the counterterrorism realm, that nearly for the past year there hasn't been a single collateral death because of the exceptional proficiency, precision of the capabilities that we've been able to develop." [13]

The military "ethics experts" could now crack open the champagne. Military technology had fulfilled its promises. The hour of the perfectly humanitarian and fully ethical weapon had arrived: following on the heels of war with zero deaths in one's own camp, there was now war with no civilians killed in the enemy camp. Despite Cassandra's warnings, the logic of the lesser evil, following its course, had eventually brought forth absolute goodness.

But how could such a miracle be possible? The statistical miracle lay, as it often does, in the counting system employed. It was a simple but redoubtable trick, as *New York Times* journalists Jo Becker and Scott Shane revealed: "It in effect counts all military-age males in a strike zone as combatants . . . unless there is explicit intelligence posthumously proving them innocent." [14] As an anonymous official said, "They count the corpses and they're not really sure who they are." [15]

Beneath the mirages of militarized ethics and state lies, this is the assuredly humanitarian and ethical principle of drones: the targets are presumed guilty until they are proved innocent—which, however, can only be done posthumously.

While ethics is classically defined as a doctrine of living well and dying well, necroethics take the form of a doctrine of *killing* well. Necroethics holds forth on the procedures of homicide and turns them into the objects of a complacent moral evaluation.

Once people's minds are implanted with the false proof that the drone is in principle a more precise weapon and, on that account, supposedly more in conformity with the principle of distinction, the necroethics of the drone abandons any discussion of fundamental issues and steers critics toward a debate on numbers in which, by reversing the onus of proof, those critics now have to establish empirically that this weapon, which they have just conceded in theory to be a priori more ethical, has in practice produced quite the opposite results—a fact that, once one has swallowed the original postulate, remains totally inexplicable other than by contingent circumstances such as human misuse and errors in deployment. The instrument, in other respects, remains good in itself.

Given the opacity of both the targeting criteria and the real results of the strikes, critics have tended to focus on a demand for transparency, with exact figures and precise information about procedures. The legal discussion drags on with technical quibbles from statisticians and forensics experts who, distracting public scrutiny from the human reality of the concrete effects of armed violence, further objectify and disembody the existence of the victims. In place of living human beings, we find only memoranda from jurists, columns of numbers, and ballistic analyses.[16]

I have tried to show that the precision-distinction thesis rests upon a cascade of confusions and sophisms that can and should first be challenged on principle. Contrary to the widespread legend, the drone is in reality related to a nondiscriminatory weapon of a new kind: by ruling out the possibility of combat, the drone destroys the very possibility of any clear differentiation between combatants and noncombatants.

I believe it is important to make such clarifications and carefully examine the validity of opposing arguments in the light of their own categories. However, doing so involves a risk, for necroethics is characterized not only by a number of particular theses but also and perhaps above all by a particular style of both thinking and writing. This style, which combines the dryness of academic writing with the juridico-administrative formalism of bureaucratic rationality, by its vocabulary alone engenders a massive euphemization and derealization of the violence that constitutes its true subject. What, actually, is "collateral damage"? What does a "humanitarian weapon" actually do? What bodies lie buried beneath these words?

What is the dream?

I dream that my legs have been cut off, that my eye is missing, that I can't do anything . . . Sometimes I dream that the drone is going to attack, and I'm scared. I'm really scared.

After the interview is over, Sadaullah Wazir pulls the pant legs over the stubs of his knees till they conceal the bone-colored prostheses. . . .

Did you hear it coming?

No.

What happened?

I fainted. I was knocked out.

As Sadaullah, unconscious, was shifted to a more serviceable hospital in Peshawar where his shattered legs would be amputated, the media announced that, in all likelihood, a senior al-Qaeda commander, Ilyas Kashmiri, had been killed in the attack. The claim would turn out to be spurious, the first of three times when Kashmiri would be reported killed.

Sadaullah and his relatives, meanwhile, were buried under a debris of words: "militant," "lawless," "counterterrorism," "compound" (a frigid term for a home). Move along, the American media told its audience, nothing to see here. Some 15 days later, after the world had forgotten, Sadaullah awoke to a nightmare.

Do you recall the first time you realized your legs were not there?

I was in bed, and I was wrapped in bandages. I tried to move them, but I couldn't, so I asked, "Did you cut off my legs?" They said no, but I kind of knew. . . .

When you ask Sadaullah, or Karim, or S. Hussein and others like them what they want, they do not say "transparency and accountability." They say they want the killing to stop. They want to stop dying. They want to stop going to funerals—and being bombed even as they mourn. Transparency and accountability, for them, are abstract problems that have little to do with the concrete fact of regular, systematic death.[17]

IV

The Principles of the Philosophy of the Right to Kill

17

Indelicate Murderers

> We restrict this right to kill legally to the executioner and the soldier. . . . [T]heir functions only approach each other in diverging: they touch each other in the same way that in a circle 1° touches 360°, precisely because they cannot be farther apart.
>
> —Joseph de Maistre

The law and the philosophy of law make arid reading. Nevertheless, at a time when legal discourse has become part and parcel of the weapons of warfare, it would be imprudent to disregard it altogether.

Many of the sorts of questions raised today by armed drones constitute a direct continuation of those raised two decades ago by the "war without risks" waged in the skies above Kosovo. At that time, Michael Walzer was wondering: is risk-free warmaking (that is, risk-free for the one making it) permissible?

He begins by noting that in the long tradition of the theory of just warfare, one finds nothing that rules out warfare at a distance: "So long as they can aim accurately at military targets, soldiers have every right to fight from a safe distance."[1] But Walzer continues with a reference to Camus that provides him with a subtle, dialectical way into another thesis. "In his reflections on rebellion, Albert Camus argues that one cannot kill unless one is prepared to die. . . .

153

But that argument does not seem to apply to soldiers in battle, where the whole point is to kill while avoiding getting
killed. And yet, there is a wider sense in which Camus is
right."[2] One gathers that this "wider sense" bears upon the
very principles of warfare, considered at a moral or meta-
legal level. Walzer then returns to Camus's maxim—which,
as we shall see, he at least introduces at the wrong point, if
not completely misconstrues—in order to formulate his own
thesis: "They have to be, as Camus suggests, prepared to die,
but that is consistent with taking measures to safeguard their
lives. . . . But what is not permissible, it seems to me, is what
NATO did in the Kosovo war, where its leaders declared in
advance that they would not send ground forces into battle,
whatever happened."[3] Then he drives the point home: "This
is not a possible moral position. *You can't kill unless you are
prepared to die.*"[4] The right to kill in this war thus seems in
principle to depend upon a willingness to expose the lives
of one's own soldiers, or at least not a priori excluding that
possibility.

It is worth noting that the position that Walzer defines
here traps the war leaders in a kind of double bind: on one
hand, they are morally bound to minimize the risks to their
own soldiers, but on the other, they are morally prohibited
from eliminating that risk altogether. As soon as one succeeds
in fully satisfying the first imperative by achieving zero risk,
one hits bottom, in every sense of the term, since that virtuous minimization turns into its contrary and becomes the
most extreme of moral scandals. This would be reaching a
forbidden limit. However, that is not exactly what Walzer
says. For him, this applies less to what soldiers do in an effort to eliminate risk for themselves than to the way their
leaders declare that they will not put their soldiers in harm's
way—which leaves open the question of whether doing so

without declaring it would be more allowable. Anyhow, as he sees it, the problem consists in setting up the principle of "zero casualty warfare" in one's own camp as a *moral norm*. But why? It boils down to considering "that those lives are expendable and these are not."[5] Therein lies the root of the scandal: by suggesting that the lives of the enemy are completely dispensable while ours are absolutely sacrosanct, one introduces a radical inequality in the value of lives, and this breaks with the inviolable principle of the equal dignity of all human lives.

I think Walzer is quite right to say that that is the presupposition of this imperative, and he is equally right to be scandalized by the idea. But I also think that he stops only halfway through the analysis. Why is it indeed unacceptable to disengage absolutely (a priori) the power to kill from the risk of dying as one kills? The author wants to break away from a fundamental principle of ontological equality. The weight of the terms that he employs indicates his essential resistance. What he lays his finger on is an extreme case that he has to reject. But the reason it is so scandalous is not solely moral but also theoretical: the gut reaction of a theory faced with a phenomenon that, if accepted wholeheartedly, would threaten to destroy it utterly.

Walzer implicitly provides the key to the problem and does so in a kind of citational Freudian slip in which he refers to *L'Homme révolté*. For in this text, Camus is reflecting not on warfare but on something else. The chapter, entitled "Delicate Murderers," concerns the conditions of terrorist political assassination, not warfare. Camus's characters, young Russian idealists of the early twentieth century, intend to commit assassinations in reprisal for the harsh repression enforced by the tsarist regime. However, they come up against a contradiction, a case of conscience:

Necessary and inexcusable—that is how murder appeared to them. Mediocre hearts, confronted with this terrible problem, can take refuge by ignoring one of the terms of the dilemma. . . . But these extreme hearts, with whom we are concerned, forgot nothing. From their earliest days they were incapable of justifying what they nevertheless found necessary, and conceived the idea of offering themselves as a justification and of replying by personal sacrifice to the question they asked themselves. For them as for all rebels before them, murder is identified with suicide. A life is paid for by another life, and from these two sacrifices springs the promise of a value. Kaliayev, Voinarovsky, and the others believe in the equal value of human lives. . . . He who kills is only guilty if he consents to go on living. . . . To die, however, cancels out both the guilt and the crime itself.[6]

Contrary to Walzer's interpretation of this text, the thesis is not that one must risk one's life in order to have the right to kill, but that assassination, nonetheless inexcusable, can only be envisioned if, at the moment of becoming an assassin, one is instantly wiped out along with one's victim. In this nihilist logic, it is a matter not of *risking* death but of *definitely* dying.

It is remarkable that Walzer makes this reference to assassination the basis of a moral critique of the immunization of the national combatant in warfare at a distance. It is a thesis that relates to the ethics of assassination, not the ethics of warfare. On the surface, of course, what he is saying is that it is morally necessary to accept the principle of one's own exposure to risk in order to be able to kill in warfare. But, in truth, his palimpsest of citation is very well chosen, for how is it possible to justify homicide in a noncombat situation? For those seeking to justify such activities, there is only one place to turn: doctrines on political assassination. That is the lesson Walzer provides as a reader of Camus. On the surface, Walzer certainly does appear to make a clear misinterpretation, for he twists the nihilist maxim in order to turn it into the moral motto of classic warfare: "One cannot kill unless one is prepared to die." However, at an underlying level, he is making another point: the agents of "war without risks" are in reality like assassins who use bombs to kill their targets; unlike idealistic terrorists, they have chosen to be ready to kill only if they are certain that themselves will not die.

As Camus predicted, "Other men to come consumed with the same devouring faith as these, will find their methods sentimental and refuse to admit that any one life is the equivalent of another." [7] And he went on to warn that then would come "the time of philosopher-executioners and of state terrorism." [8]

18

Warfare Without Combat

As to the code of war, I don't know what it is. The code of
murder seems to me a strange concept. I expect that we'll
soon have a jurisprudence for highwaymen.

—Voltaire

The history of the philosophy of law and war is marked by
many arguments about weapons that are licit and those that
are not and the criteria by which they can be distinguished.
One classic discussion concerns the use of poisons: given that
these are a means of assassination, can we use them as a
weapon of war?

Grotius appears embarrassed by this question and replies
in a convoluted two-stage fashion. On one hand, if one refers solely to "the law of nature," once it is permissible to
kill—that is to say, once a person deserves death—all that
counts is the result, so what do the means matter?[1] Nevertheless, poison does pose a particular difficulty. It is an under-
handed weapon. One cannot see it coming. It kills the enemy
without his knowing. In this respect, it deprives him of his
"power of defending himself."[2] Accordingly, "the Laws of
Nations, if not of all, at least of the best, have long been, that
it is not lawful to kill an enemy by poison."[3]

The true motive for such a prohibition was basely materi-
alistic: the reason it was in the interest of princes to prohibit

poison was because this weapon, unlike others, was directed against themselves in particular.[4] All the same, the criterion suggested for the rationalization of this prohibition was interesting: what was forbidden was the use of a weapon that deprived the enemy of the freedom to defend himself.

One historian of law, François Laurent, has provided an instructive commentary on this text:

Can one employ poison? Grotius has no hesitation in replying that, according to the laws of nature, it is lawful to do so: once an enemy deserves death, he says, what does it matter what means are used to provide it? He nevertheless hastens to add that the Law of Nations has eventually disapproved of poisoning and he admits that is it more honorable to kill in a way that allows the enemy to defend itself. He should have said that poisoning is unlawful. What misled Grotius in this whole discussion was a mistaken idea of justice. In his view, war is a judgment in which the belligerent parties are the judges and the vanquished is guilty and so deserves death; on that account, any means are lawful—the poison by which Socrates died just as much as a sword or a rope; if necessary one may even resort to an assassin. . . . We reject this doctrine, for it is as false as it is dangerous. No, the victor is not a judge, nor is the vanquished guilty. Warfare is a duel in which the most perfect legal equality must reign. Neither party is either judge or guilty; or else, it has to be that both are, together, at once the judges and the guilty parties: which is absurd. The possibility to defend oneself is thus more than a matter of nobility; it is a right and any means of killing that prevents the exercise of that right is unlawful. Otherwise the duel or war degenerates into an assassination.[5]

Historically, there are two radically opposed paradigms for the legal conceptualization of war. The first, of a penal nature, assimilates it to a legitimate punishment. The enemy is a guilty party that deserves to be punished. Armed violence is his sentence. Such a relationship is completely unilateral: the idea that the condemned party can call upon a right to defend himself seems absurd. The second model, which inspires existing law, is, on the contrary, based on the principle of *an equal right to kill* and, through the notion of the combatants' legal equality, is connected (but not confused) with the model of a duel. The founding principle of the *jus in bello* is that of an equal right to kill each other without this being a crime.

According to Laurent, the latter schema implies the right to the possibility of defending oneself. It is not clear what the positive attributes of this right are, but negatively, at least, it would prohibit the use of weapons that a priori suppressed that possibility. It would amount to something like a right not to be deprived of combat—that is to say, not a chivalric right to combat using equal weapons, but something more like a right to the chance of combat.

War is one of the rare activities in which one can kill without crime. It is presented as a moment when, in certain conditions, homicide is decriminalized. At a normative level, this is fundamentally what the word "war" means. A combatant who kills while respecting the clauses of *jus in bello* is granted legal immunity.

But there is a fundamental question that needs to be asked: in the name of what principle or meta-principle can the law of armed conflicts decriminalize homicide? On what normative basis can this setting aside of the prohibition on killing be founded?

Samuel von Pufendorf explains, "The custom of nations holds that the belligerents mutually in a formal war are upon an equal footing so far as concerns the justice of the war, when they make peace," and so "the damage caused by either side is forgiven, as if it had been done by agreement." [6] This is the thesis that there exists between belligerents some kind of war pact. "A similar agreement is entered into by those who leave the decision of their disputes to the outcome of duels . . . inasmuch as each of them, willingly and by agreement, entered a combat the law of which was either to kill or be killed." [7] Of course, this is a legal fiction, but the law is, in its very essence, founded upon such fictions.

The right to kill with impunity in war thus seems to be based upon a tacit structural premise: if one has the right to kill without crime, it is because that right is granted mutually. If I agree to confer upon another the right to kill me or my people with impunity, that is because I count on benefiting from the same exemption if I myself kill.[8] The decriminalization of warrior homicide presupposes a structure of reciprocity. The killing is allowed only because it is a matter of *killing each other.*

This has an important implication: whatever the legitimacy of the initial declaration of war, regardless of any marginal respect for the *jus ad bellum* (the right to wage war), and so even if the attack is "unjust" (but who will decide about that?), the belligerents find themselves benefiting equally from the *jus in bello* and, along with this, from an equal right to kill each other according to the rules. A nineteenth-century jurist invokes a classic image when he writes: "The legal equality assured to each of the belligerents by the laws of warfare is, to them, the same as the equality of weapons that was granted to the champions of single combats." [9] In the absence of equal weapons in single combat (for war is not a sport), the equality of the combatants here consists in their mutual right to kill each other.

But what happens to that right when there is no longer

any effective possibility of reciprocation? In practice, "the basic equality of moral risk: kill or be killed"[10] in traditional war was replaced by something akin to a "turkey shoot."[11] War degenerates into a putting-to-death. This is the situation introduced by the exclusive use of drones in asymmetrical warfare.

It could perhaps be claimed that this mutual right remains. But it must also be agreed that the right is no longer any more than formally mutual. What is the worth of a right to kill one another without crime when only one of the two protagonists can still enjoy the real content of that founding permission? Deprived of its substance, that right no longer has anything but a ghostly existence, as empty of reality as the undiscoverable cockpit of the drone is empty, with no human occupant to target.

In a false pretense, one-way-only armed violence persists nevertheless in claiming to be "war" even though it is a war without combat. It claims to be able to apply to situations of execution or slaughter—categories forged in the past for situations of conflict. But in doing so, projecting upon absolutely unilateral situations a *jus in bello* that was devised and intended for relations of relative reciprocity, it inevitably founders upon categorical errors.

In the discourse of "applied military ethics," the whole discussion is reduced to the question of whether or not the use of armed drones can conform to the principles of the law of armed conflicts: is the use of this weapon potentially in conformity with the principles of distinction and proportionality? But what is forgotten is that because this weapon rules out combat and because it transforms war from being possibly asymmetrical into a unilateral relationship of death-dealing in which the enemy is deprived of the very possibility of fighting back, it surreptitiously slips out of the normative framework initially designed for armed conflicts.

To apply norms designed for a conflict to slaughtering practices, and to be willing to pursue the discussion without
questioning the presupposition that these practices still stem
from within that normative framework, ratifies a fatal confusion of genres. As a result, the ethic of combat shifts and
becomes an ethic of putting to death, a necroethic that makes
use of the principles of *jus in bello* in order to convert them
into criteria of acceptable murder: an ethic for butchers or
executioners, but not for combatants.

But this phenomenon, which we have already seen in action, also corresponds to a profound crisis in the legal theory
of war. The difficulty, which is of a meta-legal nature, is that
once all reciprocity is in effect lost, so too the classic basis of
the right to kill without crime disappears for whoever still
claims it.

In an article entitled "The Paradox of Riskless Warfare,"
Paul Kahn has warned that this form of warfare threatens to
erode the traditional basis of the right to kill.[12] He explains
that as soon as one leaves behind a "relationship of mutual
risks" and the "requirement of reciprocity" is broken, war is
no longer war: it turns into a kind of police action. Kahn adds
that, quite apart from that reciprocal relationship, the right
to kill with impunity in war stemmed from an original right
to legitimate defense.[13] If one has the right to kill without
crime, it is—according to him—by reason of a right to self-
defense in the face of imminent peril. If all physical dangers
to oneself disappear, that right disappears too.

It is perhaps not necessary to introduce any notion of self-
defense, as he does, in order to justify the decriminalization of
murder in the law of war. As I have already pointed out, the
classic thesis is different: the rational basis for exoneration
from the crime of murder, at least in one traditional sense,
is the tacit pact of warfare described by Pufendorf. From
that point of view, the right to kill without crime is founded

purely upon its *mutual* character, its reciprocity. Even within this minimal schema, the meta-legal crisis still remains, for when the possibility of reciprocity becomes purely formal, the basis for crimeless homicide tends to evaporate.

In such a situation, how can the supporters of a right to assassinate from the air maintain their position? The solution lies in nothing less than a forceful distortion of the law of warfare. To find a basis for a right to unilateral murder, there is only one theoretical possibility: to make the *jus in bello* follow from the *jus ad bellum*, making the former conditional upon the latter in a monopolistic way modeled upon an unconventional melding of police and penal practice, so as to reserve for the "just warrior" the right to kill without committing a crime.

This is what is proposed by Strawser and also by philosopher Jeff McMahan, both of whom totally reject the thesis of "the moral equality of the combatants" and replace it by a unilateral right to kill founded upon a concept of *justa causa*. "The warrior fighting for a just cause is morally justified to take the life of the enemy combatant," writes Strawser, "whereas the unjust fighter is not justified, even if they follow the traditional principles of *jus in bello* [such as only targeting combatants and the like], to kill the justified fighter." [14] I have the right to kill, you do not. Why? Because I am just and you are unjust. I am good, you are bad, and only the good have the right to kill the bad. That, by and large, is what the puerile logic of this type of reasoning boils down to. The enemy's reply to this will of course be that he is the good one, the opponent is the bad one, so it is in truth he who has the right to kill the other . . . and so it will continue until one of the two ends by winning the day, thereby providing, through force, irrefutable proof of his own right. Since I have killed you, you can see perfectly well that I was the

good one. By contrast, the opposite thesis, that of the combatants' *legal* equality—which is what dictates the existing law
for armed conflict (and which is not, it should be stressed,
a *moral* equality, for the latter criterion is completely irrelevant here)—takes into full account the constitutive aporia
in the definition of just warfare and in consequence awards
equal rights and duties to the belligerents, irrespective of
their self-proclaimed "morality" (which, of course, nobody
doubts). In short, not content simply to deprive the enemy
of the material possibility of fighting, drone partisans intend
also to deprive him—explicitly this time—of any right to
fight at all, even at the cost of annihilating the law along
with him. All this does at least have the merit of coherence.
As Walzer pointed out, "Without the equal right to kill, war
as a rule-governed activity would disappear and be replaced
by crime and punishment, by evil conspiracies and military
law enforcement." [15]

All this constitutes a deliberate theoretical offensive in the
current "lawfare"—a neologism that highlights the legal aspects of waging war, as fought by lawyers using memoranda
as their weapons. But it is also implicit in the material nature
of the weapon. The effects of airpower on the juridical and
political categorization of the enemy was something that Carl
Schmitt, in his day, had accurately pinpointed. His analysis
of the effects of "autonomous aerial warfare," in which "the
lack of relation between military personnel in the air and
the earth below, as well as with inhabitants thereon, is absolute," is still applicable today to the armed drone: "Bombing
pilots use their weapons against the population of an enemy
country as vertically as St. George used his lance against the
dragon. Given the fact that war has been transformed into
a police action against troublemakers, criminals, and pests,
justification of the methods of this 'police bombing' must be

intensified. Thus, one is compelled to push the discrimination of the opponent into the abyss." [16] The verticalization
of armed violence implies a tendency toward the absolute
hostilization of the enemy, both politically and juridically.
He is no longer positioned, in any sense of the term, on the
same ground as oneself. [17]

19

License to Kill

If you do something for long enough, the world will accept it. . . . International law progresses through violations. We invented the targeted assassination thesis and we had to push it.

—Daniel Reisner, former head of the
Israeli Defense Forces Legal Department

Within what legal framework do drone strikes take place today? Where the United States is concerned, it is impossible to say. Everything is blurred. The administration refuses to reply to the question, even in court.[1] A speech given by Harold Koh, legal adviser to the State Department, in 2010 before the American Society of International Law is symptomatic of this calculated opacity. He performs a kind of belly dance, maintaining ambiguity, switching between a variety of registers, using them all at once or in turn but without ever deigning to choose between them, as if he were leaving the final decision until later. In any case, he claims, drone strikes are licit and are undertaken either "in an armed conflict or in legitimate self-defense."[2] But he does not explain exactly which of these the United States is engaged in, nor how the legal standards for the use of lethal force would differ depending on whether they were operating in the first or the second of those two situations. Philip Alston, the United Nations special rapporteur, comments, "He very casually said,

167

'Well, we are applying either the law of armed conflict or the rules governing the right to self-defense of a state.' Now, those two sets of rules are radically different." [3]

This artistic blurring has puzzled many jurists.[4] They tell politicians they must declare whether it is a matter of war or of legitimate self-defense; they must choose. However, the administration refuses to do that because the consequence of resolving ambiguities in the framework of reference would entail the prohibition of the present drone strikes or would drastically limit their lawfulness.

The problem is that those drone strikes are hard to fit into established legal frameworks. For anyone seeking to justify them legally, there are only two possible options—either the law of armed conflicts or else that of law enforcement[5] (which can loosely be defined as the law relating to the police, but which can be extended to include "military and security forces operating in contexts where violence exists but falls short of the threshold for armed conflict").[6]

To seize upon a first approximation of the difference between those two models, we must consider what it is that distinguishes the prerogatives of a soldier on the battlefield from those of a police officer on patrol when it comes to the use of lethal force. Whereas a soldier may, with impunity, "shoot to kill" at any legitimate military target, a police officer can fire only as a last resort, and only as a proportionate response to an imminent threat. Let us examine these two points in a more detailed fashion.

First, consider the hunter-killer drone used as a weapon for law enforcement. In law enforcement, one should first try to capture the individual, giving him the possibility of surrendering and even, if possible, offering him that chance. "Law enforcement authorities can use no more force than is absolutely necessary to effectuate an arrest, defend themselves, or defend others from attack," writes legal scholar

Laurie Blank.[7] The use of lethal force should remain the exception in this case: it is permissible only if it is the sole available means in the face of a threat that is "instant, overwhelming, and leaving no choice of means, and no moment for deliberation."[8] Any use of lethal force that does not respect these conditions is, "by definition, [to] be regarded as an 'extra-judicial execution.'"[9]

If the drone strikes take place within this legal framework, the argument that every effort is made to keep collateral damage to a minimum carries no weight at all.[10] It is more or less as if a police officer who has unjustifiably killed someone tries to exonerate himself by pointing out that he was careful to conform with the principles of distinction and proportionality that apply to armed warfare. It would all be a pure and simple category error.

Given that there can be no gradation in its use of force, the drone is incapable of conforming to the very specific principle of proportionality that applies in the law enforcement paradigm. As Mary Ellen O'Connell explains: "What drones cannot do is comply with police rules for the use of lethal force away from the battlefield. In law enforcement it must be possible to warn before using lethal force."[11]

Some supporters claim that drones are analogous to the bulletproof vests worn by the police.[12] They are efficient means of protecting the agents of the state police force, and such protection is legitimate. That may be so, but they are forgetting an essential difference: the wearing of a bulletproof vest does not prevent the taking of prisoners. With a hunter-killer drone, however, such an option is impossible. It is all or nothing: either shoot to kill or take no action at all. Lethal force is the only option available. This loss of operational capacity incidentally highlights the affinity between this weapon and the doctrine "kill rather than capture," which today is official policy in the White House: "Mr. Obama has avoided the complications of detention by deciding, in effect, to take no prisoners alive." [13] In this respect, the drone is a dream of a weapon. One can always claim afterward that capture with these means was "infeasible"—failing to acknowledge that this technical incapacity was deliberately organized further up the line. (One might imagine a classified advertisement that read "Exchange Guantánamo for Predator.")

With that first option closed, it was still possible to fall back on plan B: one would say that drone strikes are allowed by the law of war. Law professor Kenneth Anderson says wryly,

> Certainly, it sounded better, as a law-PR matter, to say that one was targeting "combatants." What [the Clinton, Bush, and Obama] administrations seemingly neglected to consider, as a legal matter, is that law of war treaties and customary law defining armed conflict actually have formal conditions—thresholds that must be met before all the particulars of the laws of war kick in. Armed conflict in a legal sense is *lex specialis*, and you get its very special rights, immunities, privileges, and obligations *only* if the circumstances meet either the treaty law (in the case of interstate conflict), or the customary law standards for armed conflict with a non-state actor . . . which requires sustained, persistent fighting occurring in a theater of conflict. A theater of war even if loosely defined is not simply the whole planet. [14]

And there was another problem: the CIA agents who piloted some of the American drones were civilians, so their participation in armed conflict would constitute a war crime. Within this framework, the agency personnel "could be prosecuted for murder under the domestic law of any country in which they conducted targeted drone killings." [15]

To sum up, the only two possibilities turned out to be unworkable: either (1) the strikes were a law enforcement activity, in which case they ought to conform to the restrictions that applied to them, one of which called for gradation in the use of force—something that was impossible for a drone—or (2) they were covered by the laws of war, although these laws do not apply in zones that are currently not experiencing armed conflict, such as Pakistan or Yemen, where they nonetheless operate at present.

Now it is easier to understand the embarrassed silence of the U.S. administration. It truly does find itself in a very uncomfortable legal dilemma, in which, "on the one hand, targeted killing outside of a juridical armed conflict is legally impermissible and, on the other hand, as a practical matter, no targeted killing even within the context of a 'war' with al Qaeda is legally permissible either." [16]

Kenneth Anderson, a visiting fellow at the Hoover Institution and a great partisan of assassination from the air, is worried. His concern is that with its supporters having so far failed to elaborate an appropriate legal doctrine, the practice of targeted assassinations may soon find itself compromised. As he sees it, there is an urgent need for the administration to "confront this problem while it still has intellectual and legal maneuvering space." [17]

So long as the practice of political assassination stayed clandestine, the question of its legal framework could remain of secondary importance. But now drone strikes fall within the domain of what might be called public secrets. Exposed to the light of day, as they now are, they become vulnerable, especially in a world where "in the complex intertwining of activist, government, international organization, and academic positions around these debates, perception matters a lot." [18]

The solution that Anderson favors would involve creating a third legal way, escaping from the binary nature of normative paradigms by creating a new regime of ad hoc law for these death-dealing operations, what he calls "naked self-defense"—*naked* in the sense that it can cast off the legal restrictions that ordinarily confine self-defense. Anderson evokes a type of customary law in the service of national self-defense that draws on antecedents provided by national tradition [19]—no doubt the traditions of mercs, "black ops," "technical advisers," death squads, and torture instructors. What he is now suggesting for the drones, on the basis of the ancient status of these clandestine practices that command honorable recognition, is quite simply that they should be officially sanctioned.

His reference here is to the doctrine elaborated in the late 1980s by former State Department legal adviser Abraham Sofaer: "Targeted killings in self-defense have been authoritatively determined by the federal government to fall outside the assassination prohibition." [20] To put that more clearly: if "targeted" assassinations are not crimes, that is because the government says so.

This would give rise to a curious legal hybrid, somewhere between warfare and policing, that could benefit from the liberalities of both regimes without being obliged to accept the constraints of either. Militarized manhunting would at last have found adequate legal expression in the shape of a global right of lethal policing. The United States would profit, since "self-defense gives the discretionary ability to attack anywhere in the world where a target is located, without having to make claims about a state of armed conflict everywhere and always across the world" [21]—an elegant enough solution, which, however, Philip Alston ventures to translate as "license to kill." [22]

If the position adopted by Anderson is instructive, that is because it reveals not only the legal fragility of this policy but also the growing disquiet assailing some of its agents. "The middle officials of the CIA in my estimation have doubts about that now—they see the whole activity moving the way that detention and interrogation did after 9/11," writes Anderson. "The advocacy folks would like to make Predator drone attacks as legally uncertain as detention and interrogation—and indications, at least in my experience, are that it does not take much uncertainty about what the future might hold in the way of [Eric] Holder-style announcements, the possibility of indictments or arrests in Spain or other jurisdictions, and all that stretching into a long and unknown future, to induce changes in behavior by US personnel." [23] You have been warned. . . .

V

Political Bodies

20

In War as in Peace

The sovereign thus provides for the preservation of man's days when he declares war as soon as it becomes necessary for the safety of his people. He makes war! But how can one speak of preserving human life when one speaks of war,—war, the aim of which is to destroy life, or at least in which death is inevitable! How amazing and, at first sight, incomprehensible!

—Abbé Joly

The invention of the armed drone has revealed not only a redoubtable weapon but also, simultaneously, something else, but without our noticing it and almost by mistake: namely, a technical solution to a fundamental tension that has put a strain on the theory and practice of political sovereignty ever since the seventeenth century. This silent revolution is what I should now like to place in perspective. This involves considering not how the drone, as a new weapon, transforms the forms taken by armed violence or our relation to the enemy in these new circumstances, but rather how it tends to modify the state's relations to its subjects. To this end, we must undertake a detour by way of the history of political philosophy.

According to social contract theories, men form political societies and set up a state for themselves primarily to preserve their lives. Nevertheless, the sovereign holds over them the power of death or life, by virtue of which he can expose their lives in war. The theoretical difficulty lies in the discrepancy between those two principles: the founding imperative to protect their lives and the overriding right to have them die.[1] In consequence, sovereignty appears to be affected by a kind of multiple-personality disorder. In passing from a state of peace to a state of war, the relations between the sovereign and his subjects undergo a complete change.

There are two different schemas. The first seems to correspond to the state that we call "normal," that of a protective or security-based sovereignty—what might be called the *protectorate*. In this case, political authority is structured by what Hobbes calls "the mutual relation between protection and obedience."[2] The sovereign protects me, and it is because he protects me that he has the right to force me to obey him. Schmitt condensed this into the formula "Protego ergo obligo": I protect, so I am obliged.[3] The power of protection is the basis for commanding. The political relationship is presented as an exchange: so long as protection descends from the sovereign to his subjects, obedience rises up from the subjects to the sovereign. It is this two-way arrow that characterizes legitimate political authority, unlike in other, unilateral relationships that insist upon obedience without supplying protection in return.

But what happens when the state goes to war? Then, according to Hobbes, "each man is bound by nature, as much as in him lieth, to protect in war, the authority, by which he is himself protected in time of peace."[4] The protective relationship is reversed. In peacetime, the sovereign protects me; in wartime, I protect the sovereign. The phenomenon is one of a reversion of the protective relationship. In this new schema, the two arrows are aligned in a single direction, from the subjects to the sovereign. Now those protected must protect a protector who no longer protects them. As soon as war breaks out, the maxim of sovereignty is no longer, at least directly, "Protego ergo obligo," but the reverse: "Obligo ergo protegor"—I am obliged, so I am protected.

This reversal of Schmitt's maxim reveals the hidden principle of political domination, which the state of war betrays when it exposes it to daylight. Beneath the apparent text—"I protect you, so I must be obeyed"—lies another, "You must obey me so that I am protected," and that is the case even if I don't protect you from anything anymore, above all not from myself. It is from that interpretative turnaround that all the critical theories of protective powers take off.

But if one sticks with contract philosophies, one can immediately see the difficulties that they pose. When the sovereign exposes the lives of his subjects to warfare, he is no longer protecting them, so upon what can the duty of obedience of those subjects be based?

One answer is that what is committed to protecting when one protects a fallen protector is the very *possibility* of protection that was set up as the original purpose of a political society.[5] Historically, this clears the way for a dialectic of sacrifice, according to which, as Rousseau states, "whoever wills the end, also wills the means, and these means are inseparable from certain risks and even certain losses."[6] Far from the protection of lives ruling out their exposure, it is that very protection that justifies the exposure, in accordance with a protection debt or vital debt contracted at birth and which the protective sovereign can call in at any moment if the circumstances demand it. Your life is not something that you can withhold from the state, as if it had preceded the latter; your life is, on the contrary, the state's product, which it has gifted to you on certain conditions.[7]

Despite such replies, the connection between protective sovereignty and warring sovereignty remained a cross that modern political philosophy had to bear. The fact that

Hegel, for his part, refused to dialectize it indicates how very radical that tension was. To claim to justify the exposure of lives by an imperative to protect those same lives seemed to him not only an unacceptable sophism but also a "grave miscalculation." The question was not whether the sacrifice was justifiable—it was—but whether it could continue to be once the principle of the protection of lives was accepted as the essential basis of state power, "for this security cannot be achieved by the sacrifice of what is supposed to be *secured*—on the contrary."[8] As Hegel saw it, the contradiction, unacceptable in those terms, revealed the full falsity of theories about a security state. To assign the state the sole purpose of maintaining "the security of goods and people" was to be mistaken about the destiny of a state and indeed about its very meaning. To expose lives to death was not a distortion of state rationality but was, on the contrary, the contingent moment in which that rationality was revealed in all its splendor. For its true nature, far from residing in a mere reproduction of life reduced to an economic-biological concept, manifested itself, as does liberty, only in confrontation with death; not in the preservation of sensible life but in its negation, in its possible sacrifice in the name of higher ends.

Consider a state that conforms to a minimal, liberal, security-oriented definition and is conceived as a safety officer for civil society. Can such a state call, without contradiction, for sacrifice in war? What Hegel tells us is that it cannot. From this thesis one could derive an interpretation quite different from what the historian Edward Luttwak has called the contradictions of the postheroic era: if liberal democracies develop "an aversion to losses," that is not because they attach too great a value to the life of their citizens but because they no longer possess anything other than a very impoverished concept of what life is, a concept according to which the preservation of physical life at all costs is more important than the safeguarding of a far superior ethical and political life.

But the opposite may well be true, for if a liberal security state found a way of doing without the sacrifices of warfare, it might, *pace* Hegel, claim to have finally and without apparent contradictions realized its announced program. And it is precisely this that tends to justify the dronization of the armed forces. One can thus grasp what is politically at stake here: reconciling the neoliberal restriction of the aims of state power to security matters with the maintenance of its prerogative to wage war. Waging war, but without sacrifices. Freely exercising war-waging sovereignty, but within the internal political conditions of sovereign security and protection. Abolishing the contradiction. Wiping off the map the second schema, which is so problematic and in which official political relations were turned inside out and became unilateral in too flagrant a manner. Exercising power, at an internal level, in war as in peace.

But there is something else here that risks being put out of action: certain modes of criticism directed against the power of war, which had likewise emerged, on the basis of that fundamental contradiction, in the modern period and had survived into our own times.

For certain currents of thinking had seized upon that political tension and, on that basis and that of the flaw that it constituted, developed discursive strategies aimed at limiting the autonomy of decision of "the king of war."

Within what limits should a sovereign legitimately exercise that right of war? The foremost limiting strategy was to be found in the area of political economy. What a population constitutes is above all *wealth*, a living wealth that must not be wasted. Arguments concerning warfare coincided with those relating to taxation: one should not levy too many taxes, and contributions should be strictly proportional to public needs.[9] Likewise, this formed the basis for a principle of savings applied to the spending of lives. In opposition to bad kings who, prompted by futile desires for personal glory, blithely sacrifice "the blood and treasures of their subjects," it was pointed out that "the blood of the people can only be shed in order to save that very people in times of extreme need." [10] The legitimate exercise of sovereignty in warfare must be limited by the strict principle of necessity.

The second major critique was based on the philosophy of law. Kant asked by what right a state may make use of its own subjects, their goods, and even their lives in order to make war.[11]

An initial reply, Kant says, one that no doubt presents itself confusedly to the minds of sovereigns, might be that, just like a chicken or sheep farmer, kings "can use, wear out, and destroy (kill)" their subjects since most of them "are his own product." So "the sovereign has the right to lead them into war as he would take them on a hunt, and into battles as on a pleasure trip." [12]

In this zoopolitical conception of sovereignty, ownership is intertwined with breeding.[13] The right to wage war, seen as a political right, appears as a right of ownership that, according to its classic attributes, allows the owner to use or abuse whatever it is that he owns. But it is also regarded as the more specific right of a producer-breeder, according to which the subjects of his power are its *products*, seen—as Kant puts it—from the point of view of their abundance. The breeder is certainly not the genitor of the beasts in his flock or herd, but it is he who ensures the domestic conditions for their growth and reproduction. The breeder-sovereign can send them to the slaughterhouse whenever he chooses to do so because they are the live result of his labors.

Kant sets the arbitrariness of a zoopolitical sovereignty in

opposition to a principle of citizenship: the sovereign can declare war only if the citizens who will risk their lives in it
have expressed their "free consent" in a republican vote.[14]
If the citizens can have a say at this point, it is not because
they generally make the decisions, but specifically because in
this decision it is their lives and the exposure of their living
bodies to the danger of death or wounding that are involved.
This introduces a very important aspect to the situation: a
form of political subjectivity set in opposition to war-waging
sovereignty, something that I shall call the *citizenship of the
living* or the *citizenship of exposable lives*. In other words,
they must have a say in the decision because they run the
risk of dying in the situation the decision may produce. It
is because war-waging sovereignty exposes the lives of its
subjects—live citizens—that they acquire a measure of control over this power that can wound or kill them. It is because
it can destroy us that we *must* have some power over it.

What we have here is a reversal in the schema of the constitutive relations implied in war-waging sovereignty. In a
republican context, as Kant explains in the case of the right
of war, it is necessary to "derive this right from the duty of
the sovereign to the people (not the reverse)." [15] The obligatory relation is reversed. In its initial version, the one that
Schmitt borrowed directly from the relations of vassaldom,
at the same time universalizing it so as to convert it into a
kind of transcendental principle of politics, the protector-
sovereign declared: "I protect you, so I am in command." But
now, with Kant, the republican citizen replies: "You, the sovereign, are exposing my life, so you are obliged to obey me."

Every protective power needs those it protects to be vulnerable, even—as all racketeers realize—to the point of actively maintaining this state of vulnerability.[16] But unlike
the discourse of protective sovereignty, which begins by
introducing the postulate of *ontological vulnerability* as the

original state of its subjects, the starting point of the present critical discourse is *political vulnerabilization*, the authority's exposure of the lives of its subjects, which becomes the basis for the possibility of it becoming the object of a critique or some kind of limitation. The vulnerability that the protectorate postulates as its founding condition is twisted against it at the political level and, inasmuch as that vulnerability is actively exposed by the destructiveness of the sovereign, it becomes opposed to the latter as a limitative principle. In the face of the claims made for the unconditional mobilization of the bodies and lives of his subjects, the voices of his living citizens are raised: *We won't do it, we don't want to die for that, not for this war, not in this fight, for it is not ours.*

This citizenship of exposable lives has constituted an important—albeit not the sole—basis for a democratic critique of the power to wage war, not only in the institutional manner forecast by Kant, namely suffrage, but also as a vector of extraparliamentary mobilization in the antiwar movements of the twentieth century, However, the dronization of the armed forces, inasmuch as it reduces the military exposure of national lives to zero, tends to somewhat deactivate that critical attitude. It would nevertheless be a mistake to believe that an "aversion to losses" is the only possible motive and the cost/benefit calculation the only relevant rationality for the development of a critical voice in the face of state violence.

21

Democratic Militarism

> We don't want to fight
> But by Jingo if we do
> We'll stay at home and sing our songs
> And leave it to the mild Hindoo.
> —British song, 1878

A sovereign, given that he never places himself in danger in a war, "can thus decide on war, without any significant reason, as a kind of amusement" or hunting party.[1] The war hunt may be defined not only by a particular kind of relationship with the enemy but also, at an earlier stage, by a mode of decision marked by the fact that the decider's life is not at stake.

In a republican regime the situation is different. Since "the consent of the citizens is required to decide whether or not war is to be declared, it is very natural that they will have great hesitation in embarking on so dangerous an enterprise. For this would mean calling down on themselves all the miseries of war."[2] When the costs of the decision are assumed by the person who makes that decision, his clearly understood interest forces him to be circumspect. This involves, as it were, a cunning ruse on the part of pacifist reason: by respecting the fundamental principles of political law and opting for a republic, one brings into play a decision-making mechanism that tends, through the interplay of its

185

own calculations, to limit recourse to warfare or possibly even to rule it out. The principle of moderation that political economy sought to impose upon a war-waging sovereign is mechanically one with the mode of functioning. What Kant called a "republic" and we hastily call a "democracy" seems to possess the virtue of being in essence a type of regime that is inclined toward peace.

Significantly enough, Kant's text was rediscovered by American political science in the 1990s. From it, despite the bloody lessons provided by the twentieth century, beginning with those of World War I, an optimistic theory of "democratic pacifism" emerged. The German of Königsberg was translated into the more familiar economic vocabulary of the theory of rational choice: whereas a dictator can externalize the costs of war even as he garners all its benefits, the citizens of a democracy must weigh both the benefits and the costs. The citizen-electors' internalization of the human and fiscal costs of war triggers political leaders' internalization of the corresponding electoral costs, so democracies tend to avoid recourse to armed force, even to the point of ruling it out completely save for exceptional emergencies.

Contemporary American political experts were surprised to discover in an eighteenth-century philosopher what looked like a plausible explanation for their own post-Vietnam situation. Given that the United States was the very incarnation of a democracy (what Kant called a republic), one could claim that it was really not surprising for that prophecy to choose this country in which to be fulfilled.

But where the German philosopher had detected reasons for hope, certain others found signs of a disturbing situation. Madeleine Albright, irritated at the time by the Pentagon's hesitation to deploy ground forces in Bosnia, acidly asked Colin Powell, "What good is this marvelous military force if we can never use it?" [3] It seemed that democracy had ended up tying the army's hands. The need to find a solution was becoming urgent.

In his hypothesis, Kant had overlooked one scenario: what would happen if one found a means to replace citizen-soldiers by other instruments of warfare? This unexpected option entailed preservation by substitution.

It was a solution that had already been attempted, albeit with means still rudimentary, in the late nineteenth century. Hobson, the great defender of British imperialism, explained in 1902 how parliamentary and colonial regimes could, at little cost, rid themselves of "dilemmas of militarism." Rather than sacrifice national lives, in order to defend the empire all that was necessary was to expand it, or to use native forces to carry out the dirty work of putting down the rebellions that were beginning to threaten imperial authority. By allowing the "mild Hindoo" to straighten things out, the lower classes in Britain would be able to avoid conscription. As a result of delegating in this way to the "lower races" of the empire, the "new imperialism" effected a class compromise within the metropolis—and this presented the added advantage of mostly averting popular antipathy toward the colonial adventures.

Hobson warned that all this went hand in hand with a different kind of political danger: "Though reducing the strain of militarism upon the population at home, it enhances the risks of wars, which become more frequent and more barbarous in proportion as they involve to a less degree the lives of Englishmen."[4] In short, as Lord Salisbury had declared a few years earlier, India could certainly serve Great Britain "as an English barrack in Oriental seas from which we may draw any number of troops without paying for them. It is bad for England because it is always bad for us not to have that check upon the temptation to engage in little wars which can only be controlled by the necessity of paying for them."[5]

As soon as the costs of war become an external matter, the very theoretical model that proclaimed the arrival of a democratic pacifism begins to predict the opposite: a *democratic militarism*.[6] When it came to approving or rejecting going to war, citizens who were now immunized against the vital demands of warfare found themselves in more or less the same position as the shallow sovereign whose irresponsibility Kant deplored. As for their leaders, they at last had a free hand.

When freed from the constraints attached to the mobilization of human combatants, a sovereign could do precisely what Kant wished to avoid: he could "lead them into war as he would take them on a hunt, and into battles as on a pleasure trip."[7] Once warfare became ghostly and teleguided, citizens, who no longer risked their lives, would no longer even have a say in it.

Whether the risks of war are transferred to natives or to machines, Hobson's views still hold. The dronization of the armed forces, just like any other procedure that externalizes those risks, alters the conditions of decision making in warfare. Because the threshold of recourse to violence is drastically lowered, violence tends to be seen as the default option for foreign policy.

In a totally coherent fashion, we today find modernized versions of a Hobson-type anti-imperialist argument in the works of a whole series of writers who set out to criticize the drones from a liberal point of view, using the tools of the economic decision-making theory. Assuming that the democratic commander in chief is a rational agent, how will the "low cost" of this weapon affect his decisions?

The main effect is to introduce a massive bias into his decision. Any agent who can take action with fewer risks to himself or his camp is likely to adopt a riskier pattern of behavior—that is to say, riskier for others. Similarly, the drone is a classic "moral hazard"—a situation in which being able to act without bearing the costs of the consequences relieves agents of responsibility for their decisions.[8]

More precisely, we are told that drones introduce a threefold reduction in the costs traditionally attached to the use of armed force: a reduction of the *political costs* associated with the loss of national lives, a reduction of the *economic costs* associated with armament, and a reduction of the *ethical or reputational costs* associated with the perceived effects of the violence that is committed.[9]

That last point is very important. What is the purpose of the discourse about the drone's necroethics? Its function is to diminish the reputational costs associated with the use of this weapon. Hence its strategic function in the political economy of warfare. The more "ethical" the weapon seems, the more socially acceptable it becomes and the more it becomes possible to use it. But that remark helps us to detect two further contradictions in the above discourse.

The first is that of the *nullity of the conditional comparison*. It is claimed that drone use is justified because it would create fewer collateral victims than other weapons that could have been used in its place. What this argument postulates is that those other means really would have been used—in other words, that the military action would have taken place anyway, and it's just a question of which weapon is used. But that is precisely what the moral hazard associated with drones renders doubtful. The sophistry becomes clear when one reflects that those other means might never have been employed because of the prohibitively high reputational costs associated with them. Another way of putting that is to say that in a situation of moral hazard, military action is very likely to be deemed "necessary" simply because it is possible, and possible at a lower cost.[10] In such cases, it is necessarily false to say that the drone has inflicted less collateral damage: as Jeremy Hammond sums up, the number of civilian victims "of course isn't lower than it would be if there weren't drone strikes, in which case precisely zero civilians would be killed in them." [11]

The second objection concerns the *cumulativeness of lesser evils*. As Eyal Weizman has commented, "Even according to the terms of an economy of losses and gains, the concept of the lesser evil risks becoming counterproductive: less brutal measures are also those that may be more easily naturalized, accepted and tolerated—and hence more frequently used, with the result that a greater evil may be reached cumulatively." [12] To claim to have produced fewer civilian victims in each strike reduces the military reputational cost of each one, making it likely that more strikes will take place and thereby increasing the total number of victims. Another way of putting it is to say that the trees of a surgical strike conceal a forest of tombs.

That moral hazard produces yet another perverse effect, this time at a strictly military level. Drones are a very imperfect substitute for troops on the ground and, as we have seen, their exclusive use results in extremely counterproductive effects in terms of counterinsurgency strategy. But if that is the case, why are they used? There may be an economic logic to explain this apparent incoherence. Jonathan Caverley suggests that "low-cost" weapons constitute a strong encouragement to replace military operations by armed forces with highly capitalized military means (in other words, to substitute material for men), even when the effectiveness of that substitution is low (in other words, when the machines do less well than soldiers), for the reduced probability of victory is counterbalanced by the considerable reduction in costs. [13]

But what would be the alternative? Amitai Etzioni, a fervent supporter of drone strikes, asks: "Would we or the people of Afghanistan and Pakistan—or, for that matter, the terrorists—be better off if they were killed in close combat? Say, knifed by Special Forces, blood splashing into their faces?"[14] To which Benjamin Friedman replies, "Actually, yes. The argument is that we make more careful judgments about lethal acts when we anticipate more costs to our troops. Free wars, . . . are more likely to be dumb wars. That doesn't mean that we should put troops in harm's way just to have more skin in the game and improve debate. But we should worry about how the absence of discernible consequences at home makes us more likely to casually bomb people. It is not pop sociology but orthodox price theory that tells us that lowering costs increases demand."[15] *Homo economicus* goes off to war, and along the way he refutes the drone.

But if one changes one's theoretical spectacles, swapping those of orthodox economics for an analysis in terms of class relations, the phenomenon takes on a different aspect. What is at stake in a tendency to substitute capital for military endeavor is not only an upset in the conditions affecting the political calculations of the democratic sovereign but also, and more fundamentally, an increased social and material autonomization of the state apparatus.

The sociologist Beverly Silver explains that in the model that prevailed up until the 1970s, the industrialization of warfare, combined with the importance of numbers and the central place of the working classes and the maintenance of mass conscription, put Western leaders in a position of close social dependency in the exercise of military power.[16]

The Vietnam crisis made crystal clear all the latent political dangers associated with such a dependent relationship. The American ruling classes came to recognize the full scope of the powerful dynamics of social radicalization that could be engendered by an unpopular imperialistic war. They

could also see to what extent the explosive synergies activated by the antiwar movement resonated with all the social
movements agitating American society.

The first response was to make concessions to the civil
rights and labor movements. But this multiform crisis also
hastened an extensive strategic reorientation. Transforma-
tions already under way in the "modes of war" accelerated.[17]
The new strategy increased the weight of highly capitalized
warfare: there was a definite break from the existing model
of conscription and an increasing reliance on private contrac-
tors and the weapons for remote warfare. The old model of
an army of citizens gave way to a "market army."[18]

The key to this mutation was fundamentally economic,
for "by making conscription and casualties less likely, capi-
talization turns arming and war into exercises of fiscal, rather
then social, mobilization."[19] However, this dynamic of cap-
italization was not independent of political choices, which
themselves were deeply intertwined with the interests of the
military-industrial complex. Niklas Schörnig and Alexander
Lembcke have shown, in this regard, how the ethical and
political discourse of "zero losses" has been very effectively
promoted by industrialists producing armaments.[20] In 2002,
one advertisement for the Boeing X-45A drone proclaimed,
"Aircrews won't have to be put at risk to complete the most
dangerous of missions."[21] The two preoccupations—that
of the industrialists wanting to sell new weapons, and that
of politicians seeking to preserve their electoral capital—
converged and interacted, each overdetermining the other.

Silver explains how the structural effect of these muta-
tions in modes of war reduced the material dependence of
the state apparatus on military work and hence likewise the
social dependence on the bodies that made up that workforce:
"As such, the growing bargaining power of workers and citizens vis-à-vis their states—an inadvertent by-product of the

inter-imperialist and Cold War rivalries of the late nineteenth and twentieth centuries—is being reversed, along with many of the economic and social benefits achieved." [22]

In fact, contrary to the optimistic claims of "democratic pacifists," implicating the lives of the population in war decisions was far from an adequate guarantee that military butcheries would be prevented. But even if it failed to rule out catastrophes, its effects were by no means minimal. The state's dependence on the bodies of the lower classes to wage war was also one of the factors that made it possible for those classes to establish a durable bargaining power. The social state was in part a product of the world wars, the price paid for the cannon fodder, compensation for the blood tax levied by the struggle. And expenses of this type were a factor when the "costs" of weaponry were being calculated.

The history of the welfare state was intertwined with that of the warfare state. As Barbara Ehrenreich explains:

In fact, modern welfare states, inadequate as they may be, are in no small part the product of war—that is, of governments' attempts to appease soldiers and their families. In the U.S., for example, the Civil War led to the institution of widows' benefits, which were the predecessor of welfare in its Aid to Families with Dependent Children form. It was the bellicose German leader Otto von Bismarck who first instituted national health insurance. . . .

Several generations later, in 2010, the U.S. Secretary of Education reported that "75 percent of young Americans, between the ages of 17 to 24, are unable to enlist in the military today because they have failed to graduate from high school, have a criminal record, or are physically unfit." When a nation can no longer generate enough young people who are fit for military service, that nation has two choices: it can, as a number of prominent retired generals are currently advocating, reinvest in its "human capital," especially the health and education of the poor, or it can seriously re-evaluate its approach to war. . . .

An alternative approach is to eliminate or drastically reduce the military's dependence on human beings of any kind.[23]

It is that second option that is winning out. What is at stake in the process of dronization is the establishment of a balance between the withering of the state's social branch and the maintenance of its armed branch. And here we come to understand concretely what lies beneath the premise of "zero losses" and the absolute preservation of national lives.

On the face of it, the drone appears as the solution to the central contradiction of the discourse of protective sovereignty: wage war without endangering the lives of one's own subjects, preserve without loss, always protect. But here comes the bad news: the promise to preserve national lives goes hand in hand with the increased social vulnerability and precariousness of many of those lives.

22

The Essence of Combatants

> To fight is one thing, to kill a man is another. And to kill him
> like that is to murder him. . . . Look here—I'm not going to
> fire on a man alone like that. Will you?
>
> —Emilio Lussu, *Sardinian Brigade*

Hegel wrote, "Weapons are nothing else than the essential being of the combatants themselves, a being which only makes its appearance for them both reciprocally."[1] If it is true that weapons constitute the essence of combatants, what is the essence of those who fight using drones?

I am my weapon: that is a counterintuitive thesis. It conflicts with concepts of instrumentalism, contradicting the idea that the nature of the subject is independent of the means of his actions. On the contrary, it affirms that the two are essentially identical. If that is the case, I cannot dissociate my intentions or ends—the things that make me what I am—from the means that I employ in order to achieve them. Ethically, what I am is expressed and defined by the nature of the weapons that I mobilize. The choice of weapons is important because it radically affects what we are, and at stake in that choice is the risk of losing our soul or essence.

But, Hegel adds, that essence can only be recognized reciprocally. To be aware of what I am as a combatant, it is not enough simply to handle the weapon; I must also know what it is like to be its object. A violent subject can seize upon his own essence only if he experiences his own violence mirrored in the weapon of his opponent.

However, with a drone, this little phenomenological mechanism is completely derailed, for at least two reasons. In the first place, this is a weapon that spares its "combatant" from having to enter into combat. So *whose* essence does the weapon constitute, then? Second, a drone deprives the violent subject of any visible or reflexive contact with his own violence, so if an armed subject can seize upon his own essence only by means of reciprocity, what happens when the weapon itself rules out the possibility of such a relationship?

The answer: "They want to turn these guys into assassins." This was, according to journalist Seymour Hersh, the heartfelt response of one high-ranking officer to the announcement of the plans that defense secretary Donald Rumsfeld had for the U.S. armed forces in the aftermath of 9/11.[2]

"The attacked State is allowed to use any means of defense," wrote Kant in the *Doctrine of Right*, "except those whose use would render its subjects unfit to be citizens. . . . It must accordingly be prohibited for a state to use its own subjects . . . as poisoners or assassins (to which class the so-called sharpshooters who wait in ambush on individual victims also belong)."[3]

The theoretical principle Kant formulates here concerns what *a state may not make its citizens do*. The principle of citizenship forbids the state from ordering its soldiers to assassinate an enemy, employing weapons that a priori deprive the enemy of any chance of fighting back. The underlying idea is that what a state can make its subjects do is limited by what that would make them become. Whatever we are made to do makes us what we are, but some metamorphoses are forbidden to a state. Kant declares that a state does not have the right to turn its own citizens into assassins. Combatants, yes; assassins, no.

But that kind of prohibition may also be problematized in another way, according to a quite different philosophical approach that is no longer juridico-political or even exactly "ethical," as we shall see—at least certainly not in the sense that this term has acquired in contemporary applied ethics.

The story is always roughly the same: a soldier targets an enemy combatant but then, when he could quite well fire, something stops him. Often it's some detail—a position, a gesture, a way of behaving, something the man is wearing—that in the end makes the soldier decide not to squeeze the trigger. The enemy lights a cigarette; dashes off strangely disheveled, clutching his trousers; strolls along dreamily in the spring sunshine; or is caught completely naked while at his ablutions. At this point the combatant who was about to fire decides not to. Thrusting his gun aside, he turns to a trench comrade and says, "To fight is one thing, but to kill a man is another. And to kill him like that is to murder him. . . . Look here—I'm not going to fire on a man alone, like that. Will you?" [4] For Michael Walzer, such cases do not, as they do for Kant, introduce the formulation of an ethico-juridical principle that would set a priori limits upon what a state can legitimately require of its soldiers. The question is posed neither at that general level nor in that register. Rather, it emerges individually, subjectively, for each soldier personally: *Am I going to shoot?*

Walzer explains that if soldiers do not shoot, it is not because of repugnance at the idea of killing in general. Rather, they see in the enemy soldiers signs that remind them with an undeniable clarity that the target is someone just like themselves, not simply an "enemy." The image of the naked soldier is emblematic of what Walzer means here. When the soldier takes off his uniform, stripping away his artificial combatant's skin, his humanity is restored to the surface and saturates the entire field of vision. In not firing at the man who now appears to him simply as a human being, the soldier intuitively recognizes his opponent's prime right: his right to life, the very right that forms the basis of civilians' abiding right never to be the direct targets of armed violence.

The philosopher Cora Diamond challenges that interpretation. She tells Walzer that this is not what soldiers themselves say in their accounts. What they say is something different: that they do not wish to fire, they do not feel like it. But they never express this using the vocabulary of rights. They do not use a moral vocabulary. Instead, they resort to certain "ideas of what is soldiering, of being in a shooting quarrel with other men, a conception of it [soldiering] as consistent with the sense of common humanity not being shattered." [5] What she vigorously denies is that there is any need "to try to force on to these cases the idea that there is a recognition of rights that lies behind the reluctance to shoot at the naked soldier." [6]

I believe that Diamond is right, although the extramoral approach that she recommends here may be ethical (and, in a different sense, political) at a much deeper and more authentic level than she chooses to acknowledge. The problem about the discourse on rights, as she correctly explains, is that it impairs our very understanding of what matters. Not firing at the naked soldier has very little to do with respect for the principles of distinction and proportionality, and to try to force such a reading of it is the surest way not to understand it at all. According to the laws of war, soldiers have a right to kill enemy soldiers who are naked, disheveled, disarmed, smoking a cigarette, or even asleep, and they know this full well. When they do not do so, their action is not of a legal nature, and neither a discourse of rights nor one of applied military ethics can grasp its meaning.

So why do they refuse to fire? In my opinion, neither Walzer nor Diamond pays enough attention to the words of the former soldier Emilio Lussu cited in the epigraph to this chapter, even though both do mention them. A soldier who does not shoot in those circumstances is not necessarily a pacifist or a conscientious objector, for he probably will not refuse to kill other men in the course of combat. On the contrary, if he abstains from firing in this particular instant, it is because he wishes to maintain the distinction, for himself and also for his comrades, between "fighting" and "killing a man, just like that." The difference to which he clings, and is right to do so, is what for him separates combat from simple killing. It is a matter of remaining a combatant and not becoming, in his own eyes, an assassin.

What matters here for him is not so much an abstract recognition of the "rights of man," but rather what the fact of "doing it like that" would imply in his own eyes. If he does it, he knows he will have to live with that action. And that is what he rejects in advance. It is a matter not of *duty* but of *becoming*. The crucial, decisive question is not "What should I do?" but "What will I become?"

I believe that within this question of what agents of armed violence become there lies a very important point: what is the subjective position that a critic of violence can adopt?

The limit of that initial position is, of course, that the refusal we are discussing is at first purely individual, self-centered, for oneself. It is a "subjectivist" obstacle. The soldier *himself* does not wish to fire but, according to one account Walzer cites, may leave it to his comrade to do what he refuses to: *You do it, if you want to.* There is a limit to this strictly self-centered refusal: *I do not feel like doing it, but I don't necessarily see anything to stop someone else from doing it.*

How does one move on from a personal refusal to a general

refusal, in other words a political one? The first move in that direction is probably a question something like the one Lussu puts to his comrade: *I won't do it. Will you?* The other soldier replies, *No. I won't either.* That personal question is already a call for identification, for a possible solidarity in a common refusal.

The next question would be to discover how subjects might take part in this kind of refusal even if they are not personally involved in armed violence and the outcome does not necessarily affect them. Everything depends on how far the "self" can be extended. Does this concern only me, or does it involve others too?

A first response might be to declare that the acts committed involve only their immediate agents and that so long as these are few in number or so long as we ourselves are not among them, it matters little; it is not our business. That is precisely what Amitai Etzioni is cynically saying about drone operators. Of the possibility that what they are made to do leads to a disturbing desensitization, even a loss of the meaning of killing, he says: "It might have the feared effects. However, we are talking about a few hundred drone drivers; what they feel or don't feel has no discernible effects on the nation or the leaders who declare war or make it drag on." [7]

Sartre, for his part, had a completely different view of such matters: "There is not a single one of our acts which does not at the same time create an image of man as we think he ought to be. . . . Our responsibility is thus much greater than we had supposed, for it concerns mankind as a whole." [8]

Perhaps that is also what Diamond means when she remarks that what is at stake in the fact of shooting or not shooting a naked soldier is the fate of our "common humanity." She goes on to say, "It was the fear that the sense of common humanity had been eroded by the Vietnam War that made that war such a divisive one for this country." [9] So antiwar sentiment developed not solely because "our boys" were dying, not solely through "an aversion to losses," but also and perhaps above all because a common humanity was involved in what was happening, and that was what was in danger of being lost.

One of the slogans brandished at the time by some of those demonstrating against the Vietnam War proclaimed: "We are not a nation of killers." It came down to rejecting that war in the name of a particular idea of what "we" were or, at any rate, of what "we" did not think we were and above all of what "we" did not wish to be assimilated to. Such a position, which contests the violence of the state on the basis of the essence of its constituent subject, certainly makes for a powerful critical position.

In a way, it has been echoed in the antiwar movements that have developed in the United States in the twenty-first century, using the slogan "Not in our name." This subjective position was that of a constituent "we" ("we the people") that by publicly disowning its leaders (but this time using a non-nationalistic formulation) refused to be complicit in armed violence sponsored by the state:

Not in our name
will you invade countries,
bomb civilians, kill more children,
letting history take its course
over the graves of the nameless. [10]

However, the Vietnam-era slogan and the more recent one are not quite the same. Beneath the family likeness, their difference takes on a decisive political importance.

What is being challenged about state violence is not only

what it is making "us" become but also the type of "us" that it presupposes.[11]

The slogan "We are not a nation of killers" identifies "we" with the nation in a way that is inevitably more mythical than real. It states (albeit in the form of a denial) a thesis that is counterfactual and challengeable, not least when one considers the genocide of Native Americans that was involved in the founding of the United States.

The slogan "Not in our name" operates by making quite a contrary gesture: instead of reaffirming a mythical assumed "we," it sets up a "we" that stands in opposition to a "you," seceding from it. In its present action of rejection, it does not fail to point out a continuing history that has already rolled over too many "graves of the nameless."

A historian of the antiwar movement has written, "While whites marched under banners proclaiming, 'We are not a nation of killers,' black Americans linked the killings in Vietnam to their own experiences. On January 3, 1966, civil rights worker Samuel Younge, a member of the Student Non-violent Coordinating Committee (SNCC), was shot and killed in Alabama when he tried to use a whites-only rest room, and SNCC's statement called his murder 'no different from the murder of the people of Vietnam. . . . In each case, the U.S. government bears a great part of the responsibility for these deaths.' "[12] The war was rejected by many black Americans, who regarded it as "a white man's war on colored people,"[13] but the position that they adopted was not that of an agent who wished to disown his action. Rather, the position from which they recognized and rejected that violence both in Vietnam and at home was that of being its *targets*.

That reminder from the past connects with a more general lesson for the present: we should not forget that when this new weapon becomes a piece of equipment for not only the military forces but also the state's police forces, it turns us into potential targets.

As always, it all begins on the periphery, in foreign lands and along frontiers. In the spring of 2012, a magazine article noted, "The latest state-of-the-art surveillance system, called Kestrel, was tested this year during operations on the US-Mexican border." [14] This was a balloon-drone, a kind of Zeppelin equipped with cameras: "Not only does Kestrel give operators real-time images, it also records every event that happens below for later recall." [15] After a month of tests, the U.S. Border Patrol announced its intention to acquire this apparatus. A representative of the company that produced it said, "We think there's a significant domestic market." [16] It soon became known that the U.S. Congress had recently ordered the Federal Aviation Administration to integrate pilotless vehicles into American airspace by 2015.[17]

Here is another press clipping from that same period: the Montgomery County sheriff's office, north of Houston, Texas, announced that it had acquired a Shadow Hawk drone and declared that it was "open to the idea of adding non lethal weapons like tear gas, rubber bullets or Taser-style rounds to the drone." [18]

This is what Marx called a scenario of "war [being] developed earlier than peace": certain social and economic relations are initially developed for military purposes, and only later are they reintroduced and developed in order to function ordinarily within civil society.[19] The army serves as a center of invention, a laboratory of experimentation for new political technologies.

One of the questions that arises is whether societies that have, for the time being, failed to rule out the use of this type of technology in wars waged on the other side of the world will eventually realize, perhaps with a jolt, that this technology is designed to be used on them too, and whether they will mobilize themselves to block its use. For it is important for them to become aware that a future of video surveillance with armed drones awaits us if we don't prevent it.

As a last resort, there is always the possibility of procuring anti-drone clothing, such as that invented by the artist Adam Harvey.[20] It is made from a special metallic fabric that renders the body practically invisible to drones' thermal imaging cameras.

23

The Fabrication of Political Automata

Only the development of robot soldiers, which, as previously
mentioned, would eliminate the human factor completely
and, conceivably permit one man with a push button to destroy whomever he pleased, could change this fundamental
ascendancy of power over violence.

—Hannah Arendt

When Theodor Adorno composed his *Minima Moralia*, in
1944, the V-1 and V-2 rockets dispatched to London by the
Nazis constituted one of the subjects of his reflections.[1] In a
long section titled "Out of the Firing Line," he wrote:

Had Hegel's philosophy of history embraced this age,
Hitler's robot-bombs would have found their place . . . as
one of the selected empirical facts by which the state of
the world-spirit manifests itself directly in symbols. Like
fascism itself, the robots career without a subject. Like
it, they combine utmost technical perfection with total
blindness. And like it, they arouse mortal terror and are
wholly futile. "I have seen the world-spirit," not on horse-
back, but on wings and without a head, and that refutes, at
the same stroke, Hegel's philosophy of history.[2]

It refutes Hegel because history has lost its head and
the world its mind. Mechanics have destroyed teleology.

A V-1 before being launched, 1944. Lysiak, "Marschflugkörper V1 vor Start," Bundesarchiv Bild 146-1973-029A-24A.

The subject has faded away. There is no longer a pilot in the plane, and the weapon is no longer the essence of anybody.

However, a few lines further on, Adorno introduces a decisive dialectical nuance into that original statement. Having emphasized that in this armed violence that involves no combat, the enemy is now relegated to the role of a "patient and [a] corpse" to which death is applied in the form of "technical and administrative measures," he goes on to say: "Satanically, indeed, more initiative is in a sense demanded here than in old-style war: it seems to cost the subject his whole energy to achieve subjectlessness."[3]

The nightmare that takes shape on the horizon is one in which weapons themselves become the only detectable agents of the violence of which they are the means. But before again rushing in to proclaim the death of the subject, we should meditate on the reflection that the ghostly planes launched by the waning Third Reich inspired in Adorno: "it seems to cost the subject his whole energy to achieve subjectlessness."

It would be a mistake to think that automatization is in itself automatic. Organizing the relinquishing of political subjectivity now becomes the main task of that subjectivity itself. In this mode of domination, which proceeds by converting its orders into programs and its agents into automata, the power, already set at a distance, renders itself impossible to seize upon.[4]

Where is the subject that holds power? Against a background of neoliberalism and postmodernity, that question has become obsessive. Adorno's words indicate a good way to resolve it: it is wherever it is working actively in order to make itself forgotten. The intense activity designed to efface it is what unfailingly singles it out: a great deal of subjective activity, involving huge efforts and enormous energy, designed to cover one's tracks, efface evidence, and wipe out any trace of a subject involved in action. The aim is to dress all this up as purely methodical functioning, a kind of natural phenomenon endowed with a similar kind of necessity, headed only by administrative systems that from time to time correct bugs, bring things up to date, and regulate access to information.

In the United States, the Department of Defense today looks forward to "gradually reducing the role of human control and decision" in the functioning of drones.[5] Although it may initially be a matter of moving into a "supervised autonomy," in the long term the aim is to establish total autonomy. At this point, human agents would be neither in the loop nor over it (in the sense of supervision), but completely out of the loop. What is envisaged is a situation in which "robots are capable of exerting lethal force without human control or intervention."[6]

The roboticist Ronald Arkin is today one of the most

active promoters of this "lethal autonomous robotics."[7] His main argument is, once again, of an "ethical" nature: robot warriors will be "potentially capable of performing more ethically on the battlefield than are human soldiers."[8] Better still, they will be able to "behave in a more humane manner than even human beings, in these harsh circumstances."[9]

To justify his work, he writes, "My personal hope would be that they will never be needed in the present or the future. But man's tendency toward war seems overwhelming and inevitable." Alas, if we cannot avoid war, at least let us use our technical abilities to try to make it more ethical, for indeed if we could manage that, it would be "a significant humanitarian achievement."[10] To be sure . . . but in what respect could those prospective robot warriors "be more humane on the battlefield than humans"?[11] For a whole series of reasons, in particular thanks to their "precision," but above all because they can *be programmed to respect the law.*

These robots would be equipped with what Arkin calls an "ethical governor," a kind of artificial conscience or mechanical superego.[12] When lethal action is suggested by some other program, this deliberation software would trawl through the rules of warfare translated into ethical logic "in order to ascertain that it constituted an ethically permissible action."[13]

Because the robots would have no emotions or passions that might upset their judgment, they would apply these rules to the letter, like cold-blooded killers. And it is precisely because they "evince no fear, anger, frustration or vengeance"[14]—in other words, because they do not possess affect, an essential human property—that these machines are considered to be more humane than humans, that is to say more ethical. In order to produce authentic humanity, it is necessary to get rid of human beings, to liquidate them.

Such paradoxical discourse is not as absurd as it appears

to be. To explain it, it must be pointed out that it plays upon different meanings of the term "humanity," a word that classically has at least two meanings: on one hand, what human beings are, their essence; on the other, a norm of conduct, the fact of acting "humanely." One of those meanings is ontological, the other axiological. The very possibility of humanism lies within that semantic gap. And, in a rather bizarre fashion, it calls upon human beings to be humane—to adopt certain forms of moral behavior that conform to its ideal. But whereas the constitutive gesture of philosophical humanism consists in enfolding those two meanings together, roboethical posthumanism takes note of their discordance, even to the point of disengaging them. If humans can sometimes prove inhumane, why should nonhumans not be able to be more humane than humans, that is, better able to conform to normative principles that define humane conduct? Axiological humanity could then become a property of nonhuman agents, just so long as those artificial moral agents are programmed in accordance with the *correct* rules. So far, so good—or almost. However, the problem blows up in your face as soon as the action under consideration is homicide. Roboethicists basically declare that it's not a problem if machines decide to kill human beings. So long as those machines kill them humanely, in conformity with the principles of the humanitarian international law that dictates the use of armed force, there is no problem.

But where might problems arise? From the point of view of legal philosophy, two very important—in truth, insurmountable—problems can soon be detected.

First, to endow mechanical agents with the same right to kill that is enjoyed by combatants in warfare would be tantamount to setting homicide on the same level as the destruction of a purely material object, and that would certainly constitute a radical negation of human dignity. Once the law noticed this, in order to ban such weapons it could mobilize a third meaning of the notion of humanity, understood this time as *humankind*, which is the supreme object of its protection.

Second, the existing law on armed conflicts, by focusing on the *use* of weapons, postulates that it is possible to draw a real distinction between the weapon, conceived as a thing, and a combatant, conceived as a person who uses that thing and is responsible for how he uses it.[15] But the law's implicit ontology is blown apart by the autonomous lethal robot, for here we unexpectedly find a thing that sets about using itself. The weapon and the combatant, the instrument and the agent, the thing and the person become strangely fused into a single entity without a status.

The problem might first find expression in a crisis concerning legal categories: can certain things be considered persons? But it would also be reflected, in a purely pragmatic way, by a radical crisis affecting the *applicability* of the law. Everything would turn on the question of responsibility and, through this, on the very possibility of retributive justice associated with the laws of war.

A robot commits a war crime. Who is responsible? The general who deployed it? The technicians who programmed it? Within this little world, there would probably be a great deal of buck-passing. The military commander could always plead that he gave no orders to the robot and that, in any case, he was no longer in control of it. The state, the owner of the machine, the legal guardian of the thing, would no doubt acknowledge some responsibility, but by pleading that the damage caused stemmed from faulty fabrication, the state might place the blame on the manufacturer, who in turn might seek to blame the programmers. Then there is the matter of the robot itself. All that would need to be done would be to incarcerate the machine, dress it in male clothing for its trial, and execute it in a public place, just as in 1386 a criminal sow was executed for infanticide in a village in Calvados.[16] All of which would, of course, be as senseless and useless as beating or reprimanding a piece of furniture that one had bumped into, in order to teach it a lesson.

In short, this would involve a whole group of irresponsible people deemed responsible, and it would be very difficult to decide who had perpetrated the crime. With no person guilty of pressing the button, it would be necessary to seek out the tracks of an elusive subject amid the maze of legal and computer codes—a hunt for a subject in flight.

The paradox is that in the last analysis, when the lethal decision is purely automatic, the only human agent directly identifiable as the efficient cause of death would turn out to be the victim himself, who, as a result of making inappropriate physical movements, was unfortunate enough to set off the automatic mechanism that results in his own elimination.

Not only can there be no simple attribution of responsibility, but the description of that responsibility, diffracted amid this headless network of multiple agents, tends to become diluted. It changes from being intentional to being unintentional, from being a war crime to being a military-industrial accident. Rather, as in the case of the "junk bonds" skillfully elaborated by finance, it becomes very difficult to determine who is who or who has done what. This is a typical way of fabricating irresponsibility.

But what, the roboethics experts chorus in reply, is the point of bothering to discover possible guilty parties, given that crime has been ruled out? Strange though this objection may appear, it is important to assess the full implications of what it expresses, for what is at stake here is how to implement the legal norm. In order to get highway speed limits respected, one can either position radar devices and impose fines, or else one can install automatic speed limiters in

every vehicle. Those are two very different ways of imposing a norm: one is a sanctioning text, the other an integrated
means of technical control. Either announce the law and
establish sanctions a posteriori or else "incorporate ethical
and legal norms into weapons design."[17] However, there the
analogy peters out, for since the killer robot incorporates no
driver, there will no longer be anyone directly responsible
who can be blamed if anything happens.

That is something of which "warbot" proponents are very
much aware. But they have already made their choice between international penal justice and ethical killer robots.
"Be careful," they add; we must make sure that no excessive
"devotion to individual criminal liability as the presumptive
mechanism of accountability risks blocking development
of machine systems that would, if successful, reduce actual
harms to civilians."[18] With the law on course to become mechanical, human justice may well perish.

But to claim, as they do, that the law can be integrated
into "weapon design" itself is a gross abuse of language. All
that the roboethicists can do is integrate certain rules within
the design of certain programs, which clearly can be unin-
stalled or reprogrammed at any time. If you are capable of
doing this on your own computer, you can be sure that every
army in the world is likewise capable of doing so. The discursive operation here consists in justifying the development of
highly dangerous *hardware* by offering the option of virtuous software. Congratulations: in buying the car (or rather
the robot tank), you have also won a magnificent key ring.

This is a typical "Trojan horse" type of procedure: in the
name of the eventual prospect of ethical killer robots, you
win the acceptance of the development of killer robots pure
and simple, even though, as their supporters themselves
know full well, public opinion still is massively opposed to
them. By presenting the process of automatization as itself

automatic and ineluctable, and by generously proposing in advance to moderate its excesses, Arkin and his associates are masking the fact that they themselves are the extremely active agents of that very process,[19] effectively promoting it by providing the justifications that will be needed for it to prosper. The more widespread the legend of the ethical robot becomes, the faster the moral barriers to the deployment of killer robots give way. One might almost forget that the surest way to make the potential crimes of the cyborgs of the future impossible is still to kill them immediately, while they are as yet unhatched and there is still time to do so.[20]

Los Angeles, 2029. Above the ruins of the town, in the dark blue night, fluorescent lighting zigzags across the sky. On the ground a human combatant collapses, hit by a laser from a robot plane. The caterpillar tracks of a ghostly tank roll over a mountain of human skulls. This is the famous opening scene in "the war of machines to exterminate humanity" in James Cameron's 1984 film *The Terminator*, one of the first, fleeting cinematographic appearances of a drone, in the style of 1980s science fiction.

The utopias and dystopias of the robot are structured by the same fundamental, simplistic schema of two terms, man and machine, in which the machine either appears as the servile extension of some human sovereign or else, increasingly autonomous, begins to slip out of the control of its former masters and to turn against them. That is the scenario of *The Terminator*.

In this kind of story, after a description of the initial position of the pilot or teleoperator, which is that of an all-powerful agent, his imminent fall is announced. The human is soon to lose his central position. The drones will become robots. This switch to integral automatism is, we are told, written into the necessary evolution of the device: "in the

long term, any step toward tele-presence is a step toward robots," as Marvin Minsky prophesied in 1980.[21] This initial
centrality of the subject is followed by the announcement
of the death of the subject, who at that point loses what he
used to be believed to possess fully, namely control. Therein
lies the paradox of this model: although initially radically
anthropocentric, it is affected by a movement that inevitably
ends up by evicting the human subject.

When Walter Benjamin, in his day, analyzed the position
of a bomber pilot, he offered a more realistic approach to the
initial moment: "In the person of the pilot of a single airplane
full of gas bombs, such leadership embodies all the absolute
power which, in peacetime, is distributed among thousands
of office managers—power to cut off a citizen's light, air,
and life. This simple bomber-pilot in his lofty solitude, alone
with himself and his God, has power-of-attorney for his seriously stricken superior, the state."[22] In order to grasp what
type of agent or subject the pilot is, we need to imagine him
in his relationship to another kind of machine—not a plane
but the state apparatus, all of whose powers he momentarily
concentrates in himself, albeit from a subordinate position.
Although he may possess a slim margin for personal maneuver, the pilot only appears to be the all-powerful "master of
the machine." In reality he is already little more than the
fetishized avatar of the modern state's bureaucratic machine,
its provisional concretization reduced to one point, one hand
or one thumb. What the dronization of the fighter plane sets
out to accomplish technically is the suppression or displacement of this most imperfect link between the state apparatus
and its war machines.

In *Wired for War*, Peter W. Singer describes the following scene: A four-star general spends several hours watching from his office the images relayed back by a Predator
drone. Eventually he reaches for his telephone to give the

order to fire, and even goes so far as to specify to the pilot what type of bomb to use. This scene provides an example of the total confusion between the various levels of command, in which the general involves himself in the lowest level of tactical choices.[23] Concerned with military efficiency, Singer is alarmed by this kind of confusion of roles. At least his warning is clear: while theorists of "network-centric warfare" thought these new techniques would make a measure of command decentralization possible, "actual experience with unmanned systems is so far proving the opposite."[24]

Instead of "man" in general losing control to the "machine," here it is the lower-ranking operators who lose their relative autonomy to the higher echelons of the hierarchy. Integral robotization would further strengthen this tendency to centralize decision making, although in a manner different and certainly more discreet, but no less overdeveloped.

As roboticist Noel Sharkey (who is fiercely opposed to the development of such programs) explains, the deliberation software for an "ethical robot" must, like any other program, necessarily incorporate not only rules but also *specifications*.[25] In other words, an order to "target only legitimate targets" is an empty operation if there is no specification of what is covered by the variable term "target." Similarly, one can attempt to codify the principle of proportionality (good luck with that),[26] but it will always be necessary to specify, whether directly or indirectly, what constitutes the acceptable proportion of the number of civilians killed to the military advantage expected. In short, the parameters of the decision need to be specified, and that specification is not done by the program itself. A higher-level choice is needed—*a decision about the decision.*

The centralization of command (even if that command is now conveyed by programmatic specifications rather than by verbal orders) now takes on excessive proportions, for one single *decision about the decision*—the choice of a single value that fixes the parameters of all future automatic decisions in a particular sequence—once and for all has consequences for the unfolding of an indefinite myriad of future actions. Fixing the value of a specification for a program is far more effectively centralized than a set of separate orders—it is the equivalent of signing a single but infinitely repeatable death sentence.

In order to assist the process of decision taking, modern armies are already using software that is claimed to ensure that decisions are as closely in line with the law of war as is possible—and are therefore more "ethical." Here is an insight into how pertinent values are established: "In the opening days of the invasion of Iraq, they ran computer programs, and they called the program the Bugsplat program, estimating how many citizens they would kill with a given bombing raid. On the opening day, the printouts presented to General Tommy Franks indicated that 22 of the projected bombing attacks on Iraq would produce what they defined as heavy bugsplat—that is, more than 30 civilian deaths per raid. Franks said, 'Go ahead, we're doing all 22.' " [27]

Here, the military atrocity was, contrary to Arkin's assumption, not the result of mistakes on the part of lower-rank soldiers confused by the "fog of war" or carried away by the passions of combat. There was nothing spectacular about the point of origin of this atrocity. It was simply a matter of fixing the threshold of a relevant variable. What would be the figure corresponding to the variable "minimum carnage"? We do not know. More than thirty citizens killed? Okay. But this little decision affecting a decision, effected by a single word or one tap on a keyboard, has multiple very concrete—all too concrete—results.

What is most surprising is that this could still come as a surprise. The greatest crime lies not in an open flouting of the law but in the recesses of its sovereign application. This ordinary military atrocity lies well within the law, and except under the most imperative conditions, it does not have to emerge. Most of the time it does not need to. Contemporary forms of atrocity are hugely legalistic. They are the rule rather than the exception, not so much because the law has been suspended, but rather because it has been spelled out in accordance with the interests involved to the point where it capitulates with scant resistance. This kind of atrocity is formalistic, cold, technically rational, and backed up by particular conditions—the same elements that are supposed to make the killer robots of the future eminently ethical.

When the 1830 uprising in Paris was in full swing and it was becoming increasingly clear that the people would at last succeed in toppling the regime, the Duke of Angoulême is said to have given the following order to his aide-de-camp:

"Have the barricades destroyed."

"My lord, there are insurgents inside who will prevent it."

"Have the National Guard fire at the insurgents."

"My lord, the National Guard refuses to fire."

"It refuses? This is rebellion; have the troops fire at the National Guard."

"But the troops refuse to fire at the National Guard."

"Then order the troops to be fired upon." [28]

But of course there was nobody left to do that.

In 2003, when Northrop Grumman presented the military with the prototype of its X-47A combat drone, one officer exclaimed, "Hey, at least that plane won't talk back to me." [29]

But, contrary to what is suggested by science-fiction scenarios, the danger is not that robots begin to disobey. Quite the reverse: it is that they never disobey.

For in the list of human failings that military robots would avoid, there is one that is decisive but that Arkin forgets to mention: a capacity for insubordination.[30] Robots may be faulty or dysfunctional, but they do not rebel. The robotization of soldiers is wrongly represented as an ethical gain (although in redefining "ethical" as conforming mechanically to rules, it is reduced to being synonymous with the most lobotomized discipline or docility). In reality it constitutes the most radical of solutions to the age-old problem of army indiscipline. It rules out the very possibility of disobedience, but at the cost of simultaneously suppressing the principal source of infralegal limitation to armed violence: the critical conscience of its agents.[31]

The problem lies not with knowing whether control lies with "man" or with "machine," for that is an underdetermined formulation of the problem. What is really at stake is the problem of material and political automatization of the bodies of armed men, the essence of the state apparatus.

Theories can sometimes be summed up efficiently by an image or a drawing. The frontispiece of *Leviathan* shows a giant whose torso rises above the land. The figure is recognizable from its classic attributes: sword, crown, and scepter. But it is his clothing that attracts attention: his coat of mail is woven entirely from tiny human bodies. The state is an artifact, a machine—even the "machine of all machines"—but the components that constitute it are simply the living bodies of its subjects.

The enigma of sovereignty and that of its constitution, as well as its possible dissolution, is resolved by the question of its material: what is the state made from?

What Hobbes did, La Boétie had tried to undo, and by the same means. After all, the master who oppresses you and "for whom you go bravely to war, for whose greatness you do not

The frontispiece of Thomas Hobbes's *Leviathan.*

refuse to offer your own bodies unto death . . . where has he acquired enough eyes to spy upon you, if you do not provide them yourselves? How can he have so many arms to beat you with, if he does not borrow them from you?" [32] Therein lay the fundamental material contradiction: if power is embodied solely by our bodies, we can always refuse to offer them.

Arendt explained that, owing to this fundamental corporeal dependence, the power of the state—even in the most authoritarian of regimes—must, despite everything, be power and not pure violence. [33] There is no power without bodies. But, as she in a way acknowledged, the reciprocal statement is true: with no bodies mobilized, there is no longer any power.

A different age produces a different image. In 1924, a popularizing scientific magazine announced a new invention: a radio-commanded policing automaton. The robocop of the twenties was to be equipped with projective eyes, caterpillar tracks, and, to serve as fists, rotating blow-dealing

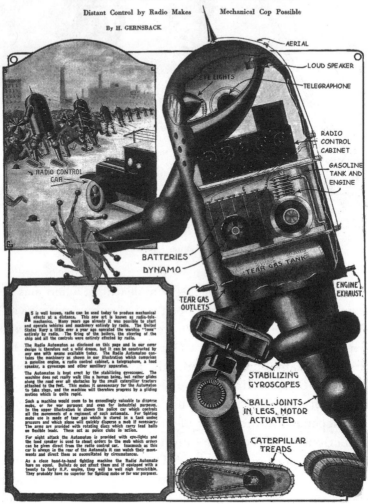

A radio-controlled police automaton. From Hugo Gernsback, "Radio Police Automaton," *Science and Invention* 12, no. 1 (May 1924): 14.

truncheons inspired by the weapons of the Middle Ages. On its lower belly, a small metal penis allowed it to spray tear gas at unruly parades of human protesters. It had an exhaust outlet for an anus. This ridiculous robot that pissed tear gas and farted black smoke provides a perfect illustration of an ideal of a drone state.

The difference between these two vignettes heralds what is at stake politically in the dronization and robotization of the armed branches of the state. The dream is to construct a bodiless force, a political body without human organs, re-placing the old regimented bodies of subjects by mechanical instruments that would, if possible, become its sole agents.

Once the state apparatus thus becomes, in effect, simply an *apparatus*, it would finally have acquired a body that cor-responded to its very essence: the cold body of a cold monster. It would at last technically fulfill its fundamental tendency. As Engels wrote, "This power, arisen out of society, but plac-ing itself above it and increasingly alienating itself from it, is the state."[34] All the same, once this stage was reached, it is also possible that its increasingly evident destiny would be to be dumped in a junkyard like any other piece of scrap metal.

EPILOGUE

On War, from a Distance

The text that you are about to read dates from 1973. At this
time, the U.S. military, beginning to learn lessons from its
Vietnam experience, was working on schemes to produce
armed drones. A number of young scientists engaged in the
antiwar movement put out a slender militant review, *Science
for the People*. They were aware of these military research
programs and produced the following anticipatory article,
warning of the perils involved:

> After the Air War a new form of warfare will appear
> much as the Air War succeeded the Ground War. We can
> call it the Remote War. . . .
>
> The central concept to Remote War is the remotely
> manned system, abbreviated RMS, which usually includes
> a remotely manned vehicle, RMV. The vehicle operator is
> located at a distant site and presented with information
> from sensors in the vehicle itself. . . .
>
> Any defense where the permanent physical limitations
> of the human body or machines physically connected with
> the human body are pitted against machines limited only
> by purely mechanical constraints, and yet controlled by a

remote director, are doomed. Remote War is a war of human machines against the human body. . . .

One side loses people; the other side loses toys. All that
is left is the shooting and dying . . . and toys don't die. . . .

The economic and psychological characteristics of Remote War determine its ultimate controller. Economi-
cally, the Remote War is much cheaper than the Air War,
besides being more effective. . . .

Because of this small cost, the U.S. Congress will have
no realistic economic restraint over the U.S. military's
conduct of Remote Wars. . . .

With respect to the U.S. Congress, this leaves the U.S.
Military free to wage Remote Wars wherever and whenever it chooses. This free hand allows the U.S. Military (or
the CIA, for that matter) to expand the American empire's
sphere of influence by forcibly crushing national movements which are considered against American interests.

The psychological characteristics of Remote Warfare
also determine its ultimate controller. Television warriors
are numbered in 1,000's, not in the 100,000's of the Air
War. The television warriors never face the prospect of
being killed in action. . . .

Psychologically, Remote Wars are easy to conceal and
the U.S. Military has to tell no one.

Characteristics of Remote Warfare could be used to
silence anti-war critics who try to stop its development.
There will be no American killed-in-action or prisoners-
of-war. Toys have no mothers or wives to protest their
loss. Remote War is very cheap. Economic critics of war-
induced expenses and inflation will have nothing to protest. With its precision killing ability, Remote War will
not harm the ecology. Ecologists who complain of envi-
ronmental devastation will have nothing to protest . . .
and so on. The only thing left to protest is the killing and

subjugation of any people the U.S. Military calls "Communists," "Gooks," . . . "the Enemy." Of course, in principle, the entire world is a potential enemy to the U.S. Military. . . .

The difference between war and peace dissolves and War is Peace.

Historically, Total Remote War continues the human heritage of war and genocide into a perpetual state of war. For America, as never before, the societal and cultural heritage of an Empire will be turned into a genocide machine. Every aspect of American industry will play an important production role. Every advance of American Science and Technology will be exploited into greater killing efficiency. . . .

The separation of illusion and reality vanishes for the television warriors. Alienation and sterilization approach perfection. After kissing their wives goodbye and battling the rush hour traffic to work, the television warriors will settle down to a day of watching TV at the Ministry of Peace. . . .

If during peace time a citizen does not support war against the Enemy, then that individual is a subversive. The individual becomes the Enemy. The next step then is to control the internal affairs of Empire . . . the establishment of a Ministry of Love.[1]

Those lines, written more than forty years ago, are alarmingly relevant today.

However, the group that published them felt it necessary to add the following:

We chose to print this article on remote warfare for two reasons. First, it increases the technical knowledge of those working against the war, making our actions more well-informed and hopefully, more effective. Second, it paints a convincing picture of the military-political thinking current among those who rule this country.

We do not, however, share the article's apocalyptic vision, nor its assumption of the ultimate superiority of those who control the most advanced technology.

Since we believe that the pessimistic and awe-stricken views presented in the article are essentially due to a lack of a proper political perspective we are presenting our analysis of the place and significance of the remote war technology within the American Reich.

First it must be pointed out that the development of the remote war technology issues from the weakness, not strength of American capitalism. In fact, this technology signifies further estrangement of the system from the American people. The Air War was developed because the American Army was no longer trustworthy. Remote warfare will come into being because this war and any future wars waged by the American Imperialists to control the world are no longer *politically* acceptable to the American people. Just as there has been an increase of social control and surveillance research to deal with resistance and lack of support at home, the American military has had to try to find technological solutions for its political problems. . . .

Second, escalation to complex (and profitable) technology is an endemic feature of American capitalism. . . .

It is important to perceive these processes freed from their ideological justification. It is not "progress" nor greater efficiency nor better satisfaction of consumers' needs that drives these processes. In the background there always looms the system's need for expansion, for operations on ever larger profits. The Remote War is an application of the same principle to another industry, the war industry.

There are a few other points in the article that deserve some comment.

First, there is little indication that the new technology will result in a lower "defense" budget. What is more likely is that the successive levels of war technology will coexist side by side, much as the missiles and the bombers do. Then there is the question of invincibility, the superhuman precision, the omniscience of sensors loaded on pilotless RPVs hooked to computer networks . . . etc. For those who are impressed by these claims we recommend paying attention to similar claims made in the past. There exists a vast difference between the results obtained under controlled conditions and the actual battle conditions. . . . The image of pinpoint destruction of individual resistors is a false one. . . .

It must be remembered that . . . bombing is a terror weapon. Its major purpose is to denude the countryside of the actual and potential guerilla supporters, and destroy the traditional social fabric of the country. . . .

Technology is *not* invincible. That is a myth which leads to passivity. It is common among scientific workers and represents a kind of technical/intellectual chauvinism. The power for social change lies with the large oppressed segments of society, and it is with them that we must join.[2]

NOTES

Prelude

1. Nancy Mancias, "Creech Air Force Base: A Place of Disbelief, Confusion and Sadness," *PINK Tank*, November 30, 2009, codepink.org/blog /2009/11/creech-air-force-base-a-place-of-disbelief-confusion-sadness.

2. See Gerald Krueger and Peter Hancock, *Hours of Boredom, Moments of Terror: Temporal Desynchrony in Military and Security Force Operations* (Washington, DC: National Defense University, 2010).

3. All the exchanges cited are taken from the official transcriptions obtained, thanks to the Freedom of Information Act, by David S. Cloud, a *Los Angeles Times* journalist. Only extracts are cited here. The original document was censored in several places before it was made public. For the whole document see documents.latimes.com/transcript-of-drone -attack (accessed April 25, 2011). For the context, see the accompanying article by David S. Cloud, "Anatomy of an Afghan War Tragedy," *Los Angeles Times*, April 10, 2011.

Introduction

1. Department of Defense, *Dictionary of Military and Associated Terms*, Joint Publication 1-02, August 2011, 109.

2. Since the 1970s, such a drone has been called a "remotely piloted vehicle" (RPV).

3. General T. Michael Moseley, quoted in Tyler Wall and Torin Monahan, "Surveillance and Violence from Afar: The Politics of Drones and Liminal Security-scapes," *Theoretical Criminology* 15, no. 3 (2011): 242.

4. The expression is that of Mike McConnell, director of national intelligence, quoted in Bob Woodward, *Obama's Wars* (New York: Simon & Schuster, 2010), 6.

5. David Deptula, on CNN's program *Amanpour*, "The Use of Drones in Afghanistan" episode, broadcast on November 24, 2009. As he later repeated in an interview: "Such reach-back allows us to keep the bulk of our footprint at home while delivering effects and capabilities to

anywhere on the globe. In other words, this system allows us to project capability without projecting vulnerability." See David A. Deptula, "Transformation and Air Force Intelligence, Surveillance and Reconnaissance: Remarks Given at the Air Force Defense Strategy Seminar, US Air Force Headquarters," Washington, DC, April 27, 2007.

6. The purpose of this technique is to establish an "unexposed power," or rather to provide that power with conditions of deployment that ensure that the vulnerability of its agents is not exposed. Before being used to describe the strategic advantage of the drone, this expression, used by Air Force strategists, was employed more generally to describe the procedures of "remote warfare," which was based on what was described as a historical tendency to favor long-range weaponry: "An examination of the long term trend, from club to spear, to bow and arrow, to catapult, musket, rifle and so on indicates a specific motivation. One wishes to be able to affect an adversary from a sufficient distance so as to avoid being similarly affected. In other words, there is a specific and rational desire to be able to project distant influence without projecting vulnerability in the same ratio. . . . The long-term military trend toward projecting distant influence without projecting vulnerability in the same ratio has favored the development of aerospace capabilities resting firmly in the ever-evolving foundation of modern technology. Advances in speed, range, agility, precision and lethality have been complemented by improvements in stealth, standoff, and information in ways that support the fullest exploitation of the third dimension in military matters. These capabilities manifest themselves in Aerospace Power." Charles D. Link, "Maturing Aerospace Power," *Air and Space Power Journal*, September 4, 2001.

7. Elaine Scarry, *The Body in Pain: The Making and Unmaking of the World* (New York: Oxford University Press, 1985), 78.

8. Department of Defense, *Report to Congress on Future Unmanned Aircraft Systems*, April 2012, www.fas.org/irp/program/collect/uas -future.pdf.

9. Chris Woods, "Drone Strikes Rise to One Every Four Days," *Bureau of Investigative Journalism*, July 18, 2011, www.thebureauinvestigates .com/2011/07/18/us-drone-strikes-rise-from-one-a-year-to-one-every-four -days.

10. "Obama 2013 Pakistan Drone Strikes," *Bureau of Investigative Journalism*, January 3, 2013, www.thebureauinvestigates.com/2013/01/ 03/obama-2013-pakistan-drone-strikes.

11. "Flight of the Drones: Why the Future of Air Power Belongs to Unmanned Systems," *The Economist*, October 8, 2011.

12. Elisabeth Bumiller, "A Day Job Waiting for a Kill Shot a World Away," *New York Times*, July 29, 2012. Between now and 2015, the Air Force will, it foresees, need more than two thousand drone pilots for armed patrols throughout the whole world.

13. John Moe, "Drone Program Grows While Military Shrinks," *Marketplace Tech Report*, January 27, 2012.

14. It is worth noting that the immediate perspective is not so much that of a small overall replacement of the classic machines by drones but rather that of a mixture of "modes of war" in which drones would occupy a preeminent position. We should also note that this tendency is not inexorable. The future is not *already* present; it plays a part in the present, which is different. But this is not in agreement with the fatalist-teleological presentation of the phenomenon that Peter W. Singer might favor. On the subject of the technical and budgetary barriers to the development of drones, he writes, "History also shows that they can't prevent the future from happening. They can only delay our effective adaptation to it." Peter W. Singer, "U-turn: Unmanned Systems Could Be Casualties of Budget Pressures" *Armed Forces Journal*, June 9, 2011. The history of twentieth-century drone projects tends, rather, to indicate the contrary: namely, a long succession of aborted projects.

15. See Jo Becker and Scott Shane, "Secret 'Kill List' Proves a Test of Obama's Principles and Will," *New York Times*, May 29, 2012. See also Steve Coll, "Kill or Capture," *New Yorker*, August 2, 2012.

16. See Medea Benjamin, *Drone Warfare: Killing by Remote Control* (New York: OR Books, 2012).

17. Ryan Devereaux, "UN Inquiry into US Drone Strikes Prompts Cautious Optimism," *The Guardian*, January 24, 2013.

18. Georges Canguilhem, *The Normal and the Pathological* (New York: Zone Books, 1991), 33 (modified translation).

19. Simone Weil, *Formative Writings* (New York: Routledge, 1999), 173.

20. Ibid., 174.

21. Ibid.

22. The phrase "state of violence" comes from Frédéric Gros, *Etats de violence. Essai sur la fin de la guerre* (Paris: Gallimard, 2006).

1. Methodologies for a Hostile Environment

1. John W. Clark, "Remote Control in Hostile Environments," *New Scientist* 22, no. 389 (April 1964): 300.

2. Ibid. "Telechir," from *tele*, "distant," and *kheir*, "hand."

3. Ibid.

4. The term "telearchic" was used by Burnet Hershey in 1944 and defined as "the remote control of mechanism by wireless.": "Telearchics— the remote control by radio of unmanned mechanisms—may have some startling advertisement before the war ends. Like all other devices, this is simply one application of the new science of electronics, child of radio and parent of television. Robot planes, guided by telearchic control, and containing television cameras, can be sent over enemy positions and flash

back a running picture." Burnet Hershey, *Skyways of Tomorrow* (New York: Foreign Policy Association, 1944), 15–16.

5. At a politico-strategic level the use of the armed drone leads back to the same kind of spatial division, the same kind of topographical division between "the safe" and "the hostile": a principle of zonage and sanctuarization. The drone and the wall function together. They interact coherently in a security model that combines a closure of the domestic space with external intervention that involves the commitment of no lives. The ideal of telecontrolled force is perfectly congruent with that of a "state-in-a-bubble." For a political philosophy of "the wall," see Wendy Brown, *Walled States, Walling Sovereignty* (New York: Zone Books, 2010).

6. Clark, "Remote Control in Hostile Environments," 300.

7. Marvin Minsky, "Telepresence," *Omni*, June 1980, 199.

8. Anonymous, "Last Word on Telechirics," *New Scientist* 22, no. 391 (May 14, 1964): 405.

9. Ibid. The end of this text produces a pastiche of Hilaire Belloc's famous sentence, "Whatever happens, we have got the Maxim gun, and they have not." Hilaire Belloc, *The Modern Traveller* (London: Arnold, 1898), 41.

2. The Genealogy of the Predator

1. G.W.F. Hegel, *Lectures on the Philosophy of History* (London: Brill, 1894), 419.

2. "The drones have no stings, being so to say imperfect bees and the newest made, the incomplete product of those that are exhausted and are now discharged from service." Pliny, *Natural History*, Book 11.11.27, trans. H. Rackham, Loeb Classical Library, vol. 3 (London: Heinemann, 1940), 449.

3. The ability to return to base is the main difference between armed drones and cruise missiles: "Although cruise missiles are closely related ancestors to UCAVs, they differ because they are one-way platforms, where UCAVs are two-way. . . . [T]he ability to return to base after completing the mission to fight another day is the primary difference between UCAVs and cruise missiles," as the latter "do not return to base when the mission is complete." Richard M. Clark, "Uninhabited Combat Aerial Vehicles: Airpower by the People, for the People, but Not with the People," thesis, School of Advanced Airpower Studies, Maxwell Airforce Base, June 1999, 4–5.

4. See Steven Zaloga, *Unmanned Aerial Vehicles: Robotic Air Warfare 1917–2007* (Westminster, MD: Osprey Publishing, 2008), 14; Jacob Van Staaveren, *Gradual Failure: The Air War over North Vietnam 1965–1966* (Washington, DC: Air Force History and Museums Program, 2002), 114.

5. John L. McLucas, *Reflections of a Technocrat: Managing Defense, Air, and Space Programs During the Cold War* (Maxwell Air Force Base:

Air University Press, 2006), 139. The drone was regarded as the low-cost weapon par excellence, in accordance with a double logic of economy, with respect to "the value of the human lives involved, and the financial costs" (*Astronautics and Aeronautics* 8, no. 11 [1970]: 43). The press, picking up on these arguments, regarded the projects for armed drones as the solution to the political contradictions of the Vietnam War: "The intensified bombings of North Vietnam since the beginning of the year has swelled the ranks of the more than 1600 American servicemen believed held prisoner in Indochina. Taking the pilots out of the bombers will remove a serious obstacle to the Nixon Administration's avowed intension to maintain American air power in South Asia." Robert Barkan, "The Robot Air Force Is About to Take Off," *New Scientist*, August 10, 1972, 282.

6. Once the war was over, that model was abandoned in favor of a return to classic fighter planes, even though armed drone projects had been both theorized and experimented. It is worth noting the 1971 Israeli experiments involving the Firebee drone with Maverick missiles. See David C. Hataway, "Germinating a New SEAD," thesis, School of Advanced Airpower Studies, Air University, Maxwell Air Force Base, June 2001, 15.

7. Ibid.

8. Jim Schefter, "Stealthy Robot Planes," *Popular Science*, October 1987, 66.

9. Ibid., 68.

10. Bill Yenne, *Attack of the Drones: A History of Unmanned Aerial Combat* (St. Paul: Zenith Press, 2004), 85.

11. Ibid.

12. "President George W. Bush Addresses the Corps of Cadets," The Citadel, Charleston, SC, December 12, 2001, www.citadel.edu/root/pres bush01.

3. The Theoretical Principles of Manhunting

1. Todd Smith, "Cyber-Hunting," *Outdoor Life*, September 2007, www.outdoorlife.com/articles/hunting/2007/09/cyber-hunting.

2. See Mark Matthews, "State Lawmakers Bag Online Hunting," *Slate*, September 28, 2005.

3. See Kris Axtman, "Hunting by Remote Control Draws Fire from All Quarters," *Christian Science Monitor*, April 5, 2005.

4. Ibid.

5. "President Speaks at FBI on New Terrorist Threat Integration Center," February 14, 2003, fas.org/irp/news/2003/02/wh021403b.html.

6. Eyal Weizman, "Thanatotactics," *Springerin*, June 4, 2006 (a variant on the chapter "Targeted Assassinations: The Airborne Occupation," in *Hollow Land: Israel's Architecture of Occupation*, [London: Verso, 2007], 239–58), www.springerin.at/dyn/heft.php?id=49&pos=1&textid

234   NOTES TO PAGES 32–39

=1861&lang=en). On the Israeli strategy of targeted assassination and its excesses, see also Ariel Colonomos, "Les assassinats ciblés: la chasse à l'homme" in *Le Pari de la guerre—guerre préventive, guerre juste?* (Paris: Denoël, 2009), 202–40.

7. Weizman, "Thanatotactics."

8. Rowan Scarborough, *Rumsfeld's War: The Untold Story of America's Antiterrorist Commander* (Washington: Regnery, 2004), 20.

9. Seymour Hersh, "Manhunt," *New Yorker*, December 23, 2002.

10. See Steven Marks, Thomas Meer, and Matthew Nilson, "Manhunting: A Methodology for Finding Persons of National Interest," thesis, Naval Postgraduate School, Monterey, June 2005, 19.

11. Kenneth H. Poole, "Foreword," in George A. Crawford, *Manhunting: Counter-Network Organization for Irregular Warfare*, Joint Special Operations University Report, September 2009, vii.

12. Crawford, *Manhunting*, 7.

13. Ibid., 19.

14. Ibid., 13.

15. John R. Dodson, "Man-hunting, Nexus Topography, Dark Networks and Small Worlds," *Iosphere*, 2006, 8.

16. See Sarah Kreps and John Kaag, "The Use of Unmanned Aerial Vehicles in Contemporary Conflict's Legal and Ethical Analysis," *Polity*, no. 44 (April 2012): 282.

17. Crawford, *Manhunting*, 12.

18. "Manhunting, its theorists tell us, has implications and applications beyond the immediate need to combat terrorism. The ability to interdict individual human targets or to disintegrate human networks provides a key capability to combat threats posed by non-state actors . . . or corporations with interests inimical to those of the U.S." Thus defined, the list is likely to be lengthy. Ibid., 12.

19. Jean André Roux, *La Défense contre le crime: répression et prévention* (Paris: Alcan, 1922), 196.

4. Surveillance and Annihilation

1. Julian E. Barnes, "Military Refines 'A Constant Stare Against Our Enemy,'" *Los Angeles Times*, November 2, 2009.

2. Ibid.

3. Ibid.

4. Sierra Nevada Corporation, "Wide-Area Airborne Persistent Surveillance: The Unblinking Eye," presentation to the NATO-ISTAR symposium, November 2012.

5. See Arnie Heller, "From Video to Knowledge," *Science and Technology Review*, Lawrence Livermore National Laboratory, April–May 2011.

6. See David Axe and Noah Shachtman, "Air Force's 'All-Seeing Eye' Flops Vision Test," *Wired*, January 24, 2011.

7. Quoted in Joe Pappalardo, "The Blimps Have Eyes 24/7: Overhead Surveillance Is Coming," *Popular Mechanics*, May 17, 2012.

8. Axe and Shachtman, "Air Force's 'All-Seeing Eye' Flops Vision Test."

9. As an information engineer reports, "The data-processing infrastructure for national security is not designed for the amounts and types of data being generated by unmanned aerial drones." As a result, "advanced and accurate analysis techniques are urgently needed by the people who are tasked with categorizing, indexing, annotating, and drawing conclusions from the petabytes of data collected daily in theatre operations." Heller, "From Video to Knowledge."

10. "Too Much Information: Taming the UAV Data Explosion," *Defense Industry Daily*, May 16, 2010.

11. Heller, "From Video to Knowledge."

12. Sharon Weinberger, "How ESPN Taught the Pentagon to Handle a Deluge of Drone Data," *Popular Mechanics*, June 11, 2012.

13. Ibid.

14. Ibid.

15. Walter Benjamin, *Theories of German Fascism*, in *Selected Writings Vol. 2, 1927–1934*, trans. Rodney Livingstone et al. (Cambridge, MA: Belknap Press, 1999), 313.

16. Within the framework of "The Mind's Eye" program.

17. Barnes, "Military Refines 'A Constant Stare Against Our Enemy.'"

18. "Too Much Information."

19. Derek Gregory, "From a View to a Kill: Drones and Late Modern War," *Theory, Culture & Society* 28, no. 7–8 (2011): 208.

20. Derek Gregory, "Lines of Descent," *Open Democracy*, November 8, 2011, www.opendemocracy.net/derek-gregory/lines-of-descent.

21. As Wall and Monahan point out, "drones are both predicated upon and productive of an actuarial form of surveillance. They are employed to amass data about risk probabilities and then manage populations or eliminate network nodes considered to exceed acceptable risk thresholds. In part, drones are forms of surveillance in keeping with the precepts of categorical suspicion and social sorting that define other contemporary surveillance systems." Tyler Wall and Torin Monahan, "Surveillance and Violence from Afar: The Politics of Drones and Liminal Security-scapes," *Theoretical Criminology* 15, no. 3 (August 2011): 240.

22. Weinberger, "How ESPN Taught the Pentagon to Handle a Deluge of Drone Data."

23. Derek Gregory, "From a View to a Kill," 195.

24. As two researchers working on a program on the automatization of the analysis of video images point out, "The automatic detection of anomalous and threatening behavior has recently emerged as a new area of interest in video surveillance: the aim of this technology is to disambiguate the context of a scene, discriminate between different types

of human actions, eventually predicting their outcomes 'visual intelligence.' " Alessandro Oltramari and Christian Lebiere, "Using Ontologies in a Cognitive-Grounded System: Automatic Action Recognition in Video Surveillance," in *Proceedings of the Seventh International Conference on Semantic Technology for Intelligence, Defense, and Security*, Fairfax, 2012.

25. See Heller, "From Video to Knowledge."

26. ARGUS-IS—the acronym for "Autonomous Realtime Ground Ubiquitous Surveillance Imaging System"—is a project of DARPA, the famous U.S. agency for military research.

27. The Gorgon Stare system, developed by the Air Force thanks to its 645th Aeronautical System Group, better known as "Big Safari," adopts the same principle as the ARGUS system but gears it down. Its creators promise that, thanks to this, it will be possible to observe overall, as well as in detail, "a whole city, so there will be no way for the adversary to know what we're looking at, and we can see everything." Ellen Nakashima and Craig Whitlock, "With Air Force's Gorgon Drone 'We Can See Everything,' " *Washington Post*, January 2, 2011. Gorgon Stare was conceived as a persistent surveillance system designed for the MQ-9 Reaper, but it could eventually proliferate on a multitude of platforms.

28. *Eyeborgs* is an astonishing sci-fi/action B movie directed by Richard Clabaugh in 2009.

29. David Rohde, "Reuters Magazine: The Drone Wars," Reuters, January 26, 2012, www.reuters.com/article/2012/01/26/us-david-rohde -drone-wars-idUSTRE80P11I20120126.

30. Stanford International Human Rights and Conflict Resolution Clinic, *Living Under Drones: Death, Injury and Trauma to Civilians from US Drone Practices in Pakistan*, September 2012, p.81ff, livingunder drones.org/wp-content/uploads/2012/10/Stanford-NYU-LIVING-UNDER -DRONES.pdf.

31. Ibid.

32. Ibid., 83.

33. Ibid., 81.

34. Ibid., 87.

5. Pattern-of-Life Analysis

1. Jo Becker and Scott Shane, "Secret 'Kill List' Proves a Test of Obama's Principles and Will," *New York Times*, May 29, 2012.

2. Harold Koh, "The Obama Administration and International Law," speech given at the American Society of International Law's annual meeting, March 25, 2010, www.state.gov/s/l/releases/remarks/139119.htm.

3. Human Rights Clinic at Columbia Law School, Center for Civilians in Conflict, *The Civilian Impact of Drones: Unexamined Costs, Unanswered Questions*, September 2012, 8, civiliansinconflict.org/uploads /files/publications/The_Civilian_Impact_of_Drones_w_cover.pdf.

4. Ibid., 9. See also Daniel Klaidman, *Kill or Capture: The War on Terror and the Soul of the Obama Presidency* (Boston: Houghton Mifflin Harcourt, 2012), 41.

5. David S. Cloud, "CIA Drones Have Broader List of Targets," *Los Angeles Times*, May 5, 2010.

6. Quoted in Anna Mulrine, "UAV Pilots," *Air Force Magazine* 92, no. 1 (January 2009).

7. US Army, *Field Manual 3-60: The Targeting Process*, November 2010, B-3.

8. Tony Mason, Suzanne Foss, and Vinh Lam, "Using ArcGIS for Intelligence Analysis," Esri International User Conference, 2012, proceedings .esri.com/library/userconf/feduc11/papers/tech/feduc-using-arcgis-for-intelligence-analysis.pdf.

9. Keith L. Barber, "NSG Expeditionary Architecture: Harnessing Big Data," *Pathfinder* 10, no. 5 (September–October 2012): 10.

10. Quoted in Adam Entous, "CIA Drones Hit Wider Range of Targets in Pakistan," Reuters, May 5, 2010.

11. Cloud, "CIA Drones Have Broader List of Targets."

12. Quoted in Ken Dilanian, "CIA Drones May Be Avoiding Pakistani Civilians," *Los Angeles Times*, February 22, 2011.

13. Winslow Wheeler, "Finding the Right Targets," *Time*, February 29, 2012.

14. Becker and Shane, "Secret 'Kill List' Proves a Test of Obama's Principles and Will."

15. Center for Civilians in Conflict, *Civilian Impact of Drones*, 34. See also Scott Shane, "Contrasting Reports of Drone Strikes," *New York Times*, August 11, 2011.

16. Kate Clark, *The Takhar Attack, Targeted Killings and the Parallel Worlds of US Intelligence and Afghanistan*, Afghanistan Analyst Network Thematic Report, June 2011, 12, aan-afghanistan.com/uploads/201105 11KClark_Takhar-attack_final.pdf.

17. Gareth Porter, "How McChrystal and Petraeus Built an Indiscriminate Killing Machine," *Truthout*, September 26, 2011.

18. Ibid.

19. Joshua Foust, "Unaccountable Killing Machines: The True Cost of US Drones," *The Atlantic*, December 30, 2011.

20. Sadaullah Wazir, quoted in Madiha Tahir, "Louder Than Bombs," *New Inquiry*, July 16, 2012, thenewinquiry.com/essays/louder-than-bombs.

6. Kill Box

1. The geographer Derek Gregory explains the "need to analyse not only the 'forever war' but also what we might call the 'everywhere war.'" Derek Gregory, "The Everywhere War," *Geographical Journal* 177, no. 3 (September 2011): 238.

2. Steven Marks, Thomas Meer, and Matthew Nilson, "Manhunting: A Methodology for Finding Persons of National Interest," thesis, Naval Postgraduate School, Monterey, June 2005, 28.

3. See Blackstone, *Commentaries on the Laws of England* (New York: Garland, 1978), 3:213.

4. To do this fully, however, it would be necessary, in contradiction to contemporary law, to resuscitate the archaic category of "common enemies of humanity." See Daniel Heller-Roazen, *The Enemy of All: Piracy and the Law of Nations* (New York: Zone Books, 2009).

5. "Deputy Secretary Wolfowitz Interview with CNN International," broadcast on November 5, 2002.

6. Douhet, *Command of the Air*, 57.

7. See Eyal Weizman, *Hollow Land: Israel's Architecture of Occupation* (London: Verso, 2007), 239.

8. Ibid., 237.

9. Eyal Weizman, "Control in the Air," Open Democracy, May 2002, www.opendemocracy.net/conflict-politicsverticality/article_810.jsp.

10. The expression is used by a now forgotten author of the 1940s, Burnet Hershey, *The Air Future: A Primer of Aeropolitics* (New York: Duell, Sloan and Pearce, 1943).

11. Weizman thus recalls that, in the course of the permanent status negotiations at Camp David, Israel, while conceding the territory, insisted upon conserving "the use of the airspace and electromagnetic space and their supervision" above the Palestinian territories. Weizman, "Control in the Air."

12. Alison J. Williams, "A Crisis in Aerial Sovereignty? Considering the Implications of Recent Military Violations of National Airspace," *Area* 42, no. 1 (March 2010): 51–59.

13. Stephen Graham, "Vertical Geopolitics: Baghdad and After," *Antipode* 36, no. 1 (January 2004): 12–23.

14. *Joint Publication 3-24, Counterinsurgency Operations*, October 5, 2009, VIII-16.

15. Air Land Sea Application Center, *Field Manual 3-09.34 Multi-Service Tactics, Techniques and Procedures (MTTPs) for Kill Box Employment*, June 13, 2005, I-5.

16. Ibid., I-1.

17. *Joint Publication 3-24, Counterinsurgency Operations*, October 5, 2009, II-19.

18. In 1996, a report on the prospective future military use of armed drones declared with foresight, "In the far-term, UAVs would both gather target location data and attack the targets in autonomous areas of operation (kill boxes)." See Air Force Scientific Advisory Board, *UAV Technologies and Combat Operations, 3-4, SAF/PA 96-1204*, 1996, 3-4.

19. Quoted in James W. MacGregor, "Bringing the Box into Doctrine: Joint Doctrine and the Kill Box," United States Army School of

Advanced Military Studies, United States Army Command and General Staff College, Fort Leavenworth, Kansas, AY 03-04, 43.

20. James A. Thomson to Donald H. Rumsfeld, memorandum, February 7, 2005, quoted in Howard D. Belote, "USAF Counterinsurgency Airpower: Air-Ground Integration for the Long War," *Air and Space Power Journal* 20, no. 3 (Autumn 2006): 63.

21. Ibid.

22. U.S. Army, *Unmanned Aircraft Systems, Roadmap, 2010–2035*, 65.

23. Kenneth Anderson, "Self-Defense and Non-International Armed Conflict in Drone Warfare," *Opinio Juris*, October 22, 2010, opiniojuris .org/2010/10/22/self-defense-and-non-international-armed-conflict-in -drone-warfare.

24. Michael W. Lewis, "How Should the OBL Operation Be Characterized?," *Opinio Juris*, May 3, 2011, opiniojuris.org/2011/05/03/how -should-the-obl-operation-be-characterized.

25. Michael W. Lewis, "Drones and the Boundaries of the Battlefield," *Texas International Law Journal* 47, no. 2 (June 2010): 312.

26. Gregory, "The Everywhere War," 242.

27. As we well know by now, the possession of American nationality is no protection against targeted assassination. But the American citizen killed in Yemen by a drone strike in September 2011, Anwar al-Awlaki, was perhaps, in the eyes of those who decided on his death, not or no longer either a full citizen or really American. Nor, apparently, was his sixteen-year-old son, born in Denver, and killed one week later by a strike designed to complete the job. See Tom Finn and Noah Browning, "An American Teenager in Yemen: Paying for the Sins of His Father?," *Time*, October 27, 2001.

28. Human Rights Watch, "Letter to Obama on Targeted Killings and Drones," December 7, 2010, www.hrw.org/news/2010/12/07/letter -obama-targeted-killings.

29. Mary Ellen O'Connell, "Unlawful Killing with Combat Drones: A Case Study of Pakistan, 2004–2009," abstract, Notre Dame Law School, Legal Studies Research Paper no. 09-43, 2009.

30. Ibid.

31. As Kenneth Anderson recalls, critics were alarmed by the fact that "the emergence of technologies for targeted killing using drones . . . has the possibility of disturbing and undermining a mostly tacit underpinning to the laws of war: an implied geography of war." Kenneth Anderson, "Targeted Killing and Drone Warfare: How We Came to Debate Whether There Is a 'Legal Geography of War,'" in *Future Challenges in National Security and Law*, ed. Peter Berkowitz, Research Paper no. 2011-16, Hoover Institution, Stanford, CA, 3.

32. On this concept, see Katherine Munn and Barry Smith, *Applied Ontology: An Introduction* (Heusenstamm bei Frankfurt: Ontos Verlag, 2008).

7. Counterinsurgency from the Air

1. Che Guevara, *Guerrilla Warfare* (Lincoln: University of Nebraska Press, 1985), 61.

2. Philip S. Meilinger, "Counterinsurgency from Above," *Air Force Magazine* 91, no. 7 (July 2008): 39.

3. Carl Schmitt, *The Concept of the Political*, trans. George Schwab (New Brunswick, NJ: Rutgers University Press, 1976), 52.

4. Quoted in Barry Bearak, "Death on the Ground, U.S. Raid Kills Unknown Number in an Afghan Village," *New York Times*, October 13, 2001.

5. Charles J. Dunlap, "Air-Minded Considerations for Joint Counterinsurgency Doctrine," *Air and Space Power Journal*, Winter 2007, 65.

6. Charles J. Dunlap, "Making Revolutionary Change: Airpower in COIN Today," *Parameters*, Summer 2008, 58.

7. Quoted in ibid., 58.

8. Ibid.

9. Angelina M. Maguinness, "Counterinsurgency: Is 'Air Control' the Answer?," *Small Wars Journal*, June 2009, smallwarsjournal.com/blog /journal/docs-temp/261-maguinness.pdf.

10. F.S. Keen, "To What Extent Would the Use of the Latest Scientific and Mechanical Methods of War Affect the Operations on the North-West Frontier of India?," *Journal of the United Service Institution of India* 53, no. 233 (1923): 400, quoted in Andrew Roe, "Aviation and Guerilla War: Proposals for 'Air Control' of the North-West Frontier of India," *Royal Air Force Power Review* 14 no. 1 (2011): p. 55. See also Derek Gregory, "From a View to a Kill: Drones and Late Modern War," *Theory, Culture & Society* 28, nos. 7–8 (2011): 189.

11. Maguinness, "Counterinsurgency." Emphasis added.

12. Ibid.

13. Richard Andres, "The New Role of Air Strike in Small Wars: A Response to Jon Compton," *Small Wars Journal*, July 2008, smallwars journal.com/blog/the-new-role-of-air-strike-in-small-wars.

14. Arendt had warned: "In the realm of politics, where secrecy and deliberate deception have always played a significant role, self-deception is the danger par excellence; the self-deceived deceiver loses all contact, not only with his audience but with the real world which will catch up with him, as he can remove only his mind from it and not his body." Hannah Arendt, "Lying in Politics," in *Crisis of the Republic* (New York: Harcourt, Brace, Jovanovich, 1989), 36.

15. David Kilcullen and Andrew McDonald Exum, "Death from Above, Outrage Down Below," *New York Times*, May 17, 2009.

16. Ibid.

17. Ibid.

18. Ibid.

19. David Galula, *Counterinsurgency Warfare in Theory and Practice* (Westport, CT: Praeger Security International, 2006), 4.

20. David Kilcullen, "Counterinsurgency Redux," *Survival* 48, no. 4 (December 2006): 117.

21. Ibid., 113.

22. David Kilcullen, *Counterinsurgency* (Oxford: Oxford University Press, 2010), 188.

23. "Counterinsurgency," in *Joint Publication 1-02 Department of Defense Dictionary of Military and Associated Terms*, 2010, 69.

24. Kilcullen, "Counterinsurgency Redux," 6.

25. Kilcullen, *Counterinsurgency*, 186.

26. Ibid., 187.

27. David Kilcullen, "Countering Global Insurgency," *Journal of Strategic Studies* 28, no. 4 (August 2005): 605.

28. Peter Matulich, "Why COIN Principles Don't Fly with Drones," *Small Wars Journal*, February 2012, smallwarsjournal.com/jrnl/art /why-coin-principles-dont-fly-with-drones.

29. Quoted in Shuja Nawaz, *FATA—A Most Dangerous Place: Meeting the Challenge of Militancy and Terror in the Federally Administered Tribal Areas of Pakistan*, Center for Strategic and International Studies, January 2009, 18, csis.org/files/media/csis/pubs/081218_nawaz_fata _web.pdf.

30. *Joint Publication 3-24, Counterinsurgency Operations*, October 5, 2009, xv.

31. Dunlap, "Making Revolutionary Change," 60.

32. Ibid.

33. Ibid., 59.

34. Andres, "The New Role of Air Strike."

35. Joshua S. Jones, "Necessary (Perhaps) but Not Sufficient: Assessing Drone Strikes Through a Counterinsurgency Lens," *Small Wars Journal*, August 2012, smallwarsjournal.com/blog/necessary-perhaps-but-not -sufficient-assessing-drone-strikes-through-a-counterinsurgency-lens.

8. Vulnerabilities

1. Louis de Baecker, *De la langue néerlandaise* (Paris: Thorin, 1868), 40.

2. Felice, *Encyclopédie ou Dictionnaire universel raisonné des connaissances* (Yverdon, 1781), III:570.

3. Ibid.

4. Mark Mazzetti, "The Drone Zone," *New York Times*, July 6, 2012.

5. "DoD News Briefing with Lt. Gen. Deptula and Col. Mathewson from the Pentagon," July 23, 2009, www.defense.gov/transcripts/tran script.aspx?transcriptid=4451.

6. Siobhan Gorman, Yochi J. Dreazen, and August Cole, "Insurgents Hack U.S. Drones," *Wall Street Journal*, December 17, 2009.

7. UPI, "Israel Encrypts UAVs as Cyberwar Widens," June 12, 2012.

8. Noah Shachtman, "Computer Virus Hits U.S. Drone Fleet," *Wired*, July 10, 2011.

9. Lorenzo Franceschi-Bicchierai, "Drone Hijacking? That's Just the Start of GPS Troubles," *Wired*, July 6, 2012.

10. Qiao Liang and Wang Xiangsui, *Unrestricted Warfare* (Panama City: Pan American Publishing, 2002), 93.

11. Trent A. Gibson, "Hell-Bent on Force Protection: Confusing Troop Welfare with Mission Accomplishment in Counterinsurgency," master's thesis, Marine Corps University, Quantico, VA, 2009, 6.

12. See Mike Davis, *Buda's Wagon: A Brief History of the Car Bomb* (London: Verso, 2007), 190.

13. To the principle of the nonexposure of lives at the scene of hostilities is added the principle of making the base of operations secure: "the US homeland must remain a secure base from which the Air Force can globally project power"—which means "ensuring the protection of US facilities and infrastructures used for power projection." Steven M. Rinaldi, Donald H. Leathem, and Timothy Kaufman, "Protecting the Homeland Air Force: Roles in Homeland Security," *Aerospace Power Journal*, Spring 2002, 83.

14. Francis Fukuyama, "Surveillance Drones, Take Two," *Democracy, Development, and the Rule of Law* (blog), September 12, 2012, blogs.the-american-interest.com/fukuyama/2012/09/20/surveillance -drones-take-two.

15. See the Team BlackSheep video from November 30, 2010, on YouTube at www.youtube.com/watch?v=M9cSxEqKQ78 and the Team BlackSheep website at www.team-blacksheep.com.

16. "Terrorists' Unmanned Air Force," Defensetech, May 1, 2006, defensetech.org/2006/05/01/terrorists-unmanned-air-force. Dennis Gormley considers that the most probable scenario would be the conversion "of kit airplanes or other manned civil aircraft as 'poor man's' UAVs." Dennis Gormley, "UAVs and Cruise Missiles as Possible Terrorist Weapons," Occasional Paper no. 12, Center for Nonproliferation Studies, 2003, 8.

17. Report DIIR SCID 010-17-0410, November 2006. See "Iraq War Logs: Al Qaida's New Suicide Bombing Tactics," *The Guardian*, October 22, 2010, www.guardian.com/world/iraq/warlogs/C39190D3-0310 -47E3-A50A-27B20C4A81B.

9. Drones and Kamikazes

1. The dream used to be to use radio control to free the mechanical from the organic, precision from error and the swift impact of fear. In 1934, Major General John Fuller regarded this as a teleological principle that necessarily led to armies of ghost planes: "Discipline, training and

skill can reduce fear, but they cannot annihilate it. Therefore, it seems to me that the next great war invention will be the unmanned aeroplane, a flying bomb or torpedo directed toward its target by wireless. Then we shall see, so I think, the most speedy form of war as yet imagined." John Frederick Charles Fuller, "Speed in Modern Warfare," in Stephen King-Hall et al., *The Book of Speed* (London: Batsford, 1934), 138.

2. See Walter Benjamin, "Das Kunstwerk im Zeitalter seiner technischen Reproduzierbarkeit," *Gesammelte Schriften* VII (Frankfurt am Main: Suhrkamp, 1989), 359. My thanks go to Marc Berdet for this reference.

3. Ibid.

4. Vladimir K. Zworykin, "Flying Torpedo with an Electric Eye" (1934), in *Television*, ed. Arthur F. Van Dyck, Robert S. Burnap, Edward T. Dickey, and George M.K. Baker (Princeton: RCA, 1947), 4:360.

5. Ibid.

6. Richard Cohen, "Obama Needs More Than Personality to Win in Afghanistan," *Washington Post*, October 6, 2009.

7. Richard Cohen, "Is the Afghanistan Surge Worth the Lives That Will Be Lost?," *Washington Post*, December 8, 2009.

8. "Suicide Bombers: Dignity, Despair and the Need for Hope—Interview with Eyad El Sarraj," *Journal of Palestine Studies* 31, no. 4 (Summer 2002): 74, quoted in Jacqueline Rose, "Deadly Embrace," *London Review of Books*, November 4, 2004, 21–24, www.lrb.co.uk/v26/n21/jacqueline-rose/deadly-embrace.

9. Rose, "Deadly Embrace."

10. Hugh Gusterson, "An American Suicide Bomber?," *Bulletin of the Atomic Scientists*, January 20, 2010, www.thebulletin.org/american-suicide-bomber. Talal Asad added: "Insofar as military interventions by Western powers continue this colonial tradition, it should be evident that their primary aim is not the protection of life as such but the construction and encouragement of specific kinds of human subjects and the outlawing of all others." Talal Asad, *On Suicide Bombing* (New York: Columbia University Press, 2007), 36.

11. "So what happens if the perpetrator of death dealing dies of his own free will at the very moment of his crime? What, in other words, if crime and punishment are united? . . . Revenge always justifies itself as fighting back, which is why it requires that crime and punishment be separated in time. It is when this eventalization is impossible, as in suicide bombing, that a fundamental sense of identity—of witnesses who identify with the dead and depend on retributive justice to produce a sense of satisfaction—may be radically threatened and horror may seize them." Asad, *On Suicide Bombing*, 90.

12. Gusterson, "An American Suicide Bomber?"

10. "That Others May Die"

1. Raoul Castex, *Synthèse de la guerre sous-marine* (Paris: Challemel, 1920), 121.

2. Voltaire, *An Essay on Universal History, the Manners* (London: Nourse, 1759), 1:220.

3. Talal Asad, *On Suicide Bombing* (New York: Columbia University Press, 2007), 35.

4. David Bell, "In Defense of Drones: A Historical Argument," *New Republic*, January 27, 2012.

5. Ernst Jünger, *Le Noeud gordien* (Bourgeois, 1995), 57.

6. Asad, *On Suicide Bombing*, 35.

11. A Crisis in Military Ethos

1. John Kaag and Sarah Kreps, "The Moral Hazard of Drones," *The Stone, New York Times* blog, July 22, 2012.

2. According to Rousseau's famous expression, in *The Social Contract* I, ch. III. See Rousseau, *The Essential Writings* (New York: Random House, 2013), 95.

3. Général Cardot, *Hérésies et apostasies militaires de notre temps, Paris/Nancy* (1908), 89, quoted in François Lagrange, "Les combattants de 'la mort certaine'. Les sens du sacrifice à l'horizon de la Grande Guerre," *Cultures et conflits*, no. 63 (2006): 63–81.

4. General Dragomiroff, quoted in Count P. Vassili, *La Sainte Russie* (Paris: Firmin-Didot, 1890), 134.

5. Mao Zedong, "Problems of Strategy in Guerrilla War Against Japan" (May 1938), *Selected Works* (Peking: Foreign Languages Press, 1965), 2:81–82.

6. Hegel, *Outlines of the Philosophy of Right*, para 327 add. (New York: Oxford University Press, 1982), 309.

7. This is the expression used by British air chief marshal Brian Burridge (Jane Mayer, "The Predator War," *New Yorker*, October 26, 2009).

8. See Edward N. Luttwak, *Le Grand Livre de la stratégie: de la paix et de la guerre* (Paris: Odile Jacob, 2002).

9. See John L. McLucas, *Reflections of a Technocrat: Managing Defense, Air, and Space Programs During the Cold War* (Maxwell Air Force Base: Air University Press, 2006), 141.

10. This can be heard, along with the extract that accompanies it, at www.youtube.com/watch?v=t8-kNPKNCtg.

11. On this theme, see Franck Barrett, "The Organizational Construction of Hegemonic Masculinity: The Case of the US Navy," *Gender, Work and Organization* 3, no. 3 (1996): 129–42.

12. Walter Benjamin, "Theories of German Fascism," in *Selected*

Writings 1927–1934 (Cambridge, MA: Harvard University Press, 1999), 2:313.

13. *JDN 2/11: The UK Approach to Unmanned Aircraft Systems*, quoted in Walter Pincus, "Are Drones a Technological Tipping Point in Warfare?" *Washington Post*, April 24, 2011.

14. Al Kamen, "Drone Pilots to Get Medals?," *Washington Post*, September 7, 2012. This medal has now been created. See Andrew Tilghman, "New Medal for Drone Pilots Outranks Bronze Star," *Military Times*, February 13, 2013.

15. Quoted in Greg Jaffe, "Combat Generation: Drone Operators Climb on Winds of Change in the Air Force," *Washington Post*, February 28, 2010.

16. Mark Mazzetti, "The Drone Zone," *New York Times*, July 6, 2012.

17. On this notion and paradox, now to be found in similar forms in many other professional activities, see Christophe Dejours, *Souffrance en France, la banalisation de l'injustice sociale* (Paris: Seuil, 1998), 108f.

18. Leah Libresco, "Brave Enough to Kill," *Unequally Yoked* (blog), July 19, 2012, www.patheos.com/blogs/unequallyyoked/2012/ 07/brave -enough-to-kill.html.

19. Alfred de Vigny, *Lights and Shades of Military Life* (London: Colburn, 1840), 1:18.

20. Jane Addams, "The Revolt Against War," in *Women at The Hague: The International Congress of Women and Its Results* (Urbana: University of Illinois Press, 2003), 35.

21. Ibid., 34.

22. Ibid., 35.

12. Psychopathologies of the Drone

1. Scott Lindlaw, "Remote Control Warriors Suffer War Stress: Predator Operators Prone to Psychological Trauma as Battlefield Comrades," Associated Press, August 7, 2008.

2. Ibid.

3. Discussion forum for the military community at www.military times.com, "Thread: UAV Operators Suffer War Stress," accessed May 2011.

4. Ibid.

5. Blake Morlock, "Pilot Is in Tucson; His Aircraft's over Iraq Battlefield," *Tucson Citizen*, August 30, 2007.

6. Matt J. Martin and Charles W. Sasser, *Predator: The Remote-Control Air War over Iraq and Afghanistan* (Minneapolis: Zenith, 2010), 31.

7. Peter W. Singer, *Wired for War: The Robotics Revolution and Conflict in the 21st Century* (New York: Penguin, 2009), 332.

8. Mark Mazzetti, "The Drone Zone," *New York Times*, July 6, 2012.

9. "Come in Ground Control: UAVs from the Ground Up," Airforce Technology, November 17, 2010, www.airforce-technology.com /features/feature101998.

10. Ortega set out the results of his study in "Combat Stress in Remotely Piloted/Unmanned Aircraft System Operations," a lecture given in January 2012 at the Brookings Institution, along with Peter W. Singer. The audio of his remarks is available at www.brookings.edu/events/2012 /02/03-military-medical-issues.

11. Ibid.

12. Ibid.

13. "And we haven't really studied exactly which pieces of the guilt portion of that there are. We know there are when there's a bad thing that happens. They internally begin to talk about things. We're actually trying to put more chaplains inside of the secure environment as well, and more medical technicians, enlisted medics." Ibid.

14. *Diagnostic and Statistical Manual of Mental Disorders*, 4th ed. (Washington, DC: American Psychiatric Association, 1994), 309.81.

15. Ibid.

16. U.S. Marine Corps, *Combat Stress—Army Field Manual (FM) 90-44/6-22.5*, 2000.

17. Karl Abraham, in *Psycho-Analysis and the War Neuroses*, ed. Ernest Jones (London: International Psycho-Analytical Library Press, 1921), 24.

18. Ibid.

19. Ibid., 247. It is worth noting that Freud's thesis is not as mild on the subject of the "repugnance at killing" as is Grossman's (which I shall be considering later). Instead of postulating a resistance to killing as a major anthropological fact, Freud stresses the conflict between contradictory versions of the ego and the threat represented by the urge to kill that is liberated by war conditions.

20. "The conflict is between the soldier's old peaceful ego and his new warlike one, and it becomes acute as soon as the peace-ego realizes what danger it runs of losing its life owing to the rashness of its newly formed, parasitic double. It would be equally true to say that the old ego is protecting itself from a mortal danger by taking flight into a traumatic neurosis or to say that it is defending itself against the new ego which it sees is threatening its life." Sigmund Freud, "Introduction to *Psychoanalysis and the War Neuroses*," in *The Standard Edition of the Complete Psychological Works of Sigmund Freud* (London: Hogarth Press, 1955), 17:245.

21. See Rachel MacNair, *Perpetration-Induced Traumatic Stress: The Psychological Consequences of Killing* (Westport, CT: Praeger/Greenwood, 2005).

13. Killing from a Distance

1. Harun Farocki, "Phantom Images," *Public* 29 (2004): 17. Filmmakers of the 1920s, in order to suggest scenes filmed from humanly impossible points of view (for example, beneath a speeding train), invented the idea of "phantom shots." A drone camera, fixed beneath the nose of the machine, does not restore the equivalent of what used to be seen by pilots seated at their controls. The drone's camera focuses perpendicularly upon the ground, not upon the horizon. Its vertical, overarching viewpoint is by no means a replica of the horizontal viewpoint of a pilot or that of a gunner from his glassed-in position in the body of the plane. So it is not the equivalent of the earlier subjective view. To designate this ambiguous form, Farocki suggests coining a new term: "We can interpret films that adopt the perspective of a bomb as *subjective phantom images*" (ibid., 13). The expression adequately conveys the nature of the images captured by a drone: those too are "subjective phantom images."

2. Farocki's suggestion makes it possible to add an important nuance to Paul Virilio's remark that "for men at war, the function of the weapon is the function of the eye," for he adds, "The war machine appears . . . as an instrument of representation." Paul Virilio, *War and Cinema: The Logistics of Perception*, trans. Patrick Camiller (New York: Verso, 1989), 20.

3. Mathieu Triclot, *Philosophie des jeux vidéo* (Paris: La Découverte, 2011), 94, with the following difference, however: here the actionable sign is reinforced by another kind of instrumental realism since, once it is set in action, it also sets up action in distant parts of the world.

4. Stáca, *Ancient Laws and Institutes of England, II, Glossary* (London: Eyre & Spottiswoode, 1840), n.p.

5. Ibid., 59.

6. Ibid., 107.

7. Ibid., 118.

8. At this point, I should like to insert a long theoretical note on this concept of pragmatic co-presence. Whereas local presence is defined by the relation between an entity and a place (a relation of localization), co-presence is defined solely by a relation between entities (whether beings or events). To be co-present means to be in the presence of one another. As a general rule, of course, co-presence presupposes co-localization (to be co-present means to be in the same place). However, that is not always the case; in fact, it is at precisely this point that the major break introduced by tele-technologies occurs.

While co-presence may be defined as a "presence at," it is nevertheless not necessarily a "presence for," as one regularly experiences: one can be co-present without being aware that one is. Another was there but I had not yet seen him. In other words, co-presence does not presuppose a consciousness of being co-present. It is not reducible to a subjective feeling. Things, inanimate material objects, may well be co-present.

But neither is co-presence simply coexistence. For two entities to be said to be coexistent, it is enough that they exist at the same time, simultaneously. But co-presence assumes more than that, namely the possibility for one term to affect the other or to be affected by it (a relation of causality). In other words, co-presence is defined by an instantaneous but not necessarily actualized possibility of a real relationship. Yet another way of putting this is to say that co-presence is defined by the *accessibility of one term to the other*. To be co-present they must be within reach of each other. Two armies are in the presence of each other when they are within range, and that is the case even when not a shot has been fired. It is this notion of range that distinguishes co-presence, as a pragmatic concept, from mere co-existence. Over and above the mere simultaneous existence of two entities, co-presence presupposes that one of them is within range of the other. Upon the indefinite background of objective coexistence, which happens as soon as several entities exist at the same time, there are certain spheres of determinate co-presence. A field of pragmatic co-presence is defined by the inclusion of one entity within the causal field of another. For humans or animals, that causal field corresponds to the field of action and perception or to its kinesthesic field. The pragmatic perimeter of co-presence is defined by the *possible* zone within which one may be affected by perceiving or being perceived, or by the zone within which action may possibly take place (one may take action or be subjected to action). There are as many fields within range as there are dimensions of possible co-presence. One may be within the range of sight, hearing, touch . . . And the fields of range that correspond to those different aspects or those different dimensions of co-presence have extensions that vary. As a general rule, the more limited the distance, the more the co-presence is complete thanks to the number of senses that are involved. Different dimensions cover variable complementary zones, so experiences of co-presence are more or less rich depending on whether they combine more or fewer dimensions of co-presence and whether a greater or smaller number of fields of range overlap. When related to the strata of the experienced world, distance is not purely quantitative but is affected by qualitative thresholds that correspond to the disappearing limits of a variety of kinesthesic ranges. From this point of view, what differentiates between a close proximity of two bodies and a great distance between them is the richness of the combined dimensions of co-presence. He was there at the station platform and I could speak to him and embrace him one last time, but the train moves away and now I can only see him in the distance. The co-presence that was rich and multidimensional has been impoverished and reduced solely to the optical range. The notion of a certain range, when limited in certain respects, determines our notions of distance and closeness. The closest proximity is when all the various ranges correspond. But successively, in a series of shifts, as I move away, I move beyond the limits of several fields of co-presence. I cross a number of boundaries, sensing qualitative stages in the distancing which, as I move farther away, manifest themselves in a progressive loss of the effects and dimensions of co-presence. The extension of the ranges of co-presence varies from one aspect to another: for example, the field of optic perception is usually more extensive than that of tactile perception. The eye can generally see farther than the hand can reach. In fact, the kinesthesic field decomposes into a number of different fields of varying extension that are somehow enclosed within one another in concentric spheres. The relationship of pragmatic co-presence is more rich or less rich, more or less complete depending on its range. Distance and proximity are thus not simply metric notions: they not only correspond pragmatically to the time that it takes to cross the intermediate space but, within the zone of co-presence itself, are established by thresholds that correspond to more or less full collections of co-presence dimensions. And this depends on whether or not we are within range of the other involved being or that being is within range of us in the relationship under consideration (and those collections of co-presence dimensions may be as numerous as are the many modes of relations possible between bodies, living bodies included). The whole spectrum of co-presence dimensions is therefore not limited to the palate of the various senses. For example, it includes one dimension that is of central importance in the present context and that could be called either the lethal zone or, reciprocally, the zone of vulnerability. This is the zone that would originally have been defined by the reach of the claws, limbs, or teeth of the prey and the predator and the relative speeds and endurance of their movements and strengths. In other words, at a pragmatic level it is necessary to replace the strictly numerical notion of distance by a notion of range or reach the length of which determines the limits and extension of the sphere of possible co-presence.

The span of the respective reaches of the individuals or entities involved may also vary. Typically, the field of vision of the one may be more extensive than that of the other. As a result, the paradoxical consequence may be that, if I have a better view, I may, so to speak, be in the presence of the other before he is in my presence. That is a paradoxical consequence because it amounts to saying that co-presence is not necessarily reciprocal. The prey and its predator lurking in the shadows are co-present even if the former is not yet aware of this (or even if the prey cannot yet see the predator). For there to be co-presence, all that is necessary is that one of the terms involved should be included in at least one field in range of the other. There are paradoxical forms of unilateral co-presence in which entity A can act upon or be affected by entity B, while entity B is not in a reciprocal position. Here, the prefix "co-" indicates no reciprocity in the relationship but simply a common inclusion. There is

co-presence only if the two terms are included within the same percep
tual or operative field. To be co-present means to be included in the same
pragmatic sphere. Yet one term may be enough. In such a case one could
speak of a unilateral co-presence, defined as the nonreciprocal inclusion
of one term within the range field of the other. So co-presence may involve not only different range fields, as a result of its differing dimensions, but also different morphological structures depending on whether
or not the relation is or is not reciprocal. What I mean by a structure of
co-presence is a relationship of either reciprocal or non-reciprocal inclusion of one entity within the range-field of another. The structure of the
co-presence determines what, for each entity, it is possible or impossible
to do to the other within this relationship. This structure fixes the constitutive pragmatic rules of the relationship (for example: it is possible
to see one another without being able to speak to one another, but if my
voice carries farther than yours does, I can speak to you without being
able to hear you). Structures and fields of co-presence can be combined in
variable ways, so on this basis, using different combinations it would be
easy to create grids of co-presence configurations, a typology of possible
co-presence forms, which would reveal rare or unexpected cases. The fictitious case of an invisible man, for example, would find a place in such
a typology: this would be a case of non-reciprocal co-presence within the
optical field but reciprocal within the tactile or lethal field. Such configurations can become the object of struggles in which each side tries
to modify the rules to its own advantage. There is a wide range of more
or less effective tactics designed to render non-reciprocal a structure of
co-presence that seems initially reciprocal. Both the animal world and
the history of warfare and weaponry abound in such tactics. For example,
one can try to increase one's range so as to strike one's opponent without
the latter being able to reciprocate, owing to his lack of equivalent equipment. It is also possible, even if one is included in the perceptual field
and operation zone of one's opponent, to try to make oneself unnotice-
able by using camouflage or other ploys to make oneself invisible. But
there is a difference between on the one hand simple schemes which,
leaving the general structure of co-presence unaffected, merely try to upset its conditions and, on the other hand, attempts to modify the structure
of co-presence radically, by making it unilateral.

Ordinarily, in the case of bodies without instruments, co-presence
implies co-localization. But that is not necessarily the case where tele-
technologies are involved. Fundamentally, what they make it possible to
do is detach the pragmatic relations of co-presence from their condition
of corporeal co-localization.

However, tele-technologies are not well named. Contrary to what that
name implies, they are fundamentally defined as techniques for operating *at a distance*. Of course it is possible to telephone to the other side
of the world, but it is also possible for two people who are very close to

each other, standing on the same pavement, to speak to each another on mobile phones. The key property of tele-technologies is that they function equally well at both close and long range. It is, in fact, this particular property that distinguishes them from more ancient devices that are founded on other principles. One can observe distant objects through binoculars, but everything becomes blurred if one points the instrument at objects close by. A telephone, likewise, is not a speaking trumpet. Just try having a conversation through megaphones set up in the same room. . . . While the tele-technologies make it possible to discount distance, they nevertheless do not rule out using the same instruments at short range, so what distinguishes them is not so much distance as the fact that they function equally well at short range. The difference between mobile phones and speaking trumpets or between binoculars and video cameras is the following: on one hand, we have techniques designed to extend the range within the spatial continuity of a zone of co-localization (these are, strictly speaking, techniques for distance, in the sense of a continuous distance, which use physical space directly, as a material medium); on the other hand, we have techniques for the delocalization of pragmatic co-presence, which suppress the condition of bodily co-localization. It is important to distinguish clearly between the two types of technique: on the one hand, procedures for extending the field within range by *amplifying certain phenomena* (including increasing the volume, blowing up the image, projecting farther, etc.); on the other, procedures of co-presence based on the principle of *retransmitting a signal* from one point to another (capture-transmission-reproduction). In this second schema, the degree of physical distance or proximity between those two points makes no difference to the success of the effect of co-presence. With tele-technological apparatuses, the sphere of co-presence is determined by the zone covered by the signal rather than by the range of the sensorimotor fields of the body itself or of its instruments. All that matters is the connection between each point and the transmission network. What really characterizes tele-technologies is the fact that they free co-presence from the condition of the co-localization of its terms within the same continuous region of space that serves as the physical medium for operations: all that is necessary is that each term be in a zone that is covered by the network. Correlatively, tele-presence will be defined, not so much by presence at a distance, but rather as co-presence that is independent of the co-localization of its terms: co-presence by connection, so that the continuum of an immediate kinesthetic field is not necessary for the operation to take place.

It is fair to say that the principal effect of tele-technologies is to dissociate co-presence from its condition of co-localization. They produce modified pragmatic equivalents of ordinary co-presence, but this is dislocated from its conditions of a physical co-localization of bodies. The terms are no longer co-present in the sense of a co-localization in the same continuous region of space. They are co-present only in the sense of an interconnected simultaneity. What tele-technologies produce for their operators may be described as a *dislocated experience*, in two senses of the expression. In the first place, co-presence and co-localization are dissociated. To dislocate is to disconnect, dismantle, undo, disarticulate. There is a disconnection between presence and the physical co-localization of bodies. Presence is no longer closely connected with the place where a body is, nor is it entirely lodged within the body. These are, so to speak, phenomena of an unearthed co-presence. It is no longer necessary to be physically within the same restricted region in order to be able to speak to one another. Physical co-localization and pragmatic co-presence used to be linked together in a necessary conditioning relationship. But that is no longer the case: and, as a result, the question of the place of the action, which used to be quite simple, becomes more complicated. Where does the action take place? Where does a telephone conversation take place? Action unfolds in several places at the same time. It happens both here and there. The event is no longer atomic. It is divided between the extremities in which it is effected.

Second, there is a dislocation in the sense of a bursting apart, a dissociation between dimensions of co-presence that are immediately associated in an ordinary experience. There are now experiences of partial, disarticulated co-presences. In the early twentieth century, people who were present when the earliest telephones came into general use described a telephone conversation as "a diminished presence" or a "partial presence." The idea was not that while speaking on the telephone one was partially localized on the other end of the telephone line, as if a bit of oneself was over there (everyone knew where they were, in what place, while they were telephoning). Rather, it was felt that the co-presence between the two interlocutors was diminished, only partial, because it was reduced to just a part of its dimensions (you could hear and speak but not see, touch, or feel; there were just voices, faceless and bodiless. This idea of a diminished presence stemmed from the phenomenon of a reduction in co-presence, that is to say a reduction in the capacity of affecting and being affected, a reduction to just one of its dimensions, with the loss of all the others that had made up a co-presence that was full and complex, in a face-to-face interaction. In this way, elements normally associated in the forms of the immediate experience were now radically disconnected, separated, disjointed. You could speak to each other but not see each other. You could strike without being struck, see without being seen. What are now dislocated are aspects that were originally indissociable from corporeal presence—aspects that a body had always presented together but which would now be able to be presented separately. You could say, very schematically, that there are at least four aspects to presence that a body combines in a single place, in the absence of other equipment: the body acts, and if one wishes to act, one does it through the body and right here; this body is perceiving and, here again, in the absence of further equipment, it is here where the body is, with all its means, that one perceives; the body is also perceptible (visible, carrying smells . . .); and, finally, this body is vulnerable, can be wounded, killed—and that is because it is alive. The body is active, perceiving, perceptible and vital and all those aspects are fixed in one and the same place, which is itself what we call the body. "The body" is the name of this immediate and seemingly indissoluble synthesis of those four dimensions or aspects of experience, which call out to one another and which, quite literally, march together. It is this immediate unity that tele-technologies radically undo, appending to the immediate synthesis another one, a technical synthesis that radically reconstructs the relations between those four aspects. They used to be linked, but now some have become independent, dissociated. The body has become dismantled and, in a partial reproduction of an organic body, it is possible to dissociate elements that the body, in its immediate unity, used to associate.

These devices thus affect both the diverse character of the dimensions of co-presence and also their structure so that, depending on the choices that govern their technical architecture, they produce new forms of experience: experiences of damaged presences, blind presences, non-reciprocal co-presences, etc. These transform the forms of co-presence by rendering certain configurations not only possible but necessary or else impossible—configurations that were not so in the immediate past.

Let us, once again, take the example of the telephone. It is, of course, possible in normal experience, to speak without seeing one another (with our eyes closed or through a closed door or in the dark), but that situation is not usually inscribed as a necessity in the structure of the experience. And it is this that the telephone changes: the device makes it impossible to see one another even as one uses it to converse. The very form of the experience is structurally changed. The particular design of tele-technological devices determines the forms of co-presence that are possible. These devices also make it possible to introduce hitherto unknown reconfigurations into the structures of experience. How do they do this? Mainly in two ways. First, the tele-technological devices can "filter" the dimensions of co-presence that they retransmit. They can sort through the immediate richness of the phenomenal assortment and select only certain aspects of it. For example, they can provide nothing but an image, or nothing but a sound. However, if equipped with adequate receivers at the other end of the line, they can add to the gamut of our sensorial capacities a dimension that was not available when working solely with a human body (for example, infra-red vision). It all depends on the technical choices available. Second, these devices can choose from among these various dimensions in order to bestow upon the co-presence a structure that is either more or less reciprocal, ranging from complete unilaterality to full reciprocity. Tele-communication devices generally adopt structures of a reciprocal nature, but that is by no means a necessity. Again, it is a matter of a decision on the design of the tele-technological device. The structural choices for the devices used by drones are, on the contrary, of a nonreciprocal nature.

The tele-technological devices both dislocate and resynthesize what one's own body, in its immediate unity, presents as going hand in hand with it. So what these new syntheses alter are the constitutive forms and structures of the experience, which are also the conditions of the inter-subjective experience. That is what drone tele-technology reconfigures radically with regard to the relationship of violence, introducing a revolution in the modes of co-presence and, at the same time, in the structure of intersubjectivity.

9. Elisabeth Bumiller, "A Day Job Waiting for a Kill Shot a World Away," *New York Times*, July 29, 2012.

10. Ibid.

11. Scott Lindlaw, "Remote Control Warriors Suffer War Stress: Predator Operators Prone to Psychological Trauma as Battlefield Comrades," Associated Press, August 7, 2008.

12. In the philosophy of warfare, there is a classic thesis concerning the relation between carrying arms and the soldier's emotional involvement. It is presented in the form of a law, which we might rename the Clausewitz-Hegel law. Clausewitz wrote as follows: "Weapons with which the enemy can be attacked while he is at a distance, are more instruments for the understanding; they allow the feelings, the 'instinct for fighting' properly called, to remain almost at rest, and this so much the more according as the range of their effects is greater. With a sling we can imagine to ourselves a certain degree of anger accompanying the throw; there is less of this feeling in discharging a musket, and still less in firing a cannon shot." Clausewitz, "Guide to Tactics, or the Theory of the Combat," *On War* (London: Kegan, 1918), 3:250. The savagery of single combat, which implied dirty feelings and hands, stood in contrast to the misty abstraction of cannon fire. According to this great account, the history of weaponry seems to go hand in hand with a triumph of reason. Hegel added: "The firearm is the discovery of a death that is general, indifferent, and impersonal" (Hegel, "System der Sittlichkeit," in *Schriften zur Politik und Rechtsphilosophie* [Leipzig: Meiner, 1923], 467). Strange praise for death dealt in cold blood by subjects who are passionless, amid general abstraction. If our ears are no longer prepared for such praise, now that the drone paradoxically reembodies that representation, that is no doubt because the twentieth century has taught us to recognize its dark face. Where the Berlin philosopher saw a triumphant teleology pointing the way to a rationalization of state violence, the twentieth century, horrified, discovered something quite different. When John Ulric Nef took up this theme at the end of World War II, his tone was far less confident: "Progress has purged actual warfare of much of the emotional

anger which accompanied the struggles of olden times. Except among the infantry, killing has become so impersonal that the killer resembles a boy with a toy pistol, or a man in a bathroom stepping on cockroaches." John U. Nef, "The Economic Road to War," *Review of Politics* 11, no. 3 (July 1949): 330.

Beneath the "progress" of long-distance violence, we can now detect the barbarity of aseptic homicide. By now doubt is certainly cast upon the notion that mechanized murder and murder from behind a desk is less terrible than blood shed in passion.

13. It is thus now possible to have optic "proximity" at the same time as absolute "distance" from what is happening in every other respect. This should be compared to the perceptual experience of troops on the ground. In homicide in combat, all the senses are involved, and horror is a synesthetic sentiment: it is experienced the more violently when all the senses are assaulted and saturated at the same time.

14. Dave Grossman, *On Killing: The Psychological Cost of Learning to Kill in War and Society* (New York: Back Bay Books, 1995), 128.

15. Quoted in Jane Mayer, "The Predator War," *New Yorker*, October 26, 2009.

16. William Saletan, "Joystick vs. Jihad: The Temptation of Remote-Controlled Killing," *Slate*, February 12, 2006.

17. Milgram added: "The manifest function of allowing the victim of a firing squad to be blindfolded is to make the occasion less stressful for him, but it may also serve a latent function of reducing the stress of the executioner." And "Many expressions of language refer to the discomfort or inhibitions that arise in face-to-face attack. It is often said that it is easier to criticize a man 'behind his back' than to confront him directly." Stanley Milgram, *Obedience to Authority: An Experimental View* (New York: Harper & Row, 1974), 39.

18. Grossman, *On Killing*, 128.

19. Milgram, *Obedience to Authority*, 38.

20. Matt J. Martin with Charles W. Sasser, *Predator: The Remote-Control Air War over Iraq and Afghanistan* (Minneapolis, MN: Zenith, 2010), 31.

21. On the effects of "moral buffering" produced by the interfaces of teleoperation, see Mary Cummings, "Creating Moral Buffers in Weapon Control Interface Design," *Technology and Society Magazine* 23, no. 3 (Autumn 2004): 28–33; Mary Cummings, "Automation and Accountability in Decision Support System Interface Design," *Journal of Technology Studies* 32, no. 1 (Winter 2006): 23–31. See also, on the associated notion of "moral disengagement," Albert Bandura, "Moral Disengagement in the Perpetration of Inhumanities," *Personality and Social Psychology Review* 3, no. 3 (August 1999): 193–209.

22. Ibid. The case of the figure closest to the drone operator is probably that of the sniper. He too associates physical distance and ocular

proximity. But, unlike the latter, the drone operator is no longer physically present in the zone of hostilities.

23. At this point, I should like to add a note on the phenomenological
dimension of this sense of "shift," or swinging over that is linked to the
experience of tele presence. The form of an "instrumented experience"
that is lived through by drone operators is strange: it is a sense of being
in between. It is hard to describe this feeling, which seems to be that of
a kind of *disturbance in one's presence*. The reflections of the American
philosopher Daniel Dennett may provide a starting point: "The workers
in laboratories and plants who handle dangerous materials by operating
feedback-controlled mechanical arms and hands undergo a shift in point
of view that is crisper and more pronounced than anything Cinerama can
provoke. They can feel the heft and slipperiness of the containers they
manipulate with their metal fingers. They know perfectly well where
they are and are not fooled into false beliefs by the experience, yet it is
as if they were inside the isolation chamber they are peering into. With
mental effort, they can manage to shift their point of view back and
forth rather like making a transparent Necker cube or an Escher drawing
change orientation before one's eyes. It does seem extravagant to suppose
that in performing this bit of mental gymnastics, they are transporting
themselves back and forth." Daniel Dennett, "Where Am I?" in *Brain-
storms: Philosophical Essays on Mind and Psychology* (Hassocks, Sussex:
Harvester, 1978), 315. By focusing his attention on the movements of the
mechanical arm, the operator can to some extent adopt the point of view
of the machine that makes the operation work, and think of himself as if
he himself is over there, at work. Yet he does not really *believe* himself to
be anywhere except where his body is sitting. So his experience is not that
of a deceit or of a false belief induced by the sensory illusion. And yet it
is "as if" he was in the place where the operations are unfolding. It is this
"as if" feeling that needs to be clarified. It is an "as if" that is not like
a belief, but neither is it an illusion. Dennett's final analogy is a subtle
one: the examples that he provides are very specific cases of paradoxical
objects. When one concentrates on a Necker cube one can see it now from
the front, now from the back, as its back surfaces become its front ones
and vice versa, depending on whether one shifts them mentally to the
front or to the back. What matters in this analogy with a tele-operator's
experience is not the idea of an interpretative indecidability so much as
that of a variation of the objective configuration of the phenomenon
as regards the mental focalizing of the subject. The associated thesis is
not so much that the feeling of tele-presence is or must be illusory if it
is to exist, but rather the following: it is a matter of how the operator's
attention is focused, of how a number of choices are separated out or of
a differential prioritization of what is to count as the foreground or the
background within a single perceptual field. How can we explain this experience of a shifting point of view? What phenomenological operations

underpin it? Loomis provides a convincing explanation of this phenomenon. He thinks that tele-operators "often report a compelling impression of 'tele-presence' or 'remote presence'" (Jack M. Loomis, "Distal
Attribution and Presence," *Presence, Teleoperators and Virtual Environments* 1, no. 1 [1992]: 113). For him, what tele-operators experience is not
fundamentally different from what happens when one uses a walking
stick or a rod to feel a surface: what one *feels* then is as if it is at the tip
of the rod, not in the hand that grasps the rod. One adopts the point of
view of the rod, Basically, tele-operators do the same when they adopt
the point of view of the mechanical arms that they control. This kind of
phenomenal shifting in one's point of view, when one adopts the point of
view of the instrument, which may also be described as a phenomenon of
a projection or translocation of perceptual data, is not in any way specific
to such a technical device or even to the use of instruments. The common
basis upon which it operates is what, in psychology, is called "projection."
This general phenomenon, which comes about through the sensual organs themselves has also been described as "externalization," "translocation," or "distal attribution." The sensations, despite being perceived
here, in my body, are assigned elsewhere, referred to another place. To
describe what happens in a subject's consciousness in such a case, Loomis
mobilizes the concepts of a *focal consciousness* and a *subsidiary consciousness*. The former designates attention paid by the forefront of the mind,
while the latter refers to a whole collection of small remaining perceptions in the background of one's consciousness. When the handling of
his instrument results in the tele operator's "subsidiary consciousness of
the chain of mediation fading to the point of becoming transparent," the
subject may develop a "focal consciousness of the distal." Yet even if he
no longer *needs* to concentrate in order to act, the feeling of his hand's
contact with the rod persists in a muted manner. Even if the instrumental
mediation has become, as it were, transparent, something remains in the
background, at least in the form of tiny perceptions deep down in the
tele-operator's subsidiary consciousness. But should the palm of my hand,
for example, be hurt by a forgotten splinter on the surface of the rod, the
latter would immediately invade the field of my focal consciousness, at
the same time relegating the stone that it has tapped to the spectrum
of my subsidiary consciousness. That, in essence, is what happens in the
"shift in a point of view" that Dennett mentions: the object shifts from
focal consciousness to subsidiary consciousness, depending on whether
I focus on the zone of contact between my body and the instrument of
mediation—for example, the rod or the room in which I manipulate the
levers—or I subsidiarize those elements in order to direct my attention to
the object that I am targeting through this intermediary.
    This involves a way of forgetting the mediation, but that forgetting
is merely *pragmatic*: there is no need to think about it in order to take
action. So one is unaware of it, not in the sense of being incapable of

recognizing its role or existence (epistemic ignorance), but only in the sense of being able to disregard it in order to take action (pragmatic forgetting). This pragmatic forgetting about the mediation by no means implies a failing in the perceiving subject or, on his part, any inability to perceive or recognize his role; it is, on the contrary, the product of long efforts to appropriate the instrument and make it part of oneself so as not to have to think about it. That momentary forgetfulness of the instrumental mediation is a state that one needs to succeed in attaining. It is not an *epistemic failure* but, on the contrary, a *pragmatic success*.

In order to be able to experience a strong sense of telepresence, the subject has to be successful in effectively subsidiarizing not only his consciousness of the instrumental mediation but also that of his own local presence and all the stimuli that affect him in his immediate environment (the chair that is hurting his back, the sounds all around him, and so on).

As Loomis writes, "When the stimulation is insufficient to support 'telepresence' (the awareness of being somewhere else), the observer experiences 'subsidiary awareness' of the actual environment and a 'focal awareness' of the remote or simulated environment. . . . Speaking with someone on the telephone is an example, for we have both subsidiary awareness of being in one location communicating through a device and focal awareness of the person at the other end." Ibid., 117.

That subsidiarization is hard work and considerable efforts are necessary in order to maintain it. It is a problem that dogs ergonomists who work on the design of interfaces and the psychologists who study the work of tele-operators and how to maintain focal attention for long hours at a time or, as they themselves put it, how to facilitate and maintain the tele-operators' "situational consciousness," which is always fragile: it involves concentrating on one environment even as one is perceiving two; this is a matter of attention and of focusing mentally on one particular point of view. In the case of the Necker cube, you do not see both images at the same time. As soon as you see one, the other disappears. There is a strict alternative here: the one effaces the other. The shift in the point of view is total. But in the case of a tele-operator, although there is a shift between a focal consciousness and a subsidiary consciousness, the problem is that the one continues surreptitiously to feed off the other, for that provides the immediate framework within which the latter is held. It is necessary to separate it out, make a selection and forget about the other, which nevertheless remains there and is not decisively effaced.

For the operators, the problem is not that, faced with some kind of perfect illusion of tele-presence, they would not know anymore where they are, what is real and what might not be. On the contrary, faced with mixed and overlapping experiences of presence that are both local and distant, their problem is to cope, in a coherent fashion, with the horizons of this experience of a mixed reality. They do not take the one reality for the other but take the one together with and within the other. There is not so much a confusion, but rather an embedding, a partial superimpression or a problematic interarticulation between the two. Their experience is not of being captured in a particular presence, but rather of having two presences, the one on top of the other.

On ontological and phenomenological debates on tele-presence, see also Luciano Floridi, "The Philosophy of Presence: From Epistemic Failure to Successful Observation," *Presence: Teleoperators and Virtual Environments* 14, no. 6 (2005): 546–57.

24. Dave Lara, in Colonel Hernando J. Ortega Jr., "Combat Stress in Remotely Piloted/Unmanned Aircraft System Operations," lecture given in January 2012 at the Brookings Institution with Peter W. Singer, audio available at www.brookings.edu/events/2012/02/03-military-medical-issues.

25. Martin, *Predator*, 85.

26. Blake Morlock, "Pilot Is in Tucson; His Aircraft's over Iraq Battlefield," *Tucson Citizen*, August 30, 2007.

27. Discussion forum of the military community of the website www .militarytimes.com, "Thread: UAV Operators Suffer War Stress," consulted May 2011.

28. Warfare is an "official abrogation of civilized standards" in which one is not only encouraged but indeed forced to adopt forms of behavior that would, in other circumstances, revolt our ordinary "aesthetic and moral dispositions," which is why soldiers "undergo a very considerable readjustment of their previous attitudes of mind and standards of conduct . . . The man's previous standards of general morality, of cleanliness and aesthetic feeling, and of his relation to his fellow-man, have all to undergo a very considerable alteration." That is, they experience a double standard. Ernest Jones, "War Shock and Freud's Theory of the Neurosis," in *Psycho-Analysis and the War Neuroses*, ed. Ernest Jones (London: International Psycho-Analytical Library Press, 1921), 48.

29. John Keegan, *The Illustrated Face of Battle* (New York: Viking, 1989), 284.

30. Nicola Abé, "Dreams in Infrared: The Woes of an American Drone Operator," *Spiegel Online*, December 14, 2012.

31. Bumiller, "A Day Job."

32. Ortega, "Combat Stress" discussion.

33. Ibid.

34. Simone Weil, *The Notebooks of Simone Weil* (New York: Routledge, 2004), 348 (modified translation).

35. Ibid., 347 (modified translation).

14. Combatant Immunity

1. Wesley Clark, *Waging Modern War: Bosnia, Kosovo and the Future of Combat* (New York: Public Affairs, 2002), 183.

2. William Cohen and Henry Shelton, *Joint Statement on Kosovo After-Action Review Before the Senate Armed Service Committee*, October 14, 1999, 27.

3. Andrew Bacevich and Eliot Cohen, *War over Kosovo: Politics and Strategy in a Global Age* (New York: Columbia University Press, 2001), 21.

4. Amnesty International, *"Collateral Damage" or Unlawful Killings: Violations of the Laws of War by NATO During Operation Allied Force*, June 5, 2000.

5. Michael Ignatieff, *Virtual War: Kosovo and Beyond* (London: Vintage, 2001), 62.

6. Quoted in Nicholas Kerton-Johnson, *Justifying America's Wars: The Conduct and Practice of US Military Intervention* (New York: Routledge, 2011), 80.

7. Jean Bethke Elshtain, "Just War and Humanitarian Intervention," *Ideas from the National Humanities Center* 8, no. 2 (2001): 14. Elshtain added, "If combatant immunity is to become our new organizing principle, we shall face many more situations in the future in which we refuse to do what is necessary to meet our stated objectives and resort instead to means that may undermine not only those objectives but also the centuries-old effort to limit war, as much as possible, to combatants." Jean Bethke Elshtain "What Makes a War Just? Whose Lives Are We Sparing?" *Washington Post*, May 16, 1999.

8. Alex J. Bellamy, "Is the War on Terror Just?," *International Relations* 19, no. 3 (2005): 289, quoted in Daniel Brunstetter and Megan Braun, "The Implications of Drones on the Just War Tradition," *Ethics & International Affairs* 25, no. 3 (2011): 337–58.

9. Amos Harel, "The Philosopher Who Gave the IDF Moral Justification in Gaza," *Haaretz*, February 6, 2009.

10. Ibid.

11. Ibid.

12. Asa Kasher and Amos Yadlin, "Military Ethics of Fighting Terror: An Israeli Perspective," *Journal of Military Ethics* 4, no. 1 (2005): 3–32.

13. Ibid., 17.

14. Ibid., 20.

15. Avishai Margalit and Michael Walzer, "Israel: Civilians and Combatants," *New York Review of Books*, May 14, 2009.

16. Ibid.

17. Menahem Yaari, "Israel: The Code of Combat," *New York Review of Books*, October 8, 2009.

15. A Humanitarian Weapon

1. Kenneth Anderson, "Rise of the Drones: Unmanned Systems and the Future of War," *Written Testimony Submitted to Subcommittee on*

National Security and Foreign Affairs, Committee on Oversight and Government Reform, U.S. House of Representatives, Subcommittee Hearing, March 23, 2010, 12.

2. Avery Plaw, "Drones Save Lives, American and Other," *New York Times,* September 26, 2012.

3. Bill Sweetman, "Fighters Without Pilots," *Popular Science* 251, no. 5 (November 1997): 97.

4. Rory Carroll, "The Philosopher Making the Moral Case for US Drones," *The Guardian,* August 2, 2012.

5. Ibid.

6. Bradley J. Strawser, "Moral Predators: The Duty to Employ Uninhabited Aerial Vehicles," *Journal of Military Ethics* 9, no. 4 (2010): 342.

7. Ibid., 344.

8. Ibid., 342.

9. Ibid., 346.

10. Ibid., 351.

11. Ibid.

12. Strawser here cites the argument put forward by Rafael Armament Development Authority, owned by the Israeli government, which claims that, thanks to Spike, its new long-range precision weapon designed for use in drones, it has reached the stage of "urban warfare precision" (ibid., 351).

13. Michael Walzer, "The Argument About Human Intervention," in *Thinking Politically: Essays in Political Theory* (New Haven: Yale University Press, 2007), 245.

14. On this idea, see, as well as the reflections of Weizman, those of Adi Ophir, "Disaster as a Place of Morality, The Sovereign, the Humanitarian and the Terrorist," *Qui Parle* 16, no. 1 (Summer 2006): 95–116.

15. "Care" has a number of meanings: "care," "solicitude," and "attention." The works of Carol Gilligan and Joan Tronto have helped to place this concept at the heart of a renewed ethical approach. As in the past, the notions of psychic vulnerability and empathy and the discourse of an ethic of solicitude are here mobilized and integrated, in an apologetic fashion, into death-dealing practices.

16. Eyal Weizman, *The Least of All Possible Evils: Humanitarian Violence from Arendt to Gaza* (London: Verso, 2012), 6.

17. Hannah Arendt, "Personal Responsibility Under Dictatorship," in *Responsibility and Judgment,* ed. Jerome Kohn (New York: Schocken Books, 2003), 36, quoted in Weizman, *Least of All Possible Evils,* 27.

16. Precision

1. Leon E. Panetta, "Director's Remarks at the Pacific Council on International Policy," May 18, 2009.

2. This founding principle of just armed conflict forbids indiscriminate

attacks: only military installations should be *directly* targeted. This implies drawing a distinction between the targeting of civilian populations and combatants.

3. Bradley Strawser, "The Morality of Drone Warfare Revisited," *The Guardian*, August 6, 2012.

4. Scott Shane, "The Moral Case for Drones," *New York Times*, July 14, 2012.

5. See Jeremy R. Hammond, "The Immoral Case for Drones," July 16, 2012, www.jeremyrhammond.com/2012/07/16/the-immoral-case-for -drones.

6. Anna Mulrine, "Warheads on Foreheads," *Air Force Magazine* 91, no. 10 (October 2008): 44–47.

7. See International Human Rights and Conflict Resolution Clinic, Stanford Law School, and Global Justice Clinic, NYU School of Law, *Living Under Drones: Death, Injury and Trauma to Civilians from US Drone Practices in Pakistan*, September 2012, 10, www.livingunderdrones .org/wp-content/uploads/2013/10/Stanford-NYU-LIVING-UNDER -DRONES.pdf.

8. "Transgenders Take to the Streets Against Drones," *Express Tribune*, July 31, 2012.

9. John Brennan, "The Ethics and Efficacy of the President's Counterterrorism Strategy," Wilson Center, April 30, 2012, www.wilsoncenter .org/event/the-efficacy-and-ethics-us-counterterrorism-strategy.

10. In other words, the argument here is that, so far as the capacity for discrimination goes, the drone technology destroys the traditionally established link between visual acuteness and physical proximity. The proximity of the operator is no longer necessarily a pertinent factor in the identification of targets. Christian Enemark, "War Unmanned: Military Ethics and the Rise of the Drone," intervention at the International Studies Association Convention, Montreal, March 16–19, 2011.

11. Adam Entous, Siobhan Gorman, and Julian E. Barnes, "US Relaxes Drone Rules: Obama Gives CIA Military Greater Leeway in Use Against Militants in Yemen," *Wall Street Journal*, April 26, 2012, quoted in Center for Civilians in Conflict, *The Civilian Impact of Drones: Unexamined Costs, Unanswered Questions*, September 2012, 33, civiliansinconflict.org /uploads/files/publications/The_Civilian_Impact_of_Drones_w_cover.pdf.

12. "Civilian individuals enjoy the protection granted by the present document, except if they participate directly in hostilities and during the time of that participation." *Additional Protocol to the Geneva Conventions of 12 August 1949 Relating to the Protection of the Victims of Non-international Armed Conflicts (Protocol II), 7 December 1978*, Title IV, article 13-3.

13. John Brennan, "Ensuring al-Qa'ida's Demise," Paul H. Nitze School of Advanced International Studies, Johns Hopkins University,

Washington, June 29, 2011, in response to questions of assistance, www .c-spanvideo.org/ptogram/AdministrationCo/.

14. Jo Becker and Scott Shane, "Secret 'Kill List' Proves a Test of Obama's Principles and Will," *New York Times*, May 29, 2012. This is clearly in total violation of the principle of distinction: the status of a combatant cannot be inferred, by default, from the apparent age and sex of a figure.

15. Ibid.

16. On this theme, see Eyal Weizman, "Forensic Architecture: Only the Criminal Can Solve the Crime," in *The Least of All Possible Evils: Humanitarian Violence from Arendt to Gaza* (London: Verso, 2012), 99–100.

17. Madiha Tahir, "Louder than Bombs," *New Inquiry*, July 16, 2012, thenewinquiry.com/essays/louder-than-bombs.

17. Indelicate Murderers

1. Michael Walzer, "The Triumph of Just War Theory (and the Dangers of Success)," in *Arguing About War* (New Haven: Yale University Press, 2005), 16.

2. Ibid.

3. Ibid., 17.

4. Ibid., 101.

5. Ibid., 102.

6. Albert Camus, *The Rebel* (London: Penguin, 1971), 169 (modified translation).

7. Ibid., 138.

8. Ibid., 139.

18. Warfare Without Combat

1. Hugo Grotius, *On the Law of War and Peace* (Cambridge: Cambridge University Press, 2012), 353.

2. Ibid., 353.

3. Ibid., 353–54.

4. Grotius himself comments: "And it is probable that this rule proceeded from kings, whose life may be defended from other causes, better than the lives of other persons; but is less safe than the lives of other person" (ibid.). One warfare theorist comments: "Grotius is quite right on this point: if kings had only one chance in five of dying in the course of a campaign, it would have been a long time since there had been a war between civilized peoples." Nicolas Villiaumé, *L'Esprit de la Guerre* (Paris: Dumaine, 1866), 60.

5. François Laurent, *Histoire du droit des gens et des relations*

internationales, vol. 10, *Les Nationalités* (Paris: Librairie international, 1865), 488.

6. Samuel von Pufendorf, *De Jure Naturae et Gentium Libri Octo,* trans. C.H. Oldfather and W.A. Oldfather (Oxford: Clarendon Press, 1934), 2:767.

7. Ibid.

8. In other words, the paradoxical possibility of a conventional agreement despite hostility may be founded on uncertainty. A death pact is only conceivable because it is a pact based on chance.

9. Théodore Ortolan, *Règles internationales et diplomatie de la mer* (Paris: Plon, 1864), 1:9.

10. Michael Ignatieff, *Virtual War: Kosovo and Beyond* (London: Vintage, 2001), 161.

11. Ibid.

12. "The fundamental principle of the morality of warfare is a right to exercise self-defense within the conditions of mutual imposition of risk." Paul W. Kahn, "The Paradox of Riskless Warfare," *Philosophy and Public Policy Quarterly* 22, no. 3 (2002), digitalcommons.law.yale.edu /fss-papers/326.

13. Ibid., 3.

14. Bradley J. Strawser, "Moral Predators: The Duty to Employ Uninhabited Aerial Vehicles," *Journal of Military Ethics* 9, no. 4 (2010): 356. And see Jeff McMahan, *Killing in War* (Oxford: Oxford University Press, 2009).

15. Michael Walzer, *Just and Unjust Wars* (London: Allen Lane, 1977), 41. The triumph of this kind of philosophy regarding the law of war would have extremely grave implications. By denying an "unjust warrior" an equal right to fight, it immediately turns him into a criminal, an outlaw. By so doing, excluding him from the *jus in bello,* it also suppresses all encouragement for him to respect its principles since, whatever he does, he will not benefit from the legal protection associated with respect for the accepted rules of combat. At that point violence, on both sides, loses any kind of safeguard.

16. Carl Schmitt, *The Nomos of the Earth* (New York: Telos Press, 2003), 321.

17. There could be an alternative to that option, which would offer the advantage of preserving the perspective of a legal regulation of armed conflicts rather than converting the latter into an extension of a monopolistic right to lethal punishment. The reflections of Charles Chaumont, who was of central importance in the Ecole de Reims and one of the most productive critics of the theory of international law in the late twentieth century, might today be extremely useful in any rethinking of the law of war in the context of asymmetrical conflicts. One principle at least worth thinking about would be that of *a right to the possibility of combat.* What happens when the law prohibits tactics which, however, are the

sole resources available to one camp in order to fight? Chaumont cites the example of a guerrilla: given "the existing inequalities between the military means and the logistics of the occupiers and those of the resistants, the guerrilla endeavors to compensate for those inequalities by specific means of fighting. Surprise, ambush, sabotage, street or maquis fighting take the place of warfare in open country and the clash between comparable military units. In such procedures, the visible carrying of arms and a distinctive sign [demanded by the law on armed conflicts] may either have no meaning . . . or else truly be incompatible with success in the struggle. . . . Given such circumstances, to reject those specific procedures is to reject guerilla warfare," Charles Chaumont, "La recherche d'un critère pour l'intégration de la guérilla au droit international humanitaire contemporain" (*Mélanges offerts à Charles Rousseau* [Paris, 1974], quoted in CICR, *Commentaire des protocoles additionnels du 8 juin 1977 aux Conventions de Genève du 12 août 1949* [Dordrecht: Kluwer, 1986], 536). It would, for example, have been absurd to insist that in occupied France in 1942, Resistance combatants should move around the streets of Paris in uniform, in order to comply with the law on armed conflicts. This constitutes a typical case in which the application of an equal law (on the obligation to display a distinctive sign) to situations that are not at all equal (involving both a regular army and partisan forces) produces inequity.

Chaumont proposes a guiding principle to remedy such adverse effects. He says, "A humanitarian law, to be objective and credible, must leave to both sides equal chances in combat: if a legal norm is incompatible with this principle and makes it impossible for one side to hope for victory, the best thing is to renounce the establishment of such a law" (ibid.).

What he suggests here is not so much *a right to equal combat*, which would involve insisting on a struggle with equal weapons, but rather *an equal right to fight*. The fact that the law should not, by the norms that it imposes, make it "impossible from the start for one side to hope for victory" implies, not turning the war into a tournament—with pistol against pistol or sword against sword but, on the contrary, taking into consideration the disparity of the forces confronting each other and taking care not to increase it by imposing short-sighted laws that would confer to one side greater advantages while depriving the other side of even the possibility of fighting.

Chaumont thus breaks away from the formal equality of classic legal logic. For him, it is no longer a matter of a principle of *absolutely identical rights* for all belligerents, as it is in the existing model of *jus in bello*. On the contrary, he favors a principle of an asymmetrization of rights, on account of the inequality in the relations of power. This principle is based on a strong concept of equality—but one of a geometrical equality in rights: asymmetrical powers deserve asymmetrical rights. In a way, the supporters of a unilateral right to kill say the same thing, except of course that for them it is a matter not of re-equating the relations of strength, but of unilateralizing that strength, even if it means scuppering the law itself, in the process.

For Chaumont, it is a matter, not of bringing about an anachronistic return to a chivalric ideal but, on the contrary, of an attempt to integrate the parameters of contemporary asymmetrical conflicts within the law on armed conflicts, and to do so in a realistic way. His central preoccupation is the following: combatants deprived by law of any legitimate possibility of fighting no longer have any pressing reason to conform with the principles of a law that itself excepts them from any role except that of targets to be hit. Chaumont's concern is pragmatic: if the aim of the law on armed conflict is to encourage the parties involved to moderate their violence and, in particular, to regulate non-conventional violence, one must not, in order to include them in the law, impose upon them rules the immediate consequence of which is to exclude them from it. What are at stake are the pragmatic conditions for the effectiveness of the law in its capacity as an instrument designed to regulate armed violence in this age of asymmetrical conflicts. For a contemporary attempt to argue this case, see Michael L. Gross, *Moral Dilemmas of Modern War* (New York: Cambridge University Press, 2010), 199.

19. License to Kill

1. Adam Liptak, "Secrecy of Memo on Drone Killing Is Upheld," *New York Times*, January 2, 2013.

2. Harold Koh, "The Obama Administration and International Law," speech delivered before the American Society of International Law, Washington, March 25, 2010.

3. "UN Special Rapporteur Philip Alston Responds to US Defense of Drone Attacks' Legality," *Democracy Now*, April 1, 2010, www.democracy now.org/2010/4/1/drones.

4. Some jurists detect a dangerous indistinction. The United States, writes Laurie Blank, relies "on both armed conflict and self-defense as legal justifications for targeted strikes outside of the zone of active combat. . . . It is the United States' insistence on using reference to both paradigms as justification for individual attacks and the broader program of targeted strikes that raises significant concerns for the use of international law and the protection of individuals by blurring the lines between the key parameters of the two paradigms." Laurie R. Blank, "Targeted Strikes: The Consequences of Blurring the Armed Conflict and Self-Defense Justifications," *William Mitchell Law Review* 38 (2012): 1659.

5. See Nils Melzer, *Targeted Killing in International Law* (Oxford: Oxford University Press, 2008), 89–90.

6. Philip Alston, *Report of the Special Rapporteur on Extrajudicial,*

Summary or Arbitrary Executions, Addendum, Study on Targeted Killings, UNO, May 28, 2010, 11.

7. This defines the principle of proportionality peculiar to law enforcement—which is very different from that which prevails in the law on armed conflicts. See Blank, "Targeted Strikes," 1690.

8. Alston, *Report*, 25.

9. See Blank, "Targeted Strikes," 1668.

10. Koh, "The Obama Administration and International Law."

11. Mary Ellen O'Connell, "Lawful Use of Combat Drones," Congress of the United States, House of Representatives, Subcommittee on National Security and Foreign Affairs Hearing: Rise of the Drones II: Examining the Legality of Unmanned Targeting, April 28, 2010, 2.

12. Bradley J. Strawser, "Moral Predators: The Duty to Employ Uninhabited Aerial Vehicles," *Journal of Military Ethics* 9, no. 4 (2010): 357.

13. Jo Becker and Scott Shane, "Secret 'Kill List' Proves a Test of Obama's Principles and Will," *New York Times*, May 29, 2012.

14. Kenneth Anderson, "Predators over Pakistan," *Weekly Standard* 15, no. 24 (March 8, 2010): 32.

15. Alston, *Report*, 22. And in the other hypothesis: "Outside of armed conflict, killings by the CIA would constitute extrajudicial executions assuming that they do not comply with human rights law." Ibid., 21.

16. Kenneth Anderson, "Targeted Killing in U.S. Counterterrorism Strategy and Law," May 11, 2009. Available at SSRN: ssrn.com/abstract =1415070.

17. Anderson, "Targeted Killing," 27.

18. Kenneth Anderson, "More Predator Drone Debate in the Wall Street Journal, and What the Obama Administration Should Do as a Public Legal Position," *Volokh Conspiracy*, January 9, 2010, www.volokh .com/2010/01/09/more-predator-drone-debate-in-the-wall-street-journal -and-what-the-obama-administration-should-do-as-a-public-legal-position.

19. "American domestic law—the law codifying the existence of the CIA and defining its functions—has long accepted implicitly at least some uses of force, including targeted killing, as self-defense toward ends of vital national security that do not necessarily fall within the strict terms of armed conflict in the sense meant by the Geneva Conventions and other international treaties on the conduct of armed conflict." Anderson, "Targeted Killing."

20. Abraham D. Sofaer, "Responses to Terrorism: Targeted Killing Is a Necessary Option," *San Francisco Chronicle*, March 26, 2004.

21. Anderson, "More Predator Drone Debate."

22. "The result of this mix has been a highly problematic blurring and expansion of the boundaries of the applicable legal frameworks. . . . The result has been the displacement of clear legal standards with a vaguely defined license to kill." Alston, *Report*, 3.

23. Anderson, "More Predator Drone Debate."

20. In War as in Peace

1. Michel Foucault summed up the difficulty as follows: "Isn't life the foundation of the sovereign's right, and can the sovereign actually demand that his subjects grant him the right to exercise the power of life and death over them, or in other words, simply the power to kill them?" Michel Foucault, *Society Must Be Defended* (New York: Picador, 2003), 241.

2. Hobbes, *Leviathan* (Cambridge: Cambridge University Press, 2003), 491

3. Carl Schmitt, *The Concept of the Political* (Chicago: University of Chicago Press, 2008), 52.

4. Hobbes, *Leviathan*, 484.

5. For Hobbes, the obligations of citizens derive not only from the convention that trades obedience for effective protection, but also from "The End of the Institution of the Sovereignty" (ibid., 150), "which is the common Peace and Defence" (ibid., 126).

6. Jean-Jacques Rousseau, *The Social Contract* (Cambridge: Cambridge University Press, 2003), 64.

7. The orators of revolutionary France were mindful of this rhetoric. In 1791, Barère, in a long speech about the endangered country, declared: "The Country says, 'Citizen, it is I who commit myself to protect your personal safety, your repose and your property. What will you offer me in return for this constant boon? If I happen to be in danger, . . . will you abandon me in stormy moments in return for my unswerving protection? . . . Surely not: there will be cases when I shall ask you to sacrifice those very rights, properties and even life itself that I have always protected.'" *Réimpression de l'ancien Moniteur* (Paris: Plon, 1862), 9:82.

8. "It is a grave miscalculation if the state, when it requires this sacrifice, is simply equated with civil society, and if its ultimate end is seen merely as the security of the life and property of individuals." Hegel, *Elements of the Philosophy of Right*, §324 (Cambridge: Cambridge University Press, 2003), 361.

9. "Since the subjects are obliged to the bearing of taxes and the like burdens on no other account but as they are necessary to defray the public expenses in war or peace, it is the duty of sovereigns in this respect to draw no further supplies than either the mere necessity or the signal benefit and interest of the state shall require." Pufendorf, *Of the Law of Nature and Nations*, Book VII, ch. IX (London: Walthoe, 1729), 742–43.

10. Jaucourt, "Guerre," in *Encyclopédie*, vol. VII (Livourne, 1773), 967.

11. Kant, *The Metaphysics of Morals* (Cambridge: Cambridge University Press, 2003), 116.

12. Ibid.

13. Zoopolitics may be defined as a branch of biopolitics, specified not

only by the transference of the proceeds of animal-breeding to the political relationships, but above all, from a legal point of view, by fusing political law with some of the fundamental categories of private law, and most specifically to private property. Typically, power based on a slavery system is a striking example of zoopolitics.

14. "Only under this limiting condition can a state direct them to serve in a way full of danger to them." Kant, *Metaphysics of Morals*, 484.

15. Ibid.

16. On this theme, see Charles Tilly, "War Making and State Making as Organized Crime," in *Bringing the State Back In*, ed. Peter Evans, Dietrich Rueschemeyer, and Theda Skocpol (New York: Cambridge University Press, 1985).

21. Democratic Militarism

1. Kant, "Toward Perpetual Peace," in *Political Writings* (Cambridge: Cambridge University Press, 2007), 100.

2. Ibid.

3. Quoted in Barbara Ehrenreich, "War Without Humans: Modern Blood Rites Revisited," TomDispatch, July 10, 2011, www.tomdispatch .com/blog/175415.

4. J.A. Hobson, *Imperialism: A Study* (London: Nisbet, 1902), 145.

5. *Hansard's Parliamentary Debates*, Third Series, 1867–1868 (London: Buck, 1868), 1:406. Today this practice has by no means disappeared but continues in different forms, those of contracting and subcontracting. At the present time, the United States recruits a considerable proportion of its dispensable military in sub-Saharan Africa, by way of private military companies under contract to the Pentagon. On this subject, see the edifying report by Alain Vicky, "Mercenaires africains pour guerres américaines," *Le monde diplomatique*, May 2012.

6. See Jonathan D. Caverley, "Death and Taxes: Sources of Democratic Military Aggression," thesis, University of Chicago, 2008, 297.

7. Kant, *The Metaphysics of Morals* (Cambridge: Cambridge University Press, 2003), 116.

8. John Kaag and Sarah Kreps, "The Moral Hazard of Drones," *The Stone, New York Times* blog, July 22, 2012.

9. "By reducing accidental civilian casualties, precision drone technologies reduce the perceived moral and reputational costs of using lethal force." Rosa Brooks, "Take Two Drones and Call Me in the Morning: The Perils of Our Addiction to Remote-Controlled War," *Foreign Policy*, September 12, 2012.

10. As Walzer explains, referring on this point to the thinking of Yehuda Melzer: "Proportionality is a matter of adjusting means to ends but . . . there is an overwhelming tendency in wartime to adjust ends to means instead, that is, to redefine initially narrow goals in order to fit

the available military forces and technologies." Michael Walzer, *Just and Unjust Wars* (London: Allen Lane, 1977), 120.

11. Jeremy R. Hammond, "The Immoral Case for Drones," July 16, 2012, www.jeremyrhammond.com/2012/07/16/the-immoral-case -for-drones.

12. Eyal Weizman, *The Least of All Possible Evils: Humanitarian Violence from Arendt to Gaza* (London: Verso, 2012), 10.

13. Caverley, "Death and Taxes."

14. Amitai Etzioni, "The Great Drone Debate," *National Interest*, October 4, 2011.

15. Benjamin H. Friedman, "Etzioni and the Great Drone Debate," *National Interest*, October 5, 2011.

16. Beverly J. Silver, "Historical Dynamics of Globalization, War and Social Protest," in *Critical Globalization Studies*, ed. Richard Applebaum and William Robinson (New York: Routledge, 2005), 308. I am referring to her analysis throughout this passage.

17. On the "modes of war" concept, see Mary Kaldor, *New and Old Wars* (Cambridge: Polity Press, 2006), 17.

18. See Yagil Levy, "The Essence of the 'Market Army,'" *Public Administration Review* 70, no. 3 (May/June 2010): 378–89.

19. Jonathan Caverley, "The Political Economy of Democratic Militarism: Evidence from Public Opinion," International Relations Workshop, University of Wisconsin, March 28, 2012.

20. Niklas Schörnig and Alexander C. Lembcke, "The Vision of War Without Casualties: On the Use of Casualty Aversion in Armament Advertisements," *Journal of Conflict Resolution* 50, no. 2 (2006): 204–27.

21. *Flight International* 161, no. 4834 (June 4, 2002): 2.

22. Silver, "Historical Dynamics," 309.

23. Ehrenreich, "War Without Humans."

22. The Essence of Combatants

1. Hegel, *The Phenomenology of Mind* (London: Allen & Unwin, 1971), 404.

2. Seymour Hersh, "Manhunt," *New Yorker*, December 23, 2002.

3. Kant, *Political Writings* (Cambridge: Cambridge University Press, 2007), 168.

4. Emilio Lussu, *Sardinian Brigade: A Memoir of World War I* (New York: Grove Press, 1970), cited in Michael Walzer, *Just and Unjust Wars* (London: Allen Lane, 1977), 142.

5. Cora Diamond, *L'Importance d'être humain* (Paris: Presses Universitaires de France, 2011), 103, 106.

6. Ibid.

7. Amitai Etzioni, "The Great Drone Debate," *National Interest*, October 4, 2011.

8. Sartre, "Existentialism Is a Humanism," in *Basic Writings* (London: Routledge, 2001), 30 (modified translation).

9. Cora Diamond, "The Case of the Naked Soldiers," unpublished paper.

10. Not in Our Name, "*Pledge of Resistance*," 2001, www.notinour name.net/index.php?option=com-content&view=article&id=20&Item id=5.

11. See Judith Butler and Gayatri Chakravorty Spivak, *L'Etat global* (Paris: Payot, 2011), 57.

12. George N. Katsiaficas, *Vietnam Documents: American and Vietnamese Views of the War* (New York: M.E. Sharpe, 1992), 116.

13. Ibid.

14. Joe Pappalardo, "The Blimps Have Eyes: 24/7 Overhead Surveillance Is Coming," *Popular Mechanics*, May 17, 2012.

15. Ibid.

16. Ibid.

17. Ibid.

18. Hannah Yi, "New Police Surveillance Drones Could Be Armed with Nonlethal Weapons," *The Daily*, March 12, 2012.

19. Marx, *Grundrisse: Foundation of the Critique of Political Economy* (London: Penguin, 1973), 109.

20. Adam Harvey, "Stealth Wear," January 17, 2013, ahprojects.com /projects/stealth-wear.

23. The Fabrication of Political Automata

1. These pilotless machines were not radio controlled; they were mechanically programmed to crash on the ground once they had covered a particular distance. The *V* in their names was an abbreviation for *Vergeltungswaffen*, "reprisal weapons."

2. Theodor Adorno, *Minima Moralia: Reflections on a Damaged Life* (London: Verso, 2005), 55.

3. Ibid., 56.

4. For the expression "political automaton," see "Et vous trouvez ça drone?," Z (Marseilles), no. 2 (Autumn 2009): 141.

5. *The Unmanned Systems Integrated Roadmap FY 2011–2036*, 14.

6. Gary E. Marchant et al., "International Governance of Autonomous Military Robots," *Colombia Science and Technology Law Review* 12 (2011): 273. The Korean SGR-1 robot is one of today's precursors of these machines of the future. They are stationed along the frontier between the two Koreas, in the demilitarized zone. These stationary robots can detect a human presence thanks to their sensors (cameras, but also detectors of movement and thermal sensors), target the individual and, if the distant operator authorizes it, open fire with either a 5 mm gun or an automatic grenade launcher.

7. "Lethal autonomous robotics" (LAR). "Autonomous" here means that the platform is, itself, capable of taking the necessary decisions, without any human intervention.

8. Ronald Arkin, "The Case for Ethical Autonomy in Unmanned Systems," 2010, hdl.handle.net/1853/36516.

9. Ronald Arkin, "Ethical Robots in Warfare," *Technology and Society Magazine* 28, no. 1 (Spring 2009): 30.

10. Ronald Arkin, "Governing Lethal Behavior: Embedding Ethics in a Hybrid Deliberative/Reactive Robot Architecture" (2007), 98, hdl.handle.net/1853/22715.

11. Arkin, "Ethical Robots in Warfare."

12. Ronald Arkin, "An Ethical Basis for Autonomous System Deployment, Proposal 50397-CI, Final Report," 2009.

13. Ronald Arkin, Patrick Ulam, and Brittany Duncan, *An Ethical Governor for Constraining Lethal Action in an Autonomous System, Technical Report GIT-GVU-09-02*, 2009.

14. Arkin, "Ethical Robots in Warfare."

15. See Vivek Kanwar, "Post-Human Humanitarian Law: The Law of War in the Age of Robotic Warfare," *Harvard Journal of National Security* 2 (2011).

16. See Michel Pastoureau, *Une histoire symbolique du Moyen Age occidental* (Paris: Seuil, 2004), 33.

17. Kenneth Anderson and Matthew Waxman, "Law and Ethics for Robot Soldiers," *Policy Review*, no. 176 (December 2012).

18. Ibid.

19. For years, Ronald Arkin has been working on their development, thanks to generous financial aid from the military-industrial complex, which includes DARPA, the US Army, the Savannah River Technology Center, Honda R & D, Samsung, CS Draper Laboratory, SAIC, NAVAIR, and the Office of Naval Research, www.cc.gatech.edu/~arkin.

20. In September 2009, the physicist Jürgen Altmann, the philosopher Peter Asaro, the roboticist Noel Sharkey, and the philosopher Robert Sparrow founded the International Committee for the control of robotic weapons, the Committee for Robot Arms Control (ICRAC), which calls for the prohibition of robotic killers. Its website is at icrac.net.

21. Marvin Minsky, "Telepresence," *Omni*, June 1980, 204.

22. Walter Benjamin, *Theories of German Fascism*, in *Selected Writings, Vol. 2, 1927–1934*, trans. Rodney Livingstone et al. (Cambridge, MA: Belknap Press, 1999), 320.

23. Andrew Cockburn reports similar facts (Bush, in person, giving the order to fire on a convoy of vehicles bound for Kandahar) and notes that such direct video retransmissions give political leaders "an extraordinary—and illusory—sense of direct control." Andrew Cockburn, "Drones, Baby, Drones," *London Review of Books*, March 8, 2012, 15.

24. Peter W. Singer, *Wired for War: The Robotics Revolution and Conflict in the 21st Century* (New York: Penguin, 2009), 349.

25. Noel Sharkey, "Killing Made Easy: From Joystick to Politics," in *Robot Ethics: The Ethical and Social Implications of Robotics*, ed. Patrick Lin, Keith Abney, and George A. Bekey (Cambridge, MA: MIT Press, 2012), 123.

26. For even though the law on armed conflicts defines the principle of proportionality as a good relation between estimated collateral damages and the scale of the military advantage expected, it provides no estimated scale nor, clearly, any unit of measurement. As Sharkey points out: "There is no known metric to objectively measure needless, superfluous, or disproportionate suffering. It requires human judgment. No clear objective means are given in any of the laws of war for how to calculate what is proportionate" (Sharkey, "Killing Made Easy"). To convert the principle of proportionality into a calculation would be like adding together apples and pears without any method of recognizing them. What is the commensurability between a particular number of lost civilian lives and an expected military advantage? What could the common unit of measurement be? However, as Eyal Weizman has shown, this kind of calculation, as necessary as it is impossible, serves solely to legitimate the deaths that result, and serves this function simply by being done. See Eyal Weizman, *The Least of All Possible Evils: Humanitarian Violence from Arendt to Gaza* (London: Verso, 2012), 12ff.

27. Allan Nairn, quoted in Robert C. Koehler, " 'Bugsplat': The Civilian Toll of War," *Baltimore Sun*, January 1, 2012. See also Bradley Graham, " 'Bugsplat' Computer Program Aims to Limit Civilian Deaths at Targets," *Washington Post*, February 26 2003.

28. Ferdinand d'Esterno, *Des privilégiés de l'ancien régime en France et des privilégiés du nouveau*, vol. II (Paris: Guillaumin, 1868), 69.

29. Quoted in Matthew Brzezinski, "The Unmanned Army," *New York Times Magazine*, April 20, 2003.

30. Arkin, in an interview, forestalls the objection: "They would not always follow orders. It must be possible for the robot to refuse an order, if it is deemed to be unethical," that is to say not in conformity with the *jus in bello* adapted as software. However, the soldiers who refuse to shoot at insurgents, as in the above example, do not do so because of their commitment to the law on armed conflicts. They dissociate themselves from the power that gives the orders, not because of the form of those orders but because of their content, their political meaning. And that is certainly something that robots are incapable of doing. Sofia Karlsson, "Ethical Machines in War: An Interview with Ronald Arkin," owni.eu/2011/04/25/ethical-machines-in-war-an-interview-with-ronald-arkin.

31. This is one of the worries of the authors of a recent report: "By eliminating human involvement in the decision to use lethal force in

armed conflict, fully autonomous weapons would undermine other, non-legal protections for civilians. First, robots would not be restrained by human emotions and the capacity for compassion. . . . Emotionless robots could, therefore, serve as tools of repressive dictators seeking to crack down on their own people without fear their troops would turn on them. . . . Emotions do not always lead to irrational killing." Human Rights Watch, *Losing Humanity: The Case Against Killer Robots*, November 2012, 4.

32. Estienne de La Boétie, *Anti-Dictator: The Discours sur la servitude volontaire* (New York: Columbia University Press, 1942), 11.

33. Hannah Arendt, *On Violence* (New York: Harcourt, 1970), 151.

34. Friedrich Engels, *The Origin of the Family, Private Property and the State* (London: Lawrence and Wishart, 1972), 229.

Epilogue

1. "Toys Against the People, or Remote Warfare," *Science for the People Magazine* 5, no. 1 (May 1973): 8–10, 37–42.

2. Ibid., 42.

INDEX

Grégoire Chamayou is a research scholar in philosophy at the Centre National de la Recherche Scientifique. The author of *Manhunts: A Philosophical History*, he lives in Paris.

Janet Lloyd has translated more than seventy books from the French by authors such as Jean-Pierre Vernant, Marcel Detienne, and Philippe Descola. She lives in Cambridge, UK.

Publishing in the Public Interest